Show up ready to learn

Show up ready to work

Show up ready to play

Show up ready =

**POSITION TO WIN**

## Acclaim for Dewayne Staats...

"I had the pleasure of getting to know Dewayne at the front end of his career, when I became a member of the Houston Astros in the early 1980s and he was broadcasting our games with Gene Elston and Larry Dierker. I always knew that Dewayne was going to go far—with a style that showed knowledge, preparation and a respect for the game. It's no surprise he's one of the best in the business."

—**Nolan Ryan**, *Hall of Fame pitcher, MLB record-holder with seven no-hitters and Houston Astros executive advisor*

"The ultimate tribute paid, when a player steps on the field, comes when a member of his peer group observes, 'He's a ballplayer's ballplayer.' That says a lot, among which is included preparation, execution, and above all else, respect for THE GAME. Dewayne Staats, throughout his career, has personified these traits. He's a broadcaster's broadcaster."

—**Tony Kubek**, *2009 recipient of the Ford C. Frick Award presented to a broadcaster by the National Baseball Hall of Fame, longtime NBC commentator and star shortstop on three New York Yankees World Championship teams*

"When I think of Dewayne Staats, what stands out first is his voice. You know it's him. Some guys have more of a generic sound, but Dewayne's got this unique, commanding tone that instantly conveys to viewers the feeling that he knows what he's talking about. And he does. He's baseball literate, astute and brings years of history and experience to every broadcast—with a cache of information and a file cabinet full of stories from a wonderful career in the game."

—**Joe Maddon**, *manager of the Chicago Cubs and longtime Tampa Bay Rays skipper*

"Dewayne Staats always impressed me as true professional while he was part of the Yankees broadcast team in New York. Always prepared, knowledgeable and respectful of the game, Dewayne and Tony Kubek were a formidable team covering us during the early 1990s. Baseball and Rays fans are fortunate to have had Dewayne in the booth through the years. He's left a mark on the game we can all appreciate."

—**Don Mattingly**, *manager of the Los Angeles Dodgers, former captain and All-Star first baseman of the New York Yankees*

"A hell of a broadcaster and a dear friend. Holy Cow!"

—*The late* **Harry Caray**, *legendary voice of the Chicago Cubs*

"Dewayne Staats has been a huge influence on my life and my career. He's as steady a person as they come. And he's highly intellectual. There are a lot of broadcasters in the game—and I'd probably throw myself into that mix—that if we weren't doing sports broadcasting I'm not sure what we'd be doing. But if Dewayne weren't in sports broadcasting, there are probably eight to 10 fields he would excel in. He's a multi-dimensional, multi-talented person who we were lucky enough chose to go down the baseball broadcasting path. He's a very important person in my life. I look up to him. I respect him. And, to me, he brings a professionalism and a consistency to every broadcast that you rarely see. He's like a player who winds up with 3,000 hits by being so good, day in and day out—you can only look back and say, 'That was an unbelievable career'."

—**Todd Kalas**, *longtime Tampa Bay Rays broadcaster dating back to the start of the franchise*

"No one prepares for a game as hard as Dewayne—and it shows in his broadcasts. He is outstanding—in addition to being a quality human being and a great guy. To have worked in the markets he has along the way to Tampa Bay—Houston, Chicago, New York, ESPN—tells you how good he is at his trade. And he's got that baseball distinctive voice and comfortable style, like he's sitting down talking to friends."

—**Art Howe**, *former manager of the Mets, A's and Astros, who played for the Pirates, Astros and Cardinals*

"I'm just amazed at the things Dewayne has experienced in his career—the teams that he has covered, the people he has gotten an opportunity to work with, the big-market cities in which he has worked. He's been with the fledgling Astros, with Harry Caray in Chicago, Tony Kubek up in New York, and done the national job with ESPN. And then there were all the years with the Devil Rays before they became the Rays. He's the only voice our fans have known. It's been a long, illustrious career—not only in length of time in the booth but in what he brings to every broadcast."

—**Brian Anderson**, *color analyst for the Rays and Staats' partner since 2010*

"Walking in the booth, no matter what happened the day before, I always felt I was putting on a finely tailored coat working with Dewayne—because I knew it was going to be a perfect fit. He was ready to work every single day, completely prepared and very loyal—and I feel very fortunate to have been his on-air partner for those first 11 seasons of the franchise."

—**Joe Magrane**, *color commentator for the Devil Rays and Rays, 1998-2008*

"Dewayne is down to earth, passionate about what he does and is one of the best at his craft. He's worked in some great markets, with some great Hall of Fame broadcasters and he should be in the Hall of Fame himself one of these days. From the day I met him at ESPN in the 1990s until I came to Tampa Bay to work with him a decade later, he never changed. He's humble, very respectful of other people and of the game itself."

—**Kevin Kennedy**, *former manager of the Red Sox and Rangers, and color analyst with Staats in 2009 and 2010*

"I can't say enough about Dewayne. In my book, he's a Hall of Fame broadcaster. He probably should be there by now, but he will get there—not just because of his longevity but because of his talent."

—**Dave Nelson**, *Staats' former radio partner with WGN covering the Chicago Cubs for two seasons*

"Like most great announcers, Dewayne doesn't have an agenda when the game starts. He just rides the game, goes with the flow. He is always full of useful information and has a good sense of humor. But he doesn't pretend to be the main attraction like some puffed-up announcers. Dewayne is a very thoughtful and sensitive person. He thinks about other people before he acts, doesn't make many snap decisions. He is a person you can rely on. He won't let you down."

—**Larry Dierker**, *former color commentator with Staats and Gene Elston with the Houston Astros, a past manager of the Astros and staff ace with the Houston Colt .45s /Astros*

"Dewayne is one of the best in the game. He's one of those calm and recognizable voices. On the players' side, you don't get a chance to listen to him on a daily basis. But I think fans appreciate just how steady and constant he is. Any time a broadcaster has been around the sport that long, it says a lot about them. He's well-respected among players, managers, coaches and everyone in the game."

—**Sam Fuld**, *former Tampa Bay Rays outfielder, now with the Oakland A's*

"When you think of the Tampa Bay Rays, you think of Dewayne Staats. He does such a great job making you feel like you're sitting right there with him in the booth, taking in the game together. I grew up in St. Petersburg watching Dewayne on TV, and one of the things I admire most is that when you meet him, he's exactly the person you imagined he would be: professional, personable and just an all-around great guy."

—**Doug Waechter**, *hometown star who pitched four seasons with the Devil Rays, now part of the Sun Sports broadcast crew*

"The voice of Dewayne Staats has been bringing baseball to life for decades, delivering consistent excellence from the broadcast booth. Reading his book will put you in a *Position to Win* as well."

—**Bob Delaney,** *Vice President NBA Referee Operations, 25 year NBA official, and coauthor* Covert: My Years Infiltrating the Mob *and* Surviving the Shadows: A Journey of Hope Into Post-Traumatic Stress

"The great baseball announcers of Dewayne Staats' caliber are like epic poets, narrating the stories of heroes. That makes Staats like Homer, a terrific storyteller who can call a homer without being a homer. In *Position to Win*, the original voice of the Rays and standout author/journalist Dave Scheiber form a winning team in bringing the game and the story of a remarkable career in the booth to life."

—**Roy Peter Clark**, *best-selling author of* The Glamour of Grammar *and* Writing Tools, *Vice President and Senior Scholar, the Poynter Institute*

# Position to Win

## A Look at Baseball and Life From the Best Seat in the House

DEWAYNE STAATS with DAVE SCHEIBER

ISBN 978-0-692-48796-9

*Front and Back Cover Photographs:*
Mike Sexton

*Book Design:*
Susan Spangler
www.susanspangler.com

Published by
Advance Ink Publishing
http://advanceinkpublishing.com

*For Gabe, Zach and Evie...*

*and the gifts of posterity yet to arrive*

# CONTENTS

# FOREWORD

When I think of Dewayne Staats, what comes to mind is that distinctive, friendly voice with a touch of his Midwestern roots. He's always had a knack for bringing a baseball game to life in a way that's engaging, insightful and just plain fun. That explains why he has connected so naturally with TV viewers and radio listeners decade after decade—and why he is one of the great play-by-play announcers in Major League Baseball.

But in my book, Dewayne is so much more. He's been a wonderful friend since we began our big-league journeys in the late 1970s, at virtually the same time, with the Houston Astros.

And he's an incredibly astute baseball mind—a quality that has distinguished him on the airwaves calling games across America for the Astros, the Chicago Cubs, the New York Yankees, ESPN and, of course, the Tampa Bay Rays; and a quality that has made him a big help to me in my years as a major league general manager and personnel executive.

I could see Dewayne's sharpness right away when I was just starting out as traveling secretary for the Astros in 1978, and he was in his second season in Houston's broadcast booth.

I was 26 and had just come out of the college coaching ranks at Florida International University with a passion for baseball management. Dewayne was only 23, and clearly had a passion and talent for broadcasting.

From our many baseball discussions at the ballpark and on the road, it was evident to me that Dewayne possessed extraordinary recall, knowledge and drive. I never had any doubt that he could easily have been an outstanding general manager or director of scouting if he hadn't gone to work behind the mic. In fact, I rank Dewayne as one of the best talent evaluators that I've come across in my years helping build rosters—for the Astros, the Mets, the Rays and now the Dodgers.

During the nine years I was general manager in Houston, a stretch in which we won four division titles, I never hesitated to lean on Dewayne long-distance to get his perspective on some potential deal I might be working on or situation I was trying to work through.

Years later, it was Dewayne who opened the door for me with the Rays.

He'd seen a newspaper interview I'd done in Houston after serving as advisor for the Astros in 2005, just after we finally reached the World Series. In response to a question, I mentioned that I wasn't looking for another general manager job, but might be interested in a front-office position working with a young GM, someone looking for guidance from a person with experience in the game.

As it happened, Rays owner Stuart Sternberg and his group had just taken over that year and were looking for a person like that to assist Executive Vice President of Baseball Operations Andrew Friedman, Tampa Bay's bright new personnel man.

Dewayne saw the clip of the story and passed it on to team president Matt Silverman, and that got the ball rolling. He also did some recruiting, talking to me about how excited he was about the potential he saw in the Rays, and what a great place the Tampa Bay area was to live. That made a big difference in helping me conclude that the Rays were the right fit. I'm a firm believer that things happen for a reason, and it almost felt like destiny was at work as we came full circle in our careers—after a quarter century on different paths.

With the Rays, I once again valued having Dewayne's knowledge of players and analysis of situations. Early on, he enabled me to become more effective with Andrew and Matt as we decided what direction we wanted to go. And quite frankly, I believe he helped fast-forward the whole transformation process that we made as an organization, marked by our turnaround from a perennial losing franchise to the team that surprised baseball by reaching the 2008 World Series, en route to becoming one of baseball's most consistently successful ball clubs.

Beyond all that, Dewayne is a special person—smart and caring, with a quick wit and amiable, self-deprecating manner. He's the essence of professionalism and integrity. And he's a great family man. In fact, it was family that brought us together. We became friends back in the '70s thanks to our wives—Dee Staats and Irene Hunsicker. They'd had kids about the same time, gotten to know each other well, and arranged baby showers for one another. As a result, we all became very close.

That bond was cemented by mutual respect and admiration and would one day be strengthened by the deepest of personal challenges entwining our respective families. You will read more about that—and about resilience, faith and fortitude—later in these pages.

For now, settle back and enjoy Dewayne's amazing ride through baseball—the story of a kid who had big dreams, was driven to pursue them and wound up as one of the best in the booth.

Gerry Hunsicker
*Senior Advisor of Baseball Operations, Los Angeles Dodgers*
*Past Senior Vice-President, Baseball Operations, Tampa Bay Rays*
*Former General Manager, Houston Astros*
*Former Assistant General Manager, New York Mets*

PROLOGUE

# What's In a Title?

I feel privileged to have been in a position to witness some truly remarkable baseball moments during 40 years as a big-league broadcaster—a journey that has included nearly 6,000 games and counting, in the only career I ever dreamed of pursuing.

Along the way, I've been fortunate to have called the action in nine no-hitters—from one that broke a major-league record that still stands 35 years later—to one of the most amazing and inspirational sporting feats a person could ever hope to achieve.

I guess you could say I was doubly blessed to have been on the job when Wade Boggs ripped a home run for his 3,000th career hit as a member of the expansion Tampa Bay Devil Rays in 1999—and again when Yankees' superstar Derek Jeter logged his 3,000th hit with a homer in the Bronx in 2011. That feat has only been accomplished three times in baseball history—and I'm gratified to have called the first two.

From my perch in the broadcast booth, I've had a bird's-eye view of more thrilling and unusual baseball games than I can remember, while working with and learning from my mentor, the great Gene Elston, in Houston; being part of a lively WGN Superstation crew that covered the Chicago Cubs, with the incomparable Harry Caray leading the way; sitting beside stellar analyst and standup human being Tony Kubek, calling Yankees games for the groundbreaking MSG Network; and sharing broadcasts with so many talented commentators at ESPN and—during these past 18 years—the Rays.

But nothing compares in sheer drama and improbability to the evening of September 28, 2011, the last day of the regular season. It was just after 10 p.m. in the East—both the time zone and the American League East Division—and Tampa Bay faced a seven-run, eighth-inning deficit against the New York Yankees on what would become, without question, the wildest night in baseball history.

Die-hard Rays fans who stuck around inside Tropicana Field late on that Wednesday night, or were watching on television and resisted the urge to change the channel, or turn off the TV altogether, will never forget what they saw.

I certainly won't.

It became the stuff of instant franchise lore, to be passed down from one Rays generation to the next. And even though you may well know the outcome, I have a reason for revisiting the night now – before we go further sharing this shared ride through baseball and life in the book you hold in your hands, Position to Win.

For all practical purposes, the Rays' inspiring quest to qualify for the Wild Card looked as if it had finally come to a deflating conclusion—especially after watching Tampa Bay ace David Price get rocked by first baseman Mark Teixeira for a grand slam in the second inning and adding a solo shot in the fourth.

In the fifth, it was 7-0 and the Yankees, who had already wrapped up the division title, appeared to be coasting toward an easy albeit meaningless victory. The Rays, on the other hand, seemed inexplicably somnambulant, amid soaring hopes for a season-ending victory to clinch at least a Wild Card tie with the Boston Red Sox, or better yet—secure the playoff spot outright with a Rays win coupled with a Red Sox loss in Baltimore.

By the bottom of the eighth, however, conventional wisdom dictated that they had virtually no chance of reaching the postseason—not with that dismal 7-0 deficit still intact and not from the way things were going at Camden Yards. We'd been keeping track of that game on ESPN on the television set in our booth. And, at this particular moment, the game was mired in a rain delay in the fifth inning, with the Red Sox in the driver's seat, holding a 3-2 lead over the last-place Orioles.

Still, I remember thinking as Tampa Bay came to bat that the team often thrived in apparent no-win situations—and this one surely qualified. But even with that hopeful thought, it was hard to imagine how the Rays could possibly pull themselves out of this hole. After a record-breaking September surge, making up nine games against free-falling Boston in the Wild Card standings, and entering the game tied with the Red Sox at 90-71, the magic had apparently vanished.

Their only chances at a playoff spot now: Pray that the suddenly revived Red Sox blew their lead and lost to the lowly O's, thus forcing a one-game playoff for the Wild Card spot the next day at the Trop—or make a miraculous comeback against New York and, assuming Boston held on to win, face the Red Sox in a one-game playoff. But any way you cut it, the Rays' shot at the post-season loomed as increasingly bleak.

That's precisely when the seemingly impossible began to unfold.

You had to see it to believe it—and even then you might not. It started routinely enough with a lead-off Johnny Damon single to left field. Yet after Ben Zobrist doubled him to third and Casey Kotchman was hit by reliever Boone Logan to load the bases with none out, disheartened Rays fans in the crowd of 29,000-plus stirred to life in a cacophonous mix of cheers and clanging cowbells.

Yankees reliever Luis Ayala, the ninth New York pitcher of the night, replaced Logan, but fared no better. Sam Fuld drew a walk to make it 7-1, and Ayala followed by hitting Sean Rodriguez to bring home a second run. One out later, when B.J. Upton's sacrifice fly to left narrowed the deficit to 7-3, I glanced at my booth-mate, Brian Anderson, and raised my eyebrows without saying a word.

We were both thinking the same thing as Evan Longoria walked to the plate: One more hit could be the opening the Rays needed to get back into the game.

As if on cue, Longoria, who had enjoyed a torrid final month, took it a step further. He crushed the first pitch he saw deep into the left field seats for a three-run homer—suddenly bringing the Rays to within one run, 7-6, before the inning finally ended.

"They're going to win this thing," I told B.A. during the commercial break.

But the Yankees had other ideas. Reliever Cory Wade—getting the bullpen call with All-Star closer Mariano Rivera being rested for the playoffs—retired Zobrist on a long fly ball to center and got Kotchman on a weak grounder to third.

Down to the final out, manager Joe Maddon decided to send Dan Johnson to the plate to pinch hit. As we learned later, D.J. hadn't anticipated two quick outs, and was taking warm-up swings in the team's indoor batting cage upstairs from the dugout. A security guard had to dash up the steps to the hitting room and tell him he was up next.

You couldn't have had a better man for the moment—a player who had fought his way through the minors to find a spot on a big-league roster and come to epitomize the Rays' battles with AL East behemoths. His Tampa Bay debut in September 2008 was the stuff of legend—arriving late to Fenway Park after an all-day trek from Triple-A Durham, then delivering a game-tying, pinch-hit home run in the ninth inning to help beat Boston in a critical pennant-run contest, ultimately proving to be a key step for the Rays en route to the World Series.

And now, all eyes were riveted on the left-handed-hitting journeyman. Working the count to 2-2, he fouled off a fastball to stay alive, then saw the Wade changeup he'd been waiting for—drilling a line shot that hooked down the rightfield line, and into Rays' history. As I watched the ball disappear into the stands, just inside the foul pole to tie the game 7-7 and trigger a frenzied celebration, I had only one thought:

"Of course he did!"

Meanwhile, the Red Sox and Orioles finally resumed play after nearly a 90-minute delay. The Sox were 77-0 that season when leading after eight innings. And Baltimore—trailing 3-2 and down to its final out in the bottom of the ninth—stunned star closer Jonathan Papelbon with a pair of doubles and a single. It was just after midnight, and the Orioles had somehow come back to beat the unraveling Red Sox 4-3—simultaneously unleashing a thunderous roar from Rays fans in the Trop who were following the game on portable radios and mobile devices.

By then, the Rays and Yankees were moving into the bottom of the 12th inning. And it was only a matter of time—barely five minutes—before Longoria launched his own epic liner off reliever Scott Proctor over the low wall in left, thrusting his hands above his head as he rounded the bases in a freeze-frame, iconic image of the franchise.

A tidal wave of jubilation instantly erupted beneath the dome—a crazy finish made even more surreal by modern technology, linking two overlapping American League dramas in real time (and I'm not even including the parallel story line that night in the National League, when the Phillies came back to beat and eliminate the Braves in 13 innings).

All that counted was that the Rays had won, 8-7—and reached the playoffs in a contest forever known as "Game 162." Suffice it to say, I have never seen a more emotionally charged champagne-drenched clubhouse celebration—or long-shot win—in my life.

But let's rewind the tape back for a moment, back to the pivotal eighth inning, when the Rays trailed by seven runs. The statistical analyst will tell you there was virtually no chance the Rays could win this game by falling so far behind so early, and trailing by the same margin so late. In fact, Baseball-Reference.com, which charts such numbers among its multitude of statistics, calculated the Rays' probability of winning when Damon singled to start off the eighth inning at just one percent.

Yet the personality and mindset of these Maddon-managed Rays prepared them for precisely this kind of situation—an intrinsic belief in their ability, an unrelenting will to find a way, and a knack for taking advantage of opportunities to somehow swing the odds in their favor.

They had put themselves in a position to win. And in life, that's what you always have to do in order to have a shot at attaining your goals.

That phrase holds different meanings to different people. As I gave thought to the title of this book, I pictured my paternal grandfather, Perry Francis Staats. He grew up in Southern Missouri, in the shadow of the Mighty Mississippi. He married my grandmother when they both were young, and built the wooden house where they raised nine children and lived the rest of their lives.

They had no air conditioning, no running water, no heat, and none of the amenities we take for granted today. For my grandfather, being in a "position to win" didn't mean buying a new car or having a house in the suburbs. It meant raising his nine kids and having all of them survive into adulthood, providing them with food and clothes. It meant growing crops on 180 acres of land, with two orchards to harvest, while also overseeing a blacksmith shop and chicken coop. He had the biggest garden I ever saw, but he maintained it as a means of survival during lean times.

While the country reveled in the Roaring Twenties, my grandparents were already feeling the effects of a depressed economy in the rural Midwest. They endured 10 years of that, followed by another decade of the Great Depression in the 1930s. Those years of extreme hardship were followed by World War II, and more challenges. But they persevered through it all, always keeping an optimistic view of the future and bequeathing to their children—my father, included—their core values of hard work, determination and empathy for others.

In so doing, they put their kids in a position to win, as well. That spirit is what this book is all about, not just a look at my life story and career aspirations.

And that same spirit also applies to the many people I'm so grateful to have encountered along the way. I look at Gene Elston, the original broadcaster of the Houston Colt .45s and Astros, and the simple Iowa background from which he came. He had no real money, joined the Navy, and eventually returned to civilian life with a burning desire to be a baseball play-by-play man. He scrambled to make his own breaks, and moved up the ladder by developing an approach that was never forced or over the top, imbued with a friendly quality and descriptive style.

Harry Caray was a little more flamboyant. He came from humble roots on the streets of St. Louis, learning to trust his own instincts and sharp wits to survive—and developing a big personality that would one day set him apart as a major league broadcaster.

While I was in Chicago working with Harry, I got to see the emergence of future Hall of Fame pitcher Greg Maddux. More than any pitcher I've ever seen, the bigger the moment became, the softer he threw. Greg knew that hitters would be fired up, waiting for the fastball, and he would respond by throwing soft, softer and then softer again.

I see a direct application to life. When you're in a crisis, maintaining a sense of calm—and softer approach—is far more effective than yelling and screaming, and very possibly losing control of the situation. That's how Greg positioned himself to win. There's a lesson in that for all of us. Looking back, I was blessed to have parents who loved me and attempted to point me in the right direction, at every turn; parents who believed that faith and education were fundamental elements in my development.

I had two sets of grandparents who were salt of the earth and made me feel special. But it was my grandpa, Francis Staats, who engaged me in conversation and debate about eternal questions of truth and social justice. He was a great storyteller and gave me an appreciation for language, history and reading. And he always encouraged me to advance my station, and simply to do the right thing.

Only Grandpa Staats went far in his formal education, attending long-defunct Will Mayfield College in Marble Hill, Missouri in the early 1900s. But in varying proportions, all of my forebearers exemplified hard work, intellectual curiosity, love of God and country, and a passion for family and life.

By contrast, I grew up in a time when it was possible to find an affordable university and a means to pay for it. We had many more tools to help us succeed than the generation that came before us—and our debt to that earlier generation is impossible to calculate. It was on this sturdy foundation they provided that I could begin to build my life.

All of this put me in a position to win. The rest—as you will read in the pages that follow—was up to me.

***Dewayne Staats***
***July 2015***

CHAPTER ONE

# Voices Across the Night Sky

For a young boy with an active imagination and passion for baseball, our little gray-sided house on East George Street was nothing short of paradise. It was tucked away in a quiet neighborhood of East Alton, Illinois, a post-War industrial town just to the east of the meandering Mississippi River. I could throw a rubber ball against the cinder-block garage wall for hours at a time, pretending to pitch for the nearby St. Louis Cardinals in the seventh game of the World Series or devising all manner of major league matchups. The Cardinals of the early 1960s were certainly alluring to my eight-year-old sensibilities—a team that boasted Stan Musial in the twilight of his storied career, and the larger-than-life likes of first baseman Bill White, third baseman Ken Boyer, centerfielder Curt Flood and the impressive young battery of pitcher Bob Gibson and catcher Tim McCarver. I didn't know exactly how good this group was, but I'd read enough game recaps and seen enough photographs in the *Alton Evening Telegraph* and the *St. Louis Globe-Democrat* to acquire a working knowledge of the Cards and get a pretty good idea they were something special.

Naturally, they were well represented in my endless wall-ball endeavors. I drew a strike zone with chalk so I could call balls and strikes, and the brown rubber ball would often ricochet off the masonry surface and replicate a groundball or a lazy pop fly. I guess you could call this activity the original fantasy baseball, a game played by youthful lovers of America's pastime on walls and front porches across the land. One by one, I'd go through the lineup of whichever team was facing me. What made these showdowns even more interesting was my discovery that if I threw a pitch low enough, at just the proper trajectory, it might rebound into an arc replicating a long fly ball. This added an element of distinct excitement to the proceedings, because there also happened to be a chain-link fence 10-to-15 feet behind me, running between our house and the neighbor's. From time to time, when the ball struck a spot where the wall met the foundation at the perfect angle and went flying, I'd race back to the fence and try to make a game-saving catch, punctuating the play with my own description of the dramatic moment.

In other words, I was like any kid who couldn't wait to get the morning paper to check out the box scores in the sports section and whose waking thoughts were filled with all things baseball. Growing up in my particular nook of America's heartland, I suppose it was inevitable that I would be consumed by the game. Even though we lived in Illinois, East Alton was perched just across the Missouri state line and the Red Birds were the hometown team by default. A short distance from our house, past the tracks of the Gateway Eastern Railway, you could hear the traffic rushing by on Route 3. The thoroughfare was officially known as Lewis and Clark Boulevard, named for the explorers who, in 1804, had set up camp in neighboring Wood River and begun their historic journey through the Louisiana Purchase and the distant Northwest. The boulevard—one of numerous local landmarks named for the famous frontiersmen—ran south along the Mississippi and virtually deposited you in St. Louis thirty miles away.

Living in Illinois had its own advantages from a baseball perspective. The ups and downs of Chicago's two big-league clubs 300 miles to the northeast—the Cubs and White Sox—could easily be followed on radio and television airwaves beamed down state. Yet I was pretty much on my own when it came to my baseball obsession. My father, Perry Staats, liked the game but he was far too busy supporting our family—which consisted at the time of my mother, Beulah, my baby sister Rita, my mom's younger sister Wanda and yours truly—to have the luxury of studying standings or hanging on the fate of any ball club. He was a child of the Great Depression and knew all too well what it was like when food and money were scarce. Consequently, he took his role as household provider very seriously.

He was born into a Missouri farming family, one of nine children and the third in the long line of Staats men given the first name of Perry. My great-grandfather was Perry. My grandfather was Perry but always went by his middle name, Francis. My father changed the pattern by sticking with Perry, and when I came along on Aug. 8, 1952, I became Perry No. 4 but was always known by my middle name, Dewayne.

My dad stayed at home into his early 30s to help his father work the 180-acre farm near the rural, map-dot city of Advance, Missouri. It had been a thriving railroad town in the late 1800s and got its name from settlers who insisted on moving further West—"advancing," as it were. Advance was some 140 miles due south of St. Louis (and, in a fitting coincidence, a distance in which the midway point was the country town of Perryville). My grandfather had raised livestock, planted and harvested crops and even operated a sorghum mill to make sweetener in the absence of sugar. And he bartered constantly to supplement his assets—trading processed sorghum for a pig, for instance. The old sorghum mill wasn't operating anymore by the time I came along, but my grandfather and father still grew, sold or traded all they could coax from the soil. It was simply what you had to do in order to survive.

My dad was 32 when he and my mom married. And he knew that options for earning enough to support a growing family were limited in Advance. It was a pleasant country burg of about 600 with a town square, a Western Auto, a Ben Franklin, the Advance Bank, a medical clinic where I was born, and not a whole lot more. My father decided there was better money to be made in steel work. Just about the time I was to begin first grade, he moved us across the Mississippi to East Alton, taking a job at the Laclede Steel Mill and eventually finding a new home on East George Street. The factory would one day re-emerge in my life some half a century later with a new name and significance that I will share later in these pages. But it will always be the place that conjures images of my father's iron will and work ethic, and the growing family he and my mother raised. By the time I turned 7, Rita was born, and five years later, our little sister Sheila came into the world.

I made friends easily in school and the neighborhood and played outside until my mother called us in for dinner. But even as a grade-schooler, I was conscious of how hard my father worked. He would spend a week on the day shift, leaving the house at dawn and getting home around 3:30 p.m. Next, he'd switch to the late shift, laboring from the afternoon until 10:30 or 11 at night—and then, the following week, do the midnight to 8 a.m. shift. He was constantly rotating, so there was never any way he could settle into any kind of regular schedule. Whenever he worked the overnight shift, my mother made sure that my sister and I kept quiet in the house during the day—making us go outside to play—so he could catch up on his sleep.

As I look back, it was a good introduction to disciplined behavior, and it also gave me an early appreciation for hard work. My father got four days off following the completion of his overnight stints, but often—instead of relaxing at our house—he'd take us all back to the farm just outside of Advance to visit my grandparents. Once we were there, Dad would get right to work fixing broken machinery or helping his parents with farming chores. There really were no days off in his world. Eventually, when Sheila was old enough to start school, my mom went to work, too. To supplement my father's earnings, she took a part-time job working at the cosmetics counter and as a cashier in the local pharmacy.

Not surprisingly, my father was very careful when it came to spending the money they earned. He wanted to make sure there was always enough cash each month to pay the mortgage and keep food on the dinner table. When the Hula Hoop craze first hit in the early '60s, I remember wanting one in the worst way. He regarded it as a frivolous purchase, but he eventually gave in and bought me one after my grandfather successfully took up my cause, stating much to my ever-lasting appreciation, "You should let the boy have a Hula Hoop."

Of course, my desire to own a Hula Hoop turned out to be considerably stronger than my interest in actually using one. I became moderately proficient at twirling the plastic band around my waist, the way they did on the cool TV commercials that caught my attention, but my preoccupation with the pop culture fad quickly faded. I was more interested in playing my made-up baseball games against the garage wall or enjoying elaborate games of Wiffle ball with Johnny and Mike, two brothers about my age who lived next door. On the side of their house was an open lot with a couple of big trees in the middle—and to us, a trio of baseball-crazy boys, it was our own field of dreams.

Even with the sizable obstacles posed by the trees on our diamond, we spent many hours after school and on weekends playing our games. We devised special ground rules that applied when the balls lined off a tree or launched into the branches, determining what was a hit and what was an out. You might say the place was a harbinger of the ballpark where I would one day go to work as an adult—Tropicana Field and its famously controversial catwalks. Needless to say, I was crushed when the father of my two baseball compadres decided to move his family back to the distant Missouri farm country they had come from. My first reaction was to wonder where on earth Johnny and Mike would be able to play baseball again, far removed from the paradise of our makeshift playing field. My second was to wonder how I'd get my fill of competition now that my two teammates had essentially been traded away for no players to be named later.

My baseball infatuation continued to grow nonetheless, as I discovered the joys of watching games on television and listening on radio. When I turned 9, the Cardinals were a middle-of-the-pack club in the National League—still three years away from becoming the team that would stun the New York Yankees in seven games to win the 1964 World Series. What really caught my attention that 1961 season was the grand finale, the World Series showdown between the Yankees and Cincinnati Reds. The

Yankees won an incredible 109 games guided by manager Ralph Houk to take the AL pennant in a season that featured the battle between Mickey Mantle and Roger Maris to break Babe Ruth's seemingly insurmountable single-season home run record of 60. Anybody who followed baseball knew about that and how Maris finally hit his fabled 61st homer on the final day of the regular season.

The Reds, meanwhile, didn't boast the same glamor or excitement. They'd won the National League pennant under manager Fred Hutchinson with a more modest 93 wins, finishing four games ahead of the Los Angeles Dodgers with the help of young stars like Frank Robinson and Vada Pinson, solid veterans such as Don Blasingame and a pitching staff that featured Jim O'Toole, Bob Purkey and Joey Jay—a 21-game winner celebrated as the first Little Leaguer to reach the majors. The Series shaped up as something of a David vs. Goliath showdown, and my allegiance lay strongly with the Reds. They were a National League team like the Cardinals, and Cincinnati wasn't all that far from our neck of the woods in southwest Illinois. I felt no love for the star-studded, big-city Yankees. I knew people were calling them one of the best teams ever assembled, but that made me pull for the Reds even harder. Unfortunately, my first experience pouring my emotions into a World Series ended in disappointment, as the Yankees dispatched the overmatched Reds in five games.

But the spectacle and thrill of watching the Series on our little black and white television set, with the action rivetingly relayed to my pre-double-digit ears by Mel Allen and Joe Garagiola, had me completely hooked. I couldn't wait for the next season to begin in 1962. When it finally did, I had developed a whole new routine for keeping up with ball games. My bedroom in our place on East George was near the front of the house, just off the kitchen, and since it wasn't next to the other bedrooms, I was afforded a little more privacy. The upshot of this was that after going to bed at 8 p.m. or so—way too early in my book, especially in the summer when it was practically still light outside—I could stay up and listen to a green plastic radio that plugged into the wall next to my bed.

I'd lie there at night, turning the dial and—to my complete amazement—be able to tune in baseball games from not just St. Louis but beaming in from across the vast night sky of the Midwest. Suddenly, a whole new world had opened up for me. I'd hear the distinctive voices calling the games—Jack Quinlan, Vince Lloyd and Lou Boudreau with the Cubs; Harry Caray and Jack Buck with the Cardinals—and feel like I was listening to friends bringing me into their own conversations.

I should underscore that growing up in the St. Louis metropolitan area, on the Illinois side of the Mississippi, made rooting for the Cardinals somewhere between a requirement and a birthright. Most of my friends were avid fans of the team, but that wasn't the case with me. Though I loved watching the Cardinals play, my heart and imagination had been captured by another franchise. To my delight, I discovered that my radio, as well as a portable Silvertone transistor, could reach out across the airwaves and capture the games of the brand new Houston Colt .45s.

As a devoted new student of the game, I was well aware that the National League had expanded in 1962. This meant increasing the number of games on its schedule from 154 to 162—something the American League had done a year earlier. And it also meant bringing National League baseball back to New York with the expansion Mets, filling the void left when the Giants and Dodgers left for California four years earlier. But to me, the big news was the creation of a new team: the Colt .45s. This was something to get excited about for a kid who had developed one big TV-watching pastime beyond baseball: Westerns.

Saturday mornings always meant watching episodes of *The Roy Rogers Show*, *The Lone Ranger* and best of all—*The Gene Autry Show*, featuring the Singing Cowboy. I wasn't even aware that Autry had become owner of the expansion Los Angeles Angels in 1961. I just knew he was one heck of a cowboy, a king of the Wild West—the action-packed world of heroes and villains that offered its own kind of magic. Now, here came the Colt .45s, a baseball embodiment of Gene and the Cowboy Gang, melding the mystique of Texas and baseball—and I was instantly hooked. There was something exotic about being able to listen to one of their games from so far away—and that cemented my allegiance even further.

I'd cross my fingers that the baseball trading cards I'd buy at our neighborhood grocery store—and rush to unwrap—would include a Colt .45s player. When it did, I'd read everything on the back of the card, committing to memory all the information about the player's history and career highlights.

I couldn't wait to get my hands on sports magazines that previewed the '62 baseball season to read about the Houston team, managed by Harry Craft and boasting a roster with such names as Bob Aspromonte, Joey Amalfitano, Bob Lillis, Dick Farrell, Ken Johnson and Hal Woodeshick—all new to me. I remember scouring one magazine and noticing how the pictures of the Colt .45s players didn't feature them wearing their new ball caps. The hats they wore in the photos featured logos from the teams they had just come from; in some cases, the logo was blanked out altogether. In my mind, that oddity set them even further apart from the pack. Though I'd tuned in a broadcast of the Colt .45s by accident, all those elements made me a fan—and, from then on, I kept tuning in.

As a result, a Gene other than Autry became a big part of my radio-listening routine. It didn't take long for me to recognize the warm, dignified tone of Colt .45s play-by-play announcer Gene Elston, standing out even amid the scratchy static of a broadcast originating 850 miles south. He became my nightly guide to the team—with such dramatic and detailed descriptions of the action that I could see the plays unfolding in my mind's eye. Gene was the one who unlocked the door to this world, and my affinity for the Colt .45s was soon entwined with the dependable, friendly voice bringing the team into my home from so far away. That is why I decided one day to write Mr. Gene Elston a letter, thanking him for doing such a fine job in the broadcast booth.

Lo and behold, several weeks later, an envelope arrived in our mailbox with a Houston postmark. I virtually ripped the envelope apart to see what was inside. My heart raced as I pulled out a letter and quickly unfolded it. There it was, on official Colt .45s stationery, no less: a letter from Gene Elston himself, thanking me for writing to him with such kind words and telling me to keep in touch. I couldn't wait to show the letter to my parents, who were excited that I had shown initiative by writing the letter in the first place—and had received such a nice response.

At barely 10, this was a true game-changer. My school friends and various family members might have been pulling like crazy for the Cardinals or perhaps the Cubs, but the Colt .45s were now my team and Gene Elston was my friend—and I had the personal letter to prove it. Naturally, I devoured every bit of information I could about the players as they slogged their way through the inaugural season, en route to a reasonably respectable first-year record of 64-96 and an eighth-place finish. I could take solace in the fact that it was still infinitely better than the woeful New York Mets, dead last among 10 teams with their laughably bad mark of 40-120—not to mention the Cubs, who had finished ninth at 59-103.

My preoccupation with baseball also extended to Little League. I began playing baseball in earnest about the same time and my father, in spite of being dog-tired from working in the steel mill, was always there to take me to all the practices and watch my games. He hadn't grown up playing baseball himself because he'd simply been too busy doing his chores on the farm. Getting the job done, doing his chores—that was his life. He had always known that he would have to work hard and he embraced it. The fact is, my father was the most honest, hard-working man I've ever known. And he always maintained a positive attitude with a sense of humor, something I think influenced me along the way, too.

Somehow, he managed to make working at the steel mill a positive experience and could always find reasons to laugh amid the grueling, often tedious routine. That said, Dad believed that sports was more or less an outlet rather than a serious pursuit. He was fine with my interest in playing and following baseball, but I'm sure he regarded it as simply child's play that I would eventually leave behind for a more serious vocation. Neither of my parents had earned a college degree, and they held high hopes I one day would achieve that goal and find a steady job in a respectable field, whatever that might be. Around this time, they signed me up for piano lessons, and I practiced every day, gradually learning to play well enough to sight-read basic songs. My dad's thinking was that if all else failed, I could always make money one day playing the piano for a living.

From the start, my parents instilled a strong work ethic in me and, later, my sisters. In spite of all the hours I'd devote to my burgeoning baseball interests, I was also expected to do my chores around the house, for which I earned what seemed like a whopping payday of a dollar per week. I was also fortunate—though I didn't really appreciate it at the time—to have parents who stressed the importance of a good education. They'd grown up in rural areas and spent countless hours working on farms to help their families make ends meet. As much as my father enjoyed farm work himself, and later always looked for the silver lining in factory work, he never wanted that life for me. He knew there was only so far a factory worker could go and didn't want me to live the non-stop grind that defined his daily life.

I'm sure that message seeped into my subconscious and I always took school seriously and brought home good report cards. But that didn't stop me from building on my new-found friendship with the man whose voice reached out through my plastic radio, bringing me a nightly narrative of the fledgling Colt .45s.

CHAPTER TWO

# Heeding the Call

I distinctly recall the first time I heard three engaging new voices beaming from the land of spurs and six-shooters. That game in 1962 featured a trio whose easy, amiable banter made me feel an instant connection. From then on, whenever the Colt .45s played a night game, I tuned in from the comfort of my bed to hear Gene Elston, Loel Passe and Al Helfer describe the trials and tribulations of Houston's expansion team.

Loel was more of a P.T. Barnum type in his over-the-top delivery, punctuated with cornpone phrases like "Hot ziggety dog and good ol' sassafras tea!" But I instantly was drawn to Gene's dignified, amiable and positive manner. He was straightforward and I liked that, too. Having hit the jackpot with one letter from him, I decided to keep writing. And that's what I did. During the next few seasons, I sent several letters asking what he thought about this or that player, and was even bold enough to suggest trades the struggling expansion team could make to improve their lowly lot.

Sometime during the 1964 season, while Houston was wobbling to a 66-96 record and ninth-place finish, I went a step further. The Colt .45s had started accumulating more recognizable names on the roster—Jimmy Wynn, Rusty Staub, Nellie Fox, a hot prospect named Joe Morgan, and power-hitting first baseman Walt Bond. That name struck a chord. As a devotee of the team, I had been devouring every weekly issue of *The Sporting News*, otherwise known as the baseball bible. I studiously read every nugget on the backs of baseball cards. Somewhere in the midst of my voracious consumption of baseball news, it came to my attention that Bond, a Tennessee native, listed his home as Alton, Illinois. He was in the process of leading the team in homers and I thought, "Wow, this is the greatest thing ever."

I promptly decided I should write to Gene and see if he could put me in touch with Houston's long-ball star. I guess I was a bit forward as kids go, because I also asked if he could send me Bond's home address so I could pay him a visit. Of course, I had no idea how I could possibly make such a trip. Alton was a daunting distance from East Alton for a boy relying on a bicycle for transportation. But I suppose I planned to ride the bike to wherever Walt Bond lived, get his autograph, and perhaps strike up a conversation. To his credit, Gene eventually wrote back and explained that he couldn't provide the player's address. But he did include a handful of player autographs I'd also inquired about—a gesture that made it easier to get over striking out in my attempt to meet a hometown star.

During that same season, however, I did connect with another ballplayer whose stature far exceeded that of Houston's home run hero. On May 27, 1964, my father took me to a night game at old Busch Stadium, a.k.a. Sportsman's Park. Walking inside the stadium at dusk bordered on a spiritual experience. Beneath the floodlights atop the stadium, colors took on a surreal quality—the perfectly manicured grass in the outfield and infield was somehow greener and thicker than anywhere else on the planet. It was like entering another dimension—made even more magical on this evening because I was about to watch a one-time Dodgers sensation playing in the waning stage of his career for the arch-rival San Francisco Giants—Mr. Duke Snider.

I was well aware of the Duke of Flatbush's many feats, including averaging 42 homers, 142 RBI and a .320 batting average between 1953-1956 for the old Brooklyn Dodgers. And I knew he was sure to be immortalized as a Hall of Famer, in spite of his dwindling numbers with the Mets in 1963 and now with the Giants. All of these elements fueled my excitement over having a chance to watch him play.

There was no shortage of other reasons for a heightened sense of intrigue besides the focus on the Duke. The Cardinals were tied for third with the Pittsburgh Pirates, each one full game behind the Philadelphia Phillies and the Giants. It was shaping up as a great race in the National League, and this game would showcase two of the league's best pitchers—hard-throwing Bob Gibson for St. Louis and high-kicking Juan Marichal for San Francisco. In addition, the night featured one of the game's most electrifying players, Giants centerfielder Willie Mays, chasing down fly balls under the lights flooding that resplendent grass.

My father and I had sat in the bleachers on previous trips to Busch Stadium. On one occasion, I'd been razzed by a Cardinals fan when my Colt .45s souvenir pennant slipped down its wooden stick, thereby assuming an inadvertent half-mast position during a drubbing by St. Louis. So I was thrilled when my dad decided to upgrade our seats this time and pay $2.50 apiece for reserved seats down the right field line.

My growing sense of excitement and anticipation quickly soared when, in the top of the first, two home runs rocketed through the illuminated sky in our general direction: one belted by Giants second baseman Chuck Hiller, the other by none other than Duke Snider himself. If that wasn't enough, when I saw Snider trotting out from the dugout in the bottom of the frame to take his position in right field, I realized that he was going to be playing directly in front of me. I had no way of knowing this was going to be Duke's final year in a big-league uniform. I thought he looked great standing out there in the Giants' colors, heavy on orange and black. I'm sure that Dodger fans wouldn't have agreed with my assessment, but that was of no consequence to me.

I watched his every move, the way he bantered and laughed while warming up with teammates. He seemed almost approachable, and I began to contemplate some sort of overture. My reveries were temporarily interrupted by another resounding crack of the bat. This time, it was a blast to left by Ken Boyer, cutting the St. Louis deficit to 2-1—an astounding third homer allowed by two of the game's best pitchers in the first few innings alone.

My thoughts soon returned to Snider and an impromptu plan to get his attention. I began repeatedly yelling his name, "Duke! Duke! Duke!" By the fourth, my auditory overtures remained unrequited. In the home half of the fifth, Snider resumed his place in right and I engaged my lungs once again, trying to make my voice low-pitched but still loud enough to carry through four rows of seats, over the bullpen and within earshot of No. 4. "Duke! Duke! Duke!" I implored, still with no success. My 11-year-old vocal cords were growing weary. But with two outs, as Marichal prepared to face Gibson, I decided to give it one more try. And when Gibson struck out to end the inning, it happened. In response to my last bellow, Duke Snider turned his head to the left, looked directly at me, raised his right palm and waved. I had made contact—a young, star-struck baseball fan had exchanged a glance with a major leaguer. Snider turned and jogged back to the dugout, but my gaze remained fixed on the spot where he stood when the magic moment materialized.

Looking back, a comparatively small crowd of 14,786 had watched the Cardinals fall 2-1 on a night two future Hall of Fame pitchers dueled memorably—Marichal striking out 11, Gibson allowing just five hits. We saw four other players on various points in their journey to Cooperstown: Mays, Willie McCovey, Orlando Cepeda, and Edwin Donald Snider. But what I'll always remember—more than Duke's game-winning clout off Gibson—was the simple yet powerful manner he connected with an elated kid. It was a little wave that would ripple for a lifetime.

Meanwhile, my favorite team was further cementing my love of the game. In 1965, Houston took a giant leap—moving from Colt Stadium into what folks were calling the eighth wonder of the world, the Astrodome. And with the move came a name change to the Astros. I wasn't thrilled with having to say farewell to the Colt .45 moniker and its Wild West imagery. But by now, I felt a strong allegiance to the club regardless of what they were called.

Along with the new home and name, a new broadcaster joined the team with Gene, Harry Kalas—a man with a captivating style and delivery I immediately enjoyed. It's funny how life can create some amazing bridges to connect past and present. Completely unbeknownst to me, Harry and his wife Eileen would become parents to a baby shortly after that '65 season—and 33 years later, Todd Kalas and I would be working together on the very first telecast team covering the expansion Tampa Bay Devil Rays, starting a friendship and professional association as Rays announcers that lasts to this day.

Back in the mid-'60s, I was just a kid with a growing interest in the voices that brought the game to life. In eighth grade, my homeroom teacher gave us an assignment to write a career essay. Predictably, I wrote mine on broadcasting and my desire to make it a career. Even at 13, I think I'd begun to realize that the road to becoming a major league ballplayer wasn't going to be an easy one.

I actually was a pretty good Little Leaguer, always one of the better players on whatever team I played for. I'd even tossed a no-hitter for a team called the Astros (My coach had offered naming rights to the first player who hit a homer in practice. I was the lucky player who knocked one deep, and instantly selected the name of my beloved big-league club). My accomplishment as a young pitcher was muted by the fact that I wound up losing the game. Ironically, the disappointing twist linked me inauspiciously to a member of the Houston Astros' staff, righthander Ken Johnson, who had become the first pitcher in major league history to lose a complete-game no-hitter—a bitter fate he suffered 1-0 against the Cincinnati Reds and Joe Nuxhall in 1964.

Despite my loss, the local paper ran a picture of me throwing the unusual no-hitter, and my grandfather carried the clipping for months, proudly pulling it out of his shirt pocket as a conversation piece whenever the chance presented itself. But my moderate pitching success didn't delude me. I'd seen far better players from our neck of the woods fail to make it to the minors, let alone the top level and I thought, "If they can't get to the majors, how am I going to make it?" And perhaps, even subconsciously, that's when I began to look at sportscasting as a more attainable path-way into baseball.

All the while, my relationship with Gene Elston continued to develop. In 1966, the Astros visited the new Busch Memorial Stadium in St. Louis, and I wrote Gene in advance, asking if there was a chance I could meet him. I was ecstatic when I received his note telling me that he would be glad to have me stop by the booth to say hello. I went to the stadium far more excited about my impending meeting than the Astros-Cardinals tilt. An hour before game time, I made my way up the steps toward the press box, waiting at the ramp to the booth, which was chained off and guarded by a security worker. Just as promised, Gene walked out after receiving word that I'd arrived and shook my hand heartily.

My butterflies about meeting the man whose voice I had only heard over the airwaves disappeared as we began to talk. Because I was an avid reader of *The Sporting News*, which contained every major and minor league box score during a given week, my head was filled with the latest statistics of every player on the big-league Astros and throughout their farm system. I arrived that day with a stack of note cards, on which I had jotted down ideas for possible trades Houston could make to better their standing in the National League, and I proposed various ones to Gene. He listened and obliged me with thoughts of his own. I couldn't believe that I was actually having a baseball conversation with the man who served as a conduit of the game's magic over the past four years. I could barely concentrate on the game after that, as my thoughts continued to replay my dream encounter—one that probably couldn't have lasted more than 10 minutes but had a profound impact on me going forward.

I continued to write to Gene on and off during that season—and that led to an even greater thrill the next season. He arranged for me to sit in the radio booth when the Astros were in St. Louis, and I actually got to help the Astros radio crew keep out-of-town baseball scores for use on the post-game show. It was there I met the dean of National League technicians, Bob Green, the Astros radio engineer. One day, as he was packing up all the equipment,

Bob gave me some advice. He said, "Son, if you get into this business, make sure you're on the other side of the microphone and not my side." I couldn't possibly imagine, at that moment, that I'd end up one day on the other side of the mic, and that Bob would become a lifelong friend. I only knew how surreal—and good—it felt, at only 15 years old, to suddenly be seeing baseball from the inside.

I attended East Alton-Wood River High, a school with good resources and an established track record for excellence. The number of unionized factory jobs in our little town made it possible for middle-class and blue-collar workers to earn a living wage, creating relative prosperity, and our economic well-being laid the base for the community's first-rate public education system. The entire system was top-notch—in fact, on par academically with far bigger and richer schools upstate in the Chicago and North Shore area. This meant that I was the recipient of a high school education offering a wide variety of tracks, from vocational to the fine arts to math and science.

Pre-testing was also part of the system, gauging a student's abilities and interests before entering high school. As it turns out, I'd tested particularly well for math and science, so my curriculum was heavy with those classes. That was all well and good, except for one thing: I really didn't enjoy math and science all that much. I was more interested in English and speech—and the types of courses that would help in a broadcasting career. Midway through my high school career, I went to my counselor and asked to switch to a communications-oriented track.

I had two great teachers in this new educational setting, Richard Claridge and Tom Fearno. They encouraged me once I changed my focus, suggesting that I participate on Wood River's debate team and take part in speech competitions. They also drafted me into speech competitions, which—much to my delight—included a category in radio speaking. They'd give us pages of wire copy and we were required to produce a five-minute newscast under deadline pressure. I was one of the students they zeroed in on, and I loved the challenge of speaking in a competitive format. I liked debating as well, and found I had a knack for it. We'd compete in tournaments, pontificating on hot national topics of the times, such as whether there should be a compulsory military draft or an all-volunteer army. We never knew until the last second which end of the spectrum we'd be defending—so we kept file boxes with quotes on both sides of the issue. It was a great experience that taught us how to think on our feet and learn how to prepare. Those skills came in handy when I decided to run for senior class president, convincing my fellow students to elect me as their advocate with the school administration. More than anything, debating was terrific mental training that would serve me well in the years to come.

I did make time, amidst the academic and extracurricular load, to keep my connection strong with the Astros and my handpicked mentor, Gene Elston. In my junior year, at age 16, I took a road trip to Houston with several classmates and an American history teacher. We talked to Gene before a game and he left us all tickets so we could stay and watch. We took another trip my senior year—this time driving to New York City to watch the Astros play the Mets at Shea Stadium.

I was 17 and I remember the adrenaline rush of driving us through the Lincoln Tunnel and into the big city, immediately fighting through a sea of Yellow Cabs on the way to our modest Manhattan lodging, the Times Square Motor Hotel. Later, we made our way to the considerably more upscale Roosevelt Hotel, where all the ballplayers stayed, along with Houston's broadcast team. We immediately ran into Gene and his booth colleague Loel Passe, who were kind enough to spend time talking to us and answering all our questions about the latest trials and tribulations of the Astros. And again, Gene left tickets for us. In the coming year, as I thought more seriously about a career in broadcasting, I'd occasionally send him letters asking for advice—and I'd always get a response from him. Looking back, I realize it was incredibly generous of Gene to give all that time to a nerd of a kid from East Alton and give him so much encouragement.

I shared a budding interest in broadcasting with my best friend, Frank Akers. We'd known each other since junior high school and always wound up playing on the same Little League teams. Frank and I pooled our meager resources one year and purchased a wildly popular baseball board game called APBA. It realistically replicated performances of major league players, and we spent countless hours managing our own teams.

Frank and I were part of a varied group of about eight guys at Wood River who hung out together. Some liked sports, some gravitated to traditional academics, some were into cars, some theater. Frank and I were the baseball freaks of the contingent, and when it came time to think about college, we both wanted to find a school where we could hone our radio skills. I knew there wasn't going to be a lot of money for college from my parents; wherever I went the burden of tuition would fall largely on me. Frank and I decided to look at the same colleges, and ones we could afford.

There was a small private school in Jacksonville, Illinois called Illinois College, with a nearby local TV station. We visited it together and then made a trip to Cape Girardeau, home of Southeast Missouri State. It was known as a teacher's college, but the town featured a number of radio stations we thought might offer part-time work. That looked promising, especially after we'd spent time on campus and weaseled our way into a few of the radio stations to talk with employees and scout out opportunities. I know my dad was hoping I would pick Southeast Missouri. By then, he was entertaining thoughts about moving back to the farm outside of Advance, Missouri and building a house before he got too old. If I chose Southeast Missouri, I'd be close by.

But my two trusted high school teachers, Richard Claridge and Tom Fearno, had another idea, suggesting we take a look at Southern Illinois University Edwardsville. It was only eight miles away, had a mass communications facility for its radio and TV program, and was about to launch its first student radio station, WSIE. In the back of my mind, I'd been thinking about larger, more prestigious Northwestern and the University of Illinois, but those institutions were a fair distance from my home. I was also concerned that I might get lost in a big program, just be another kid from downstate Illinois. Furthermore, I had no idea how I'd finance my way through either of those schools.

Frank and I followed up our teachers' advice, arranged a visit to SIUE—and we were sold. It felt like a perfect fit. With my strong academics, I was able to earn a grant from the Illinois State Scholarship Commission to cover some of my costs. And in the fall of 1970, off we went to start a new chapter in life.

From the first day I was on campus, you'd find me, more often than not, working at the radio station. Frank and I basically lived in the station—one of us was always there. Most of our work on air was unpaid, and I took on a student job in the station's music library to help cover expenses. But what a learning experience! I had the opportunity to edit tape, co-produce newscasts, and handle news and sportscasts at the mic. Frank and I even did WSIE's first play-by-play sports event, calling a football game at Edwardsville High School. The star player was a kid named Morris Bradshaw, who went on to play eight seasons as a wide receiver for the Oakland Raiders.

I guess you could say that autumn evening, sitting in the bleachers doing the high school play-by-play, marked the official starting point for what would become my calling. On radios throughout our town, my own voice was suddenly being carried over the night airwaves, bringing the action to life. And maybe somewhere, a little kid was tuning in and dreaming big.

CHAPTER THREE

# Tuning in to Romance

It didn't take long for life to fall into a familiar rhythm at Southern Illinois University Edwardsville—almost always revolving around new chances to refine my style at the microphone. There was barely enough time on any given day to do all the work I was tackling at the station, not to mention handling a full load of classes. But the environment was completely energizing, fueling my desire to learn everything I could and couple it with invaluable hands-on experience.

Frank and I continued to do our two-man broadcasts of high school football games during our first fall on campus. By the time basketball season started up, we shifted our operation to include courtside broadcasts at Edwardsville High's gymnasium.

About that time, we met another student, Dennis Sullivan, who was a little older than we were and also involved in SIUE sports broadcasts. He had already done some work on commercial radio in the area, and that impressed the heck out of two wide-eyed freshmen trying to forge ahead in the business. Dennis and a handful of other upper classmen at the station encouraged us to keep taking any jobs we could to sharpen our skills. And those new connections eventually opened the door to broadcasting additional football and basketball games at a small commercial radio station in Alton, WOKZ.

That was a considerably bigger deal than calling the action on the university airwaves. I wound up as a sophomore working football games on Friday nights and Saturday afternoons for the Alton station. Then, when basketball season rolled around, I'd call two or three games a week. Somehow, I managed to go to classes, earn decent grades, and still have energy to do some news reports and sportscasts at my school station, WSIE. On top of all that, during the spring and summer I co-managed a Little League team with Frank. As jammed as my daily routine was, it was precisely what I wanted. And there was an additional pursuit I happily squeezed into my overloaded schedule.

Dee Tsimpris was a beautiful, funny and bright student from East Alton-Wood River High, just a few miles away. She was a year behind me in school, and had made quite an impression when I'd met her during my senior year. As president of my class back then, one of my job duties was to escort the retiring queen from the prior school year to the school prom, though she wasn't technically my date. At the time—this being the early 1970s—I was in a rebellious phase of sorts and had decided to defy tradition and blow off the prom altogether. But Dee, who was serving on the prom committee, prevailed on me to attend and escort the departing queen. Dee was so charming and vivacious—how could I say no? She had her own date, and I wound up taking one of her best friends, Rhonda Tweedy, to the big dance. Dee and I maintained a casual friendship for the remainder of my senior year. I was so focused on beginning college and diving head-first into a broadcasting career that it didn't dawn on me that maybe I should ask this cute young woman out on a date.

My attitude changed during my first semester at college when a mutual friend of ours, a student named Dan Paquette, pulled me aside one day and said, "You know Dewayne, you should really ask Dee out." I'll always be grateful to Dan for the little kickstart to a relationship that would soon completely alter my life. I called Dee up one day from campus—she was now a senior in high school—and, much to my relief, she seemed pleased to hear from me. Our first date was a simple one. To make sure I impressed her sufficiently, I took Dee over to the campus radio station, where I just happened to be doing a weekly radio segment that evening, co-hosting a program on billiards.

I shared the show with a man on campus named Bill Hendricks, who was so good at the sport that he taught a billiards class for the school's physical education department. Our program was called "Cue Tips" and we'd talk about the history of different pool and billiard greats, with Bill analyzing different kinds of shots.

On that particular show we began discussing how the sport was great for female participation—not only a pastime for a bunch of guys hanging around the local pool hall. And on the spur of the moment, I asked Dee if she'd come on the air to represent the women's perspective. She knew enough about playing to feel comfortable obliging. And she was great—heck, I think she could have done the show herself.

After the broadcast, we went bowling at the student center. Conversation came easily and we enjoyed each other's company. That was the start of it all—we continued to see each other, and always had a good time.

As it turned out, an extra bond we had was that Dee knew her baseball—an interest that went back to her childhood. She was the oldest of three sisters in a tight-knit Greek family and spent hours in the backyard playing makeshift baseball games with her father and uncle. Her paternal grandfather was a Greek immigrant and eventually opened one of those old soda fountain and candy stores in Wood River. He made his own candy and even created a distributing business for it. Dee helped out in the store as a little girl, and that's where she developed her own connection to baseball over the radio airwaves. Often, when there was a major league game to tune in, her grandfather had the broadcast playing in the background, and Dee would listen intently, learning the players' names and the nuances of the game—and enjoying the colorful calls of a Cardinals fixture, Harry Caray.

It was no surprise that she developed a love for the sport and the Cardinals. As it turned out, Frank's girlfriend, Joyce, also was a baseball devotee. On many occasions, Dee and Joyce would come out to sit in the stands to watch us coach our team. Frank and I had been high school seniors in 1969 when we began coaching the Little League team at our childhood rec center. We loved the diversion it provided from the pressures of schoolwork, and we continued to manage all through college. There was something pure and refreshing about coaching and helping kids learn how to play the game we had grown up loving.

The squad we coached in high school was particularly green—they reminded us of Major League Baseball's latest expansion club, the San Diego Padres, who began play that same year, 1969. We decided that the logical choice of a name for our eager yet largely inexperienced group of 8-to-10-year-olds was the Padres. When we coached the team the next year, as SIUE freshmen, our kids were starting to show signs of improvement, finishing close to .500.

We weren't geniuses as managers, but we knew we had to develop our pitching in order to succeed—not unlike a certain ball club whose games I would broadcast decades later in Tampa Bay. We had one kid named Bobby Low, who could throw strikes, so we built the team around him and tried to develop another pitcher to fill out our staff. Using that approach, we managed to take a bunch of other little guys and match them up with what they could reasonably achieve.

Our aim was to allow them to experience a taste of success in some aspect of the game. For instance, we had one boy who was smaller than everybody else and couldn't hit, but could fly on the bases. We taught him not to swing at bad pitches and to bunt. He'd bunt his way on or walk and be on third base two pitches later. That was typical of the kind of thing we'd try to do with the kids, hoping they'd leave the field feeling good about themselves—and have some fun, too.

With Dee at the games, it was all the more fun for me. She even put up with my continual habit of tuning in the big-league Astros amid the night-time radio static on San Antonio's WOAI or WWL in New Orleans so I could follow the fortunes of my favorite team. But my passion for the game was about to take on a whole new form—and it wasn't long before my own voice would begin to find a home on professional baseball broadcasts. The minor leagues soon beckoned, serving as a gateway to the career I dreamed of, accompanied by the woman I loved.

In the summer following our sophomore year, Frank and I decided to take a road trip to see what contacts we could make in the minors over two or three days. We hopped in my car, first visiting the Evansville Triplets of the American Association, a team whose announcer was popular institution Marv Bates (Marv would tragically die in the airplane crash that killed the entire Evansville basketball team in 1977). He was very kind to us, and offered to reach out to anyone on the club staff he could on our behalf.

Meanwhile, the Oklahoma City 89ers—the Astros Triple-A farm team—were playing a series in Indianapolis at old Bush Stadium, and that became another must stop. After arriving, I tracked down Larry Calton, the colorful radio guy for the 89ers who would become a member of the Minnesota Twins broadcast team several years later. Larry came from Springfield, Missouri and was a genuine character—an announcer with a folksy, high-energy delivery that was a hit with listeners and mirrored the style of Harry Caray. I struck up a conversation with him before the game and told him about my career aspirations. And without missing a beat, Larry jumped in with an invitation.

"Why don't you come on up to the radio booth and join me for the game?"

I hadn't expected to hit a home run on my first at bat. But the best was yet to come. Perhaps Larry wanted to give me a break or just take one himself. Whatever the case, he let me call a few innings of Triple-A baseball as a guest announcer. It happened so quickly I didn't have time to feel any jitters. In fact, I felt right at home at the mic. I'll always be grateful to Larry for offering me that unexpected opportunity right out of the box. Looking back, I guess you could say that I was simply following an emerging life pattern of doggedly chasing my baseball dreams—just as I had unknowingly done as a persistent kid, striking up my penpal friendship with Gene Elston, deciding I'd bicycle to Walt Bond's house in Alton, and relentlessly calling out to Duke Snider from the stands until he turned around. Now that same straightforward approach from my youth was putting me in position to win as a young man trying to make my own breaks.

I stayed in contact with Larry, who went on to work in Wichita before getting his big break with the Twins. (Years later, having moved to Los Angeles to try his hand at acting, Larry wound up broadcasting Pepperdine basketball games and somehow got slapped with a technical foul while calling the action in one contest—always the character.) Thanks to our friendship, I'd learned ahead of time that he would be leaving his job at Oklahoma City sometime at the end of the 1972 season.

That gave me a valuable jump at throwing my name in the hat with 89ers general manager Dick King. During the winter of '72 and into 1973, my junior year, I made a real pest out of myself calling Dick about the job. I sent him letters and mailed him tapes of my work, including calling the SIU Edwardsville games from the NCAA Division II College World Series in the spring of 1972. I don't remember dialing his number every week, but it was pretty close to that. To Dick's credit, he'd always take my calls and listen to me make my case. I really think that I became such a pain in his neck that he finally relented and said to me, "All right, come on out."

I couldn't believe it. My tried-and-true formula of good-natured persistence and networking had succeeded in landing my first minor league job. I'd have to put off finishing my senior year of college until the off-season, but I decided that would be no problem.

Still, there was a formidable obstacle to overcome before Oklahoma City would become a reality. Dee and I had become very serious in our relationship by now, in spite of my mountain of commitments at school and work. At SIU Edwardsville, I'd earned one of our mass communication department's first internships, leading to long hours at KMOX radio station in St. Louis. I was still calling high school football and basketball games for the little radio station in Alton, which now had added regular sportscasts to my studio assignments. To make that schedule work, I'd record a generic sportscast in the morning for the station to air during the afternoon.

In order to meet all my obligations—between going to the two radio stations, taking classes and trying to carve out time for Dee and me to see each other—I adopted a schedule of sleeping in two shifts of three hours. We would usually get together at random times during the week, but often late on a Sunday night. Our big deal would be to order a pizza and eat it on her parents' back porch under the stars.

Dee had gone right into the work force after high school during a difficult time for the Tsimpris family. Dee's mother had been diagnosed with breast cancer several years earlier, and though she appeared to be recovering well, Dee still wanted to be close to home and help out any way she could. She chose to defer college and take a job as an office assistant in a munitions supply company. Then along came my opportunity with Oklahoma City, and suddenly Dee's parents wanted to know about the status of our relationship. True to their traditional Greek Orthodox heritage, they weren't about to give their blessing to their oldest daughter following me off on my new adventure.

"What are you going to do if Dewayne goes to Oklahoma City for the baseball season?" her mother asked.

"Well, I'll go out to see him whenever I can," Dee replied innocently.

"What? And not be married?" replied her mother.

Suddenly, the topic of marriage was front and center. Dee and I had already talked about spending our lives together, but now there was an accelerated timetable. We countered that we would get married after the 1973 season. But there was simply no way Dee's parents would agree to letting her spend time visiting Oklahoma City without a wedding in the equation.

Consequently, as soon as my job was formalized, plans for our nuptials fell into place for a late March wedding—only a couple of weeks before the 89ers' season was to begin. Bear in mind: This was during Lent, a time of year when the Greek Orthodox Church forbids celebrations. But Dee's mother was not to be denied. She and her husband requested special dispensation from the church to hold the wedding. Fortunately, there was a loophole. Greek Independence Day fell on March 25, so church officials agreed to let the wedding take place on the festive holiday.

We had quite a celebration of our own. The family staged a big Greek wedding and did so on hardly any notice. Dee's mother made her daughter's dress and everything came together perfectly. All her family and friends were there, partied heartily and immediately took me into the fold. Our two families created what might have been a comical contrast: a lively, boisterous Greek clan doing traditional circle dances and a reserved farm family. I can imagine it as a precursor to the movie *My Big Fat Greek Wedding*. But truthfully, everybody had a wonderful time and felt delight in the bride and groom's happiness.

The rush precluded any possibility of a honeymoon. (That would have to wait until after the baseball season when we spent a week in Clearwater, a quarter-century before the tropical area and a new franchise named the Tampa Bay Devil Rays would lure us back.) Nine days after we became man and wife, I was driving off to Oklahoma City to begin my dream job in the booth.

Dee stayed home to tie up loose ends and then came out for a short visit. But as soon as she returned home, her mother's health took a sharp and unexpected turn for the worse. The cancer had apparently spread to her lungs. Several weeks later, I took time off from the job and drove back to Alton expecting to attend a funeral. But when I got there, Dee's mom had rallied remarkably and was able to leave the hospital. Still, Dee decided it was best she stay back home with her mom while I drove back to Oklahoma to learn the ropes of my new job.

I realized quickly that doing broadcasts was the fun part of the work with the 89ers, like recess at school. The rest of the staff and I did virtually everything else that needed to be done to run a minor league club. The whole crew pitched in. We cleaned the ballpark, painted the ballpark, wrote the press releases, distributed tickets—whatever was required short of trying to get a base hit for the team. I could hose down and sweep a ballpark with the best of them.

The 89ers were a mix of quasi-major leaguers and career farm-team players in the Cleveland Indians organization. Our manager, Frank Lucchesi, was the real deal. He'd been fired by the Philadelphia Phillies after serving as their skipper from 1970-72, and still wanted to manage. We basically had a veteran team, including "4-A" guys who had played in the majors or were hoping to get a taste of big-league life. Ozzie Blanco, a righthanded-hitting first baseman from Venezuela, belted 20 homers for us in a big ballpark with double-decked outfield fences, and an outfielder named Tommy Smith hit about .340. We had some other good players—like Mike Hedlund, a major leaguer with Kansas City trying to pitch his way back. He got a lot of attention because he was paid $27,000, which everyone thought was an outlandish amount. Later, our roster featured Alan Ashby, Duane Kiper and Rick Manning, and all three not only had long big-league careers but also all became big-league broadcasters.

Despite the talent, the 89ers were a bit of a disappointment, finishing in the middle of the pack. But for me, it was an immeasurable hands-on experience. One aspect of the job I had to master—and came to enjoy—was doing game recreations for certain Oklahoma City road games that we didn't broadcast live.

In those cases, Frank Marx, the 89ers ticket manager, and I would go to a radio studio in town and do a faux game broadcast over the airwaves. Frank would sit inside the office and place a call to a contact he had in the press box at whatever town the 89ers were playing in and scribble down notes on a yellow legal pad of what had transpired during the inning. For instance, he wrote in one game on June 2, 1973:

Smith—walk.

Johnson—walk, Smith—2.

Ford—Ground rule double (1 RBI), ball bounced, hit light pole and bounced back into the park; Smith—scores. Johnson—3.

Blanco—Ground ball to Tatis at 3rd, threw high to plate trying to get Johnson (1 RBI). Fielder's choice. Johnson—scores; Ford—3.

Then he'd hand me the piece of paper and I'd dramatize the action I read on the paper, adding proper inflection, embellishing a little by describing balls and strikes—though I didn't really know the count, and maybe adding in an argument or two along the way. I also kept a reel-to-reel tape recorder by my side, so I could play a loop of crowd noise for atmosphere. As a youngster, Frank listened to baseball recreations in New York City after the Giants and Dodgers left for California in the late 1950s—and got a huge kick now out of being part of the show. He's very kind in his assessment of my theatrical performance.

"I was awed, stunned that this kid who was new to the business could do these recreations," he recalls. "He was sitting there in front of the deejay equipment, seeing a baseball game in his mind and reporting on it like he was in the ballpark. I don't know where a guy would learn how to do that, but Dewayne clearly knew his baseball and just had a natural talent for this. Even at a young age, he had the perfect baseball voice—an inviting Midwestern accent that made you feel very comfortable listening."

My first year in Oklahoma City was total immersion into all things baseball at the professional level—and learning from the master: Dick King. He was a great guy and told me something I'll never forget: "Preparation is 95 percent of the job. And for a young broadcaster in the minors, always be ready for that first opportunity because you may never get another chance."

Dick, as I soon found out, was of Greek heritage and interested to learn that my newlywed wife had the same roots. He'd been a catcher in the minors, and—because he felt there was some prejudice against Greeks—changed his name to King from Kerabatsos. His mother was still alive though she spoke little English, and whenever Dee came to visit, she made sure to spend time sitting with her, conversing in Greek.

Anyone who worked for Dick knew he could be hard-nosed and demanding at times. But as I see it, you can learn a lot—and gain self-esteem—from meeting the challenge of a demanding situation. I was grateful to Dick for the opportunity he gave me, and also appreciative of the chance to go through "Dick King's Boot Camp."

After the '73 season, I resumed my studies at SIU Edwardsville. The school operated on the quarter system, allowing me to continue work during the off-season on my mass communications degree. All the pressure of back-and-forth responsibilities did carry a price. I came down with a brutal case of mononucleosis during my first offseason and, for the first time in my life, wound up in a hospital. If you recall, I wasn't even born in one—I came into the world in a little rural clinic. Dee's mother, Elizabeth, having beaten the odds and regained her strength, was often there by my side to make sure I had whatever I needed.

Once I had recovered and was back at 100 percent strength, I began looking forward to the start of my second season with the 89ers. But I never expected the turn of events that followed. Suffice it say, the 1974 season was a complete fiasco, in spite of the invaluable baseball education it provided me.

During the '73 campaign, Dick ran the club for a Tulsa oilman named Phil Dixon, but new ownership took the reins in '74: A local car dealer with a son reminiscent of Lumpy Rutherford, the oafish, daddy's boy character on the TV classic, *Leave It To Beaver*. The son always hung around the ballpark and part of the reason his father bought the team, it seemed to me, was to give the young man something constructive to do. He became our traveling secretary, which probably made us the only minor league team to have someone solely devoted to that job. Back then, everyone wore multiple hats—on many teams, the trainer might double as traveling secretary. But the new owner had his own agenda, tailored to keeping his son occupied. And not unexpectedly, Dick King wanted no part of the arrangement and decided to leave, soon becoming general manager of the Triple-A Wichita Aeros.

King's replacement as GM was Fred Minton, a born-again Christian who'd played briefly in the Orioles farm system. Meanwhile, former major league journeyman outfielder Don Demeter bought a partial interest in the team and did some of the color commentary at home games. The first problem arose when Fred, who didn't believe in alcohol consumption, banned beer sales from the ballpark. That was not exactly a popular move with many of the fans or a wise move for financial success. Fred's heart was in the right place with many things he did as GM, but let's face it: You can't throw beer out of a minor league ballpark and expect people to come. As you might guess, not many did.

I found myself caught in the middle of the whole mess. I was back home working on getting more credits toward my college degree when I learned the team had been sold. Unsure of my role with the new group, I put some money together and drove 800 miles to Houston to attend the Winter Baseball Meetings in December 1973.

My purpose was to introduce myself to Fred and his partners and emphasize that I wanted to return to the 89ers broadcast booth. We all went to dinner at a Chinese restaurant across the street from the Astrodome. I immediately knew Fred was a little different when the waiter asked him what he wanted to drink, and there, in the middle of a Chinese restaurant, he asked for buttermilk. I'm pretty sure that was a first in that eatery, or in Chinese restaurants, period. The good news was they definitely wanted me back in the booth in 1974. But once the season got underway, things began to sour like a glass of Fred's curdled buttermilk.

The owner's son lived in a townhouse and, according to word on the street, a young man and woman he'd let stay there for a time were on the run from the law. Rumor had it that the female guest had helped spring the guy, and somehow they both wound up staying with good old Lumpy. I thought to myself, "Really?" I began to feel I was in the midst of a baseball sitcom. In addition, we learned, Fred was not only the general manager but had experience as a counselor—and part of his current job responsibility was to work with the son, trying to help him walk the straight and narrow. But things clearly weren't working on that front. Nor were they working out for the team.

It was becoming evident that we were following a course toward disaster. Fred's no-beer policy assured that revenues took a beating, and he was fired before the season ended. Owen Martinez, the former traveling secretary of the Houston Astros, was brought in to replace Fred as our new GM but things were already spinning out of control by then. I realized I had no future in Oklahoma City and began considering the possibility of contacting Dick King about a job in Wichita. But my decision to leave was made for me before that could happen. I was actually in Wichita three or four weeks before the end of the season, getting ready to broadcast an 89ers-Aeros game. The telephone hookup back to Norman, Oklahoma was in place and I was on the line when I was abruptly informed that this would be the final 89ers broadcast.

I can't say I was shocked, given the direction events were moving, but it was not the most pleasant way to hear that my season was ending early. I couldn't believe that Martinez hadn't even bothered to tell me. I was in a tough spot. I wasn't earning a lot—about 600 bucks a month—but every dollar counted for me and my new bride back home. I returned home three weeks earlier than planned—frustrated and discouraged, but also a bit relieved to escape from the mounting mess. I reminded myself that I was still just 21 and had two years of Triple-A broadcasting experience under my belt. It was time to confer with Dee, to think about finishing my last year of college and to figure out a new plan of action for returning to a minor-league broadcast booth.

Despite the inglorious end to my first foray into professional baseball broadcasting, I felt lucky to have met some wonderful folks. One of the many people whose paths I crossed during that time, and with whom I formed a friendship, was Wichita manager Jim Marshall, a former big-league first baseman with the Orioles, Cubs, Giants, Mets and Pirates.

Jim, a native of Danville, Illinois, was working his way up the managing ladder in the American Association, a year away from becoming a coach for the Chicago Cubs. We would eventually

CHAPTER FOUR

# A Princely Opportunity

Though my budding baseball announcing career had been dealt an unexpected blow, I was sure that I'd be able find work elsewhere in the minors when the 1975 season rolled around. And once I returned home, there was no time to dwell on the bizarre turn of events in Oklahoma City.

I resumed work on my remaining classes at SIU Edwardsville and did some local sports play-by-play for the college radio station, WSIE, as well as the small station in Alton, WOKZ. I also took a broadcast performance class—putting together a newscast and sportscast in the school's practice television studio and refining my on-air delivery. Since my only professional experience to date had been on the radio, I figured I might as well try to polish my skills in case an opportunity arose to find work on TV. In its own way, that class literally changed everything.

The two cameramen in the class were TV veterans who had worked commercially in the local market, and one of them approached me after I'd finished taping a practice news show. "You know, you were pretty good there—you ought to send that tape around to some of the stations," I recall him saying. That hadn't dawned on me, but his encouragement gave me a lift, and I decided I might as well follow his advice. Coincidentally, another adjunct member of the school's broadcast program, Jim Winkle, had done some directing at a growing independent TV station in nearby St. Louis—KPLR—and passed along a tip. Jim knew the head of KPLR production, Bernie Corno, who had told him that the station was searching for a booth announcer and in the process of creating a local newscast.

I could not believe how circumstances had conspired to create what looked like a phenomenal television opportunity, fresh on the heels of my minor league radio fiasco—and I rushed my tape to the station. As background, the company was owned by a high-profile hotel magnate and entrepreneur in St. Louis named Harold Koplar, whose surname inspired the call letters of his station, KPLR. He also owned the Chase Park Plaza Hotel, where all the visiting major league teams stayed—and, in addition, a resort in the Lake of the Ozarks.

Harold had two sons, Robert and Ted. Robert was a brilliant businessman who had died tragically young, in his mid-30s, of a heart attack. Ted grew up around the station, working in virtually every department on his way up the ladder to president. He and his GM, Hal Prodder, watched the tape I'd sent over and apparently liked what they saw. Within days, they brought me in for an interview—and offered me a job.

Here I was, now just 22, and another incredible door had opened—this one in TV, despite my lack of any previous on-air experience in front of the camera. Somehow, my persistence with Dick King had helped me jump right to the top-rung of minor league broadcasting at the Triple-A level. And now, thanks to some fortuitous contacts in my broadcast performance class, I'd been put in position to move into TV—the missing element of my resume—and do so in one of America's great sports towns, a major market. Dee and I were ecstatic, and couldn't help but think there was a helping hand from above at work in all of this.

Landing the job had the added benefit of keeping me close to SIU Edwardsville, allowing me to finish my degree in 1975. I'd attend classes, do my papers and homework—and then head off to KPLR in my initial role as booth announcer. In those days, local TV stations still utilized booth announcers to break in on the hour with a station ID. In my case, the job required intoning in a deep, polished voice something to the effect of: "You're watching KPLR TV, Channel 11 in St. Louis, Missouri." That's basically what I did while the station built its news operation from the ground up. Once the KPLR news show made its debut—airing at 9:30 p.m. throughout the week ahead of the other stations in town—I moved into the job as sports anchor.

I loved the work, which included the entertaining contributions of sports reporter and St. Louis Cardinals closer Al "The Mad Hungarian" Hrabosky. Al, who worked with us in the off-season, was much more mild mannered than his animated mound presence suggested (and I'm proud to say his broadcasting career began with us, eventually leading to his current position in the Cardinals' TV booth). The station proved itself to be a feisty competitor on the local scene—as well as something of a trailblazer. KPLR employed several progressive news execs who pushed the technological envelope. We were one of the first TV stations in the country to install a satellite receiver, replacing landlines. We could get news feeds and programming feeds from all over the country on our receiver—a technological advancement that gave me access to endless sports highlights and proved enormously helpful to my sportscast.

In addition, an increasing number of baseball teams traveling to St. Louis chose to forgo setting up their own hardlines for transmitting games—and instead utilized the satellite at our station to beam the action back home. That allowed me to get all the baseball video snippets I could possibly want, mostly from visiting teams, and use them on my nightly segment. I was like a kid in a candy store. All you needed to do was give proper credit and you were good to go. For instance, when the Houston Astros were slated to come to town for a series against the Cardinals, I'd get permission from Art Elliott, the Director of Broadcasting for the Astros, to pull highlights for my sportscast. And I'd wind up airing far better game visuals on my report than my competitors in the market.

The added benefit of this arrangement was the opportunity it gave me to form a working relationship with Art, a front office exec of the Astros, a team that was still very close to my heart. I could also keep up with the steady, familiar baseball voice of Gene Elston, now broadcasting Houston's games with another legendary announcer, Bob Prince. For three decades, Bob had been the much-recognized voice of the Pittsburgh Pirates on KDKA, as well as for the Steelers and Penn State football in the

1950s. A feud with radio management, Westinghouse, had led to his firing in 1975, angering many Pirates fans and even some of Pittsburgh's players. But there was no turning back, and Bob landed a spot in the booth alongside Gene—replaced in Pittsburgh by another baseball broadcasting icon, Milo Hamilton.

The intersection of these three eventual Hall of Fame baseball broadcasters would ultimately have a direct impact on my career path. The first step in the chain occurred one night in 1976 when I was driving home from the station and picked up an Astros signal on my car radio. I immediately recognized Prince's distinctive gravelly voice, but sounding uncharacteristically flat and disinterested. There was none of the lively banter or folksy weaving of baseball stories for which he was known with the Pirates—just bare bones play-by-play: "That's strike one. ... That's a ball. ... Strike two. ... That's another ball." And I thought, "It doesn't sound like things are going very well down there. I wonder what the story is with that?"

A few nights later, while working in the KPLR newsroom, it suddenly all made sense. Word came across the KPLR wire machine—the kind that automatically typed out Associated Press and United Press International stories at a rapid-fire speed—that Bob Prince was heading back to his beloved Pittsburgh to broadcast the NHL games of the Penguins. Nobody had to tell me what that meant: the Astros would be looking for a new partner to pair with Gene Elston for the 1977 season.

Maybe, I thought, that person could be me. It wouldn't hurt that I had developed a connection with Art Elliott during the past two years, securing permission to air Astros footage on my sports report in St. Louis. In the process, Art had also become aware of my back story—that I'd done two years of play-by-play in Triple-A, had followed the Colt .45s-turned-Astros avidly through the years, and had developed a long-distance friendship with the incomparable voice of the team, Gene Elston.

I had never stopped keeping up a correspondence with Gene. As a kid, my agenda was geared to seeking player autographs, asking if he knew where Walt Bond lived in Alton—or picking his brain about Astros trade scenarios I'd envisioned. I remember once asking him, "Hey Gene, I hear the Astros had a chance to sign Tony Oliva; how could they not do that?" He could easily have brushed me off as an annoyance, but always answered my questions. And as my career began to take shape, I continued to seek his advice—most recently about broadcast techniques. For example, I'd asked him how enthusiastic should one sound on air, and his response was valuable: "Your enthusiasm will come through, but you should never manufacture it, or it won't be authentic, and people will know."

Even at this stage of my professional development, I was still picking Gene's brain about potential player transactions for the team, as if I were the general manager. "The Astros have this guy in the minors still," I'd ask. "What's the story?" And now, I had a new question for him. If I applied for the job, did he think I'd have any shot? I realized it might sound audacious for a 23-year-old sportscaster—with no Major League Baseball announcing experience whatsoever—to even consider applying for the job vacated by the one and only Bob Prince. But the more I thought about it, the more I knew I had to take a swing at this unexpected opportunity.

I tracked Gene down as quickly as I could and he confirmed that the Astros were already in the process of auditioning possible replacements. I remember him saying, "If they're putting those guys on the air, why shouldn't you get a shot?" That's all I needed to hear. I reached out to my other Astros' contact, Art Elliott, and then spoke to Dean Borda, Houston's head of broadcasting. They were both sufficiently intrigued by this eager young broadcaster—with a blend of minor league radio and local TV sports experience—to agree to a live audition. In a span of only three days, plans were made for me to fly to Chicago and do a radio audition for an Astros-Cubs game at Wrigley Field—for the record, August 26, 1976. I'd not only be working alongside my idol, Gene—but also with the crusty legend whose decision to leave the Astros created the opening in the first place, Bob Prince. Talk about pressure, mixed with giddiness.

I arranged to take that Thursday off from work and began my preparations for the trip without telling my bosses. The only person at KPLR who knew about the audition was a good friend, Gil Engler, who also attended SIU Edwardsville and now worked in the newsroom as a writer. The advice that Dick King had shared with me in my first year in Oklahoma City echoed in my head as I arrived at the hallowed ballpark on Chicago's north side: When you get your big chance, don't mess up because the opportunity might not come again.

I settled in hours before game time in the press lounge known as the Pink Poodle, writing out notes about various players and their key statistics, and underlining any nugget about the two teams that would help distinguish me in the tryout. Prince noticed me and walked over, offering reassurance in his rough-hewn timbre. "Don't worry kid, we'll screw this up together." It was a class move by an old pro, trying to loosen up the kid with a little humor. I laughed, then got back to my notes. Soon enough, Gene walked by and explained how it would work.

"Don't worry," he said. "You'll do most of the game with me and we'll work it all out." Despite their efforts to settle me down, it was impossible not to feel jittery at the thought of calling a game with the towering—if short-lived—team of Elston and Prince.

I felt confident in my knowledge of the Astros. It wouldn't be a problem expounding on the strengths and weaknesses of the team, which was on its way to an 80-82 finish in the middle of the NL West pack. They had a strong rotation with pitchers like J.R. Richard, Larry Dierker and Joaquin Andujar, along with such name position players as Bob Watson, Jose Cruz, César Cedeño and Roger Metzger. But the Cubs were another matter entirely. I had a working knowledge of the club but wasn't plugged in to the nuances of the lineup or pitching staff. I needed more information, and during batting practice, I headed down to the field to see what helpful background I might be able to gather for use in the broadcast.

I knew I had one potential ace in the hole—former Wichita manager Jim Marshall, who had left the Aeros in 1973 and joined the Cubs coaching staff in '74. Midway through a dismal season, Chicago manager Whitey Lockman was fired and Jim took over as skipper. I hadn't seen him in three years and knew he would be tied up before the game talking to the Cubs beat writers, and perhaps some from Houston. But I sought him out on the field, and he seemed both surprised and pleased to see me. When I explained the circumstances of my presence, Jim didn't hesitate.

He motioned me to follow him into the Cubs' clubhouse—past players talking at their lockers and clusters of writers looking for notebook material—and directly into his office. He settled in behind his desk and offered me a seat across from him—and then, out of the goodness of his heart, proceeded to give me a detailed scouting report of his entire team. He intuitively understood what this moment meant to me, and—I believe—respected me as a hard-working, diligent radio guy from Triple-A ball. For a young broadcaster in need of a break, Jim's analysis of his players and team was pure gold. I scribbled as fast as I could to get his thoughts down on my notepad. As I wrote, I couldn't help but remember that this was a player whose baseball card I owned as a young kid when he was a left-handed hitting first baseman for the Mets.

When Jim finished, I shook his hand and thanked him for going out of his way to help educate me. I headed upstairs to join Gene and Bob in the booth, now feeling well-armed with valuable insights into both the Astros and the Cubs—and anxious to get my make-or-break audition for the big leagues rolling. For the record, J.R. Richard was on the mound for the Astros facing Rick Reuschel, and the Astros jumped out to a 4-0 lead in the first two innings. Richard had good stuff, allowing only five hits in 8⅓ innings as Houston held on 5-3. I'd managed to hold on, too, feeling a mix of relief and accomplishment. As we packed up, I told myself, "I think you did a pretty good job here." I knew I'd prepared as well as I possibly could. I hadn't made any distinguishable flubs and felt I'd worked well with Gene and Bob throughout the game.

I rode on the Astros' team bus back to the airport and grabbed a flight back to St. Louis, replaying the broadcast in my head. I was convinced I'd given them a solid representation of what I could do, and—as badly as I wanted the job—knew all I could do now was wait and see. Gene had maintained a low-key demeanor. When he told me, "You were good," I wasn't aware at the time that such a comment actually translated into high praise. Dee and I had an apartment by now near St. Louis, about 30 miles from KPLR, and she was excited to hear how everything had gone. But the days and weeks passed with no word from Houston, and I quickly fell back into the fast pace of my work at the television station.

My boss Ted Koplar was always solidly in my corner, trying to create more opportunities for me. In addition to my nightly sportscasts, I did some play-by-play for our coverage of the St. Louis Stars of the old North American Soccer League, whose marquee player—Brazilian superstar Pele—joined a cavalcade of foreign "football" standouts to help the sport gain a foothold in the States as the league's marquee player.

Ted sent me to New York City to do a telecast in Yankee Stadium, where the Stars took on the powerhouse Cosmos. The NASL's glamor franchise featured the aging but still entertaining Pele and Italy's sensational striker, Giorgio Chinaglia, who would go on to become the league's all-time leading scorer. Our crew stayed at the five-star Pierre Hotel in Manhattan, where the room service price of a hamburger—a whopping amount in the neighborhood of $15—made my jaw drop. The big thing I remember about the Stars team was that they had a goaltender from England named James Bond, and the team gave him a jersey with 007 on the back—typical of the lively marketing for which the fan-friendly league was known.

KPLR also carried games of the hometown NHL team, the St. Louis Blues, simulcasting the coverage on KMOX radio. The play-by-play man was Dan Kelly, one of the great hockey announcers of all time. Fans could tune in to hear him call the Blues games either on TV or radio. Ted wanted to do away with the simulcast format and have me become the television play-by-play guy for the Blues, with Dan handling radio. I thought, "This may not be such a good idea—it would be a great opportunity for a young announcer, but it also could be a death knell."

I'm not saying that I couldn't have handled the assignment. I'd have prepared myself, as always, and done a credible job. But I was not an adequate replacement for Dan Kelly—not by a long shot. My gut feeling was that we'd anger countless listeners in the Midwest and parts of Canada who loved hearing him describe the action. And I don't think they'd have taken kindly to a new kid bumping him from the booth.

Though Ted worked behind the scenes to try to make it happen, the plan failed to gain the necessary traction—and boy, was I ever relieved. My career might have been over before it started and I'd have been selling real estate, if Blues fans had anything to say about it. But there were plenty of other ways for a newcomer like me to make a mark and gain recognition. I was nominated for a local Emmy for my sportscast—much to my excitement. And another show—one that I co-anchored with Ted's wife, Nancy Scanlan—actually did win an Emmy. Still, none of the unfolding opportunities and experiences compared to the possibility of getting a crack at calling games for the Astros.

Finally, when the baseball season ended in late September, I got a call. The Astros wanted me to travel to Houston to be interviewed by Art Elliott and Dean Borba. Another man would also be present at the interview—powerful general manager Tal Smith, and I took that as an encouraging sign. But I arrived in Houston with my hopes in check, not knowing who else might be competing for the job. We all went to lunch at the Astroworld Hotel, and Tal turned to me with a question. He wanted to know my opinion on the club and its players. "How good do you think we can be?" he asked me.

"Well, it depends on whether you can get a catcher or not," I answered without missing a beat. "I think the guy I'd go get is Joe

Ferguson in St. Louis." I knew from covering the team closely for KPLR that the Cardinals had two good catchers in Ferguson and Ted Simmons, and that Ferguson would be available.

"Oh, you think we should get him?" Smith replied, though I wasn't sure if he seriously valued my suggestion or was just humoring me.

"Yeah, I do. I think you could get him and he'd help you," I replied.

An aside to this recollection: The Astros wound up getting Ferguson for the upcoming season, trading aging ace Larry Dierker. Do I think I was the one who gave Tal that idea? Not at all. He was one of the most astute talent evaluators in the game, and had just returned from a two-and-a-half-year stint as executive vice president and head of baseball operations for George Steinbrenner and the New York Yankees. But I feel certain that my recommendation of Ferguson confirmed to Smith that I had an idea of what I was talking about—and that had to have helped my cause.

I returned to St. Louis, once again feeling that I'd prepared as well as I could, and had done a reasonably good job in the interview sessions. Finally, one afternoon in early December, I picked up the phone at the station—and the voice on the other end belonged to Borba.

"I think we want to ruin your life and offer you the job," he said.

I had to maintain a semblance of calm inside the newsroom, so I stifled the rush of excitement and joy I felt at hearing the news—the culmination of a long, tense process, and a dream rooted in my childhood.

"Well, consider my life ruined," I responded.

Gil was standing nearby and had an idea of what was transpiring. When I hung up, I looked over and nodded with a smile—and he walked over and gave me a victory hug. As enjoyable as it was to share the news with Dee, it was difficult to tell Ted that I'd be leaving—he was the benevolent boss who'd taken a shot on a young college student. But it wasn't like I was moving to another TV station in the market; he understood the lure of this new opportunity—and he wished me well.

I realized I hadn't even discussed money with Dean on that first call. When it finally came time to talk salary, I remembered some sage advice that Dick King had imparted. "Never give them a figure first." Consequently, when Dean asked if I had an idea what I wanted to earn, I responded: "Well, you expect me to do a major league job, and I'd expect major league money."

The truth is, baseball broadcasters weren't making great money back in those days. But that didn't concern me in the slightest. I was too preoccupied by the surreal turn of events—vaulting from limited minor league experience right into the big leagues. In no time, I was heading to Houston with barely enough money to live on, but ready to live the life of a major league play-by-play man.

## CHAPTER FIVE

# Houston, We Have Lift-Off

When I arrived in the city famous for oil and NASA in the winter of 1977, I suddenly assumed the honor—if anyone was paying attention to such things—as the youngest play-by-play man in the major leagues. I actually hadn't given this distinction much thought myself until it was brought to my attention early in the season when the Astros played the Pittsburgh Pirates.

The news came courtesy of Pittsburgh's junior play-by-play guy, Lanny Frattare, who had been mentored as a minor league broadcaster by the ubiquitous Bob Prince. Lanny got his shot in the Pirates' booth in 1976 after Prince left for Houston, becoming the junior broadcast partner of Milo Hamilton at the youthful age of 28, and proud owner of the short-lived title as big-league baseball's youngest announcer.

"Hey Dewayne, you know, I'm upset with you—I was the youngest guy until you came along!" he informed me in a tone of mock annoyance when we crossed paths.

I laughed at Lanny's playful jab about unseating him, though truly the issue of age didn't concern me. What mattered most to me, in general, was doing my best to live up to Astros' management expectations, and, in particular, to live up to the expectations of my mentor Gene Elston. The latter was no small proposition. It still seemed somewhat surreal that I would soon be working alongside Gene, and I planned to do everything in my power to make him proud. At the same time, I felt ready for this next step in my career, however young my driver's license said I was.

Excited as I was about the move, however, sad news on the home front brought me back to earth, shortly after I'd accepted Houston's offer. Dee's mother—who had seemingly beaten her cancer—suffered a relapse and was rushed to the hospital, where she lay on her deathbed. The watch began, as family members and friends crowded into her room for quiet visits and to say their good-byes.

It was painful to see Dee's mother succumb, but I was grateful I had the chance to tell her, "We got the job." I knew she would be reassured to hear that I had made it to the majors, that I had a secure place in my profession and, most important, that her daughter would be okay. In the past, her parents had wondered what I was trying to do with my career—and Dee's grandmother would underscore their concern more bluntly, saying, "He should get a real job." But now, I was glad I could say—with confidence—I was able to provide the future the family hoped for. When Dee's mother passed away, the Astros sent flowers, though I wasn't yet in Houston. It was a wonderful gesture, very touching to Dee and me and to the entire Tsimpris family—cementing my feeling that my new career move would be a strong base for our future lives.

Shortly after the first of the New Year, I made the 13-hour drive to Houston to get settled while Dee stayed home to be with her father and family. I needed to be in Texas in time for an annual extravaganza—the Astros Caravan—designed to stir up excitement over the upcoming season.

The caravan, sponsored by Chevrolet, consisted of Houston's public relations staff, a handful of players and members of the broadcast crew—all of whom piled into three Chevy vans and drove all over Texas and beyond to meet with fans. Chevy spared no detail or expense: The vans all had custom paint jobs, featuring Astros orange and yellow and the logo of an exploding star on the back windows. And our itinerary—broken into separate week-long trips over the course of a month—called for dozens of stops at Chevy dealerships, where we mingled with legions of Astros faithful, signed autographs and answered endless questions about the team.

Gene and I rode together, giving us time to get to know each other better. I noticed he was a quiet man, but what a magnet he was to the folks who came out to see us. Our trip took us to South Texas and the Rio Grande Valley, including Victoria, Corpus Christi and King Ranch. Next, we headed for San Antonio and Austin in Hill Country, and then to East Texas with stops in Huntsville and Beaumont. Louisiana was also big Astros territory, and our trip led us all the way to New Orleans and back. In addition, the plan included hitting as many small towns as possible between Houston and all of these larger cities. It was hard to get any quality sleep on the road, and we'd try to catch up on rest over the weekend, when we got home.

Everywhere we went, car dealers wanted to take us to dinner and then out on the town. The players, naturally, were the main draws. Bob Watson, one of the team's stars, always wore a three-piece suit and was more or less the spokesman of the bunch. Small wonder that he went on after retirement to become the Astros' and Yankees' general manager in the 1990s, and eventually an executive in baseball's front office.

We had a second baseman named Rob Andrews, brother of Mike Andrews (an All-Star infielder who had played for the Red Sox and White Sox), pitchers Bo McLaughlin and Joe Niekro, infielders Art Howe and Roger Metzger, outfielder Jose Cruz, and even the catcher I'd suggested as a trade acquisition, Joe Ferguson. Niekro provided the entertainment and levity, highlighted by his trick of fashioning a napkin in the form of a rocket, setting it on fire and somehow making it lift off the table. It was the perfect gimmick for a group of Astros, and made him a hit at all of our stops.

As tiring and occasionally tedious as the long drives across the Lone Star State were, I was having a blast. It was a fantastic introduction to my new team—and life in the big leagues. Then, soon after the caravan ended, we headed off to Cocoa, Florida, home of the Class A Cocoa Astros of the Florida State League—and the site of my first spring training with the major league team of my childhood dreams.

I'd been anticipating this moment from the day I got the job. There was something almost mythical about this two-month period. As a lifelong baseball fan, I was fully aware of the long, storied history of Florida's Grapefruit League. The annual rite of Spring—even though much of it overlapped winter on the calendar—was a time of unfettered hope and new beginnings for players and their ball clubs. As a rookie broadcaster, I had the same sense of eager anticipation—determined to get off to a good start and make a name for myself.

Our broadcast team arrived several weeks after the newspaper beat writers, who had traveled to Cocoa in early February when the pitchers and catchers reported to camp. We flew into tiny McCoy Field in Orlando, well before Orlando International Airport existed, and retrieved our luggage outside the terminal in a small pavilion. Disney World had only been in business for five years and central Florida still looked like one big orange grove—a pale version of the worldwide tourist destination it would soon become. From there, we drove the 50 miles to Cocoa, which, for the record, shared none of the glistening oceanfront of nearby Cocoa Beach, an allure I had envisioned. Cocoa, by contrast, seemed like a typical small Florida town out of the 1950s or early '60s, though the space industry attracted droves of tourists to witness rocket launches at nearby Cape Canaveral—and big-league baseball drew fans to watch the exhibition exploits of the Colt .45s-turned-Astros.

We checked into a two-story, cinder block building, a compound that had the look of a bland military barracks. I learned right away that Astros players referred to this place as "Stalag Hofheinz," nicknamed after Judge Roy Hofheinz, a former mayor of Houston who had helped bring baseball to the city starting in 1962, later served as a managing partner of the Astros.

The players hated the dorm-like facility, and by '77 only the rookies or newcomers made it their home base. The veterans found places away from the complex. Gene and I stayed at the compound with the younger players, sharing what only a generous stretch of the imagination could be described as a "suite"—

two bedrooms with a small bathroom in between. But that was fine with me; everything about the experience was new and exhilarating, and I was far less concerned about the quality of our accommodations than the quality of the work I would be doing.

We only had a few days before the Astros started their slate of exhibition games, stretching from the East Coast to Central Florida to up and down the West Coast. There wasn't going to be much time to catch our breath upon arriving, because we were scheduled to broadcast all 30-some games. Once again, Chevrolet was a sponsor, and one of the local Chevy dealers gave our crew a station wagon to transport us from ballpark to ballpark across the state. The car was more than spacious enough for Gene, engineer Bob Green and me to ride in comfort, with plenty of room in the back to hold Greenie's mountain of sound equipment.

I felt a wave of nervous energy the day of our first game against the Braves in West Palm Beach. But after all the buildup—picturing how things might play out and battling some pre-game nerves—my first day on the job was rained out. That actually helped get my jitters out of the way, and I couldn't have felt better about my spring training debut the next day. Gene and I were able to get into a rhythm as the exhibition season progressed, just as the players were doing on the field. The complex we stayed at had a dining hall, where everybody gathered in the evening—giving Gene, Bob and me the time to share our observations and ideas, and form a closer bond. I couldn't believe it had only been seven years since Gene had left tickets at Shea Stadium, allowing me and a handful of my high school classmates to catch an Astros-Mets game on a senior-year road trip to New York City.

Dinner hour also helped me get acquainted with the younger players, various people in the organization and members of the media who covered the team regularly. One of those media folks was the new beat writer for the *Houston Post*, Kenny Hand. We were close to the same age—both in our first year on the job—and that became the common ground on which our friendship flourished. Kenny grew up as a Houston Colt .45s fan just as I did, even though his childhood was spent in the Dallas area. At that time, Houston's franchise was the closest thing to a home team anyone in Texas had. We spent our down-time discussing every aspect of the Astros roster, or heading into town at night for a beer after a long day on the job. In the process, we forged a friendship that would last through my years in Houston and to the present day. I appreciate his kind words, spoken all these years later.

"Dewayne was a consummate professional from the time I first met him. I thought I knew baseball well, but he was just exceptional with his background and knowledge of the game. Sometimes broadcasters and beat writers have a hard time getting along in a competitive situation, especially when you're on the road a lot. But if I ever needed help from Dewayne, he was there like a friend and just a great guy to be around."

The feeling was definitely mutual, and having somebody to talk to—who was a similar age and in a similar situation—made camp all that more fun. Gene, I learned, generally liked to keep to himself after dinner. If I didn't hit a bar with Kenny in the evening, chances were I'd be out having apple pie a la mode with Bob Green—whose company I also enjoyed, in spite of his chain-smoking in the booth. Bobby had a soft spot for pie and ice cream, so, after games, we would frequently find a place to partake.

Within a week or two, I began to feel right at home in my new baseball life. I enjoyed talking to the players and asking them about themselves, hearing what they had to say about their goals for the season, or various opponents they'd be facing. One of the first guys with whom I developed a rapport was versatile infielder Art Howe, a Pittsburgh native who'd broken in with the Pirates in 1974 and went to Houston in 1976 in exchange for Tommy Helms and a player to be named later.

Art struck me right from the start as a quality individual, and apparently I made a good impression on him.

"Dewayne would come down to the field and introduce himself to the players—he came across as a great guy, and he had that classic announcer's voice. He reminded me of a young Jack Buck. And the players could identify with Dewayne a little more than

Gene, because many of us were close to the same age and from the same generation. I think the players were a little intimidated by Gene—he was a lot older and an icon in Houston. Everybody on the team gravitated to Dewayne, and appreciated how prepared he was. He'd get background on every single player and if he didn't, he'd come down from the booth and ask you questions—just to get to know you better."

Little by little, the daily routine and the faces became more familiar, and I developed an increasing sense of confidence in the booth. I phoned Dee every day and she was happy to hear that everything was going well. Later in camp, she flew in for a week and I sprang for a hotel room for us on Cocoa Beach, a much-appreciated respite from Stalag Hofheinz.

When spring training ended in Cocoa, the team embarked on a mini-barnstorming series before opening day—and we made stops in such minor league cities as San Antonio, Tulsa and Baton Rouge. The stop in San Antonio brings back a significant memory. Gene and I were taking turns calling the action. It was my segment to fill until the first pitch—and then say something like, "Okay, now we're ready to go, and here for the start of the game is Gene Elston." But for some reason, there was a long delay on the field, and I struggled to ad-lib on the mic. I hadn't studied the rosters as closely as I normally did before the game, I found myself repeating points needlessly and sounding less at ease than I'd been. To make matters worse, Gene didn't jump in to bail me out with any friendly patter. He was letting it all fall on my shoulders to fill the time, and I couldn't have been more relieved when the game finally got underway and Gene took over.

The next day, he casually brought the episode up before we reached the ballpark: "You know, when you had to fill yesterday, you basically fell flat on your ass."

Gene wasn't big on passing out praise, but this was the first time he had been remotely critical of my work. With my first regular-season broadcast almost at hand, he had tested me and I'd fallen short. It was his way as the senior broadcaster—and my mentor—of reminding me to always be focused and prepared, especially with the games about to count. And I vowed to myself that I wouldn't let that kind of stumble happen again. As unpleasant as it was to hear his assessment, he'd done me a favor with an important teaching moment on the eve of my official big-league debut.

The season was scheduled to start April 8 against the Braves, with J.R. Richard facing Andy Messersmith in a game at the Astrodome. Houston had finished just under .500 the previous season, but considering the team had lost nearly 100 games the year before, that represented progress and the prevailing sentiment was that the team should be even better in 1977. The Astros clearly seemed to be turning things around in Tal Smith's third year shaping the roster as GM, and second as team president. His handpicked skipper from the Yankees, veteran manager Bill Virdon, was also in his third season at Houston's helm, and a steadying force.

The roster boasted not only the talented players who'd come along on the caravan but standouts like outfielder Cedeño, left-fielder Cruz and, later in the season, promising outfielder Terry Puhl. The real calling card was the returning pitching staff of Richard, Andujar, Niekro, Floyd Bannister and Ken Forsch. Richard and Messersmith didn't disappoint in the opener, each throwing nine strong innings before departing with the score tied 2-2. But in the bottom of the 11th, Houston won it when Joe Ferguson—yes, the man I'd recommended trading for during my job interview—hit a walk off homer for a 3-2 victory before a modest but spirited crowd of some 25,000. Talk about a dramatic start to the season and a memorable way to usher in my career.

The Astros kept the mojo going by winning five of their first six games, but any thoughts of a playoff-caliber season soon unraveled. Eight straight losses followed and the team spent most of the remainder of the season under .500, finally pulling to 80-79 before winning on the last game of '77 to salvage an 81-81 record.

Meanwhile, that first year in the booth proved to be quite an education in the art of baseball broadcasting. When it came to being technically sound as a broadcaster, Gene was a master. He was always in control of the game and had a wonderful sense of pacing that complemented the natural ebb and flow of baseball. As a booth partner, his style and skill had an immediate impact on me and undoubtedly influenced my own emerging style.

Gene was from the old school, where baseball broadcast tandems essentially worked alone once the action got underway. He generally did not interact with others in the booth and, though I personally enjoyed bantering, I kept the chatter to a minimum when it was his turn to handle the play-by-play during the game. Every once in a while, I'd chime in with a comment or remark about something he'd just said. He never suggested I stop doing that, but that kind of give-and-take simply wasn't part of his approach.

That first year, we only did 50 telecasts out of the 162 games. The rest of the time we did radio, once again each of us basically working alone during our respective portions of the game: Gene did the first three innings, I took the middle three, and Gene took over for the final three—and we'd continue to alternate if the game went extra innings. With Gene, it was a straightforward, pure presentation without many flourishes, yet always executed in a low-key manner that put the spotlight on the game—rather than on himself.

When it was my turn to call the radio action, I emulated that minimalist style but adapted it slightly. During my portion of the broadcast, I might make reference to "engineer Bob Green in the booth"—and perhaps something Greenie and I had been talking about or what he might be doing at a given moment. Bob wouldn't necessarily make his own comment, but the mere act of bringing his name up created what I felt was an important conversational element, even though I was the only one talking.

Going solo on the mic to call a ballgame might seem strange, since we've all grown accustomed to hearing multiple voices relay the action and analysis. But the great Vin Scully always worked alone—and still does. The fact is, I did most of my minor league broadcasts in 1973 and 1974 alone, and Gene—like so many broadcasters of his era—forged his style in the minors working by himself. One upshot to this particular format was that it forced me to rely on myself heavily, and without question accelerated my development. Halfway through the season, I felt that I was getting my footing—and by and large the feedback I received was good.

There was another fundamental way that Gene influenced me during this phase—in his preparation for every game. During his early years as Houston's play-by-play man, he had also worked as the team's official statistician. He kept a little black book filled with situational statistics about every player on a particular team, along with comprehensive game notes and pertinent trends. I saw how much this helped Gene, giving him instant access to those key details during a broadcast—and I started to keep my own book.

Simply put, his organizational skills were unparalleled, and his tunnel-vision approach to the job not only helped cut down on mistakes, but infused his coverage with authority. If I wanted to gain Gene's respect and approval—and I did—there was no choice but to strive to emulate his approach. He wasn't going to say, "Dewayne, you're doing a great job!"—there was none of that. When it came to hearing overt praise, it was like crickets. Then again, I hadn't received any criticism since that exhibition game just before the season, and I could sense he was pleased with my work.

Bob Green helped me put Gene's reticent nature in perspective.

"You know, Dewayne, I've been working with him for 20 years," he told me, "and you and I have gotten dinner together on the road more times this year alone than I've had with Gene in that entire time."

This was simply Gene's way, semi-reclusive and non-effusive, but a man with a big heart who would go out of his way to help you. I remember one day how he brought a mentally challenged couple to the booth to show them a real baseball broadcast; he made sure to give us all a heads-up, and was very caring with them. And, of course, I was living proof of his kind and compassionate nature—in the generous way he had taken time to write to me, answering my childhood baseball questions and encouraging me to follow my dreams.

You might be wondering how Dee and I had managed to settle in as a young married couple amid the whirlwind pace of this first season. I need to back up a bit to explain. In the fall of 1976—before the Astros had decided to hire me—we had fallen in love with a spacious 19th-century home near the Mississippi River back home in Alton, Illinois. It was an easy drive to KPLR in St. Louis, and we decided to make an offer on the old place, which had been built in 1868. The elderly owners were moving into assisted living and their son had flown in from Arizona to help them sell the house. We thought they might want close to $70,000, which would have been far out of our price range.

When I met the son for coffee one morning to talk it over, I told him that we didn't have a lot of money but expressed how Dee and I felt about the lovely house—and that we were serious about moving fast to buy it. By the end of our meeting, he agreed to sell us the house for a price of only $27,000. Why did we want this house so badly even though moving to Houston was a legitimate possibility? I guess you could say we were hedging our bets: If I didn't get the Astros job, Dee and I would have a wonderful home near my fast-growing TV station, and I could focus on my budding career as a sports anchor.

I went straight to the bank and was approved—thanks to my KPLR job—for a 95 percent loan. I only had to put down $1,350, with a monthly mortgage of $270—unbelievably low for even 1976. We moved our belongings in, and promptly rented out the upstairs to a teacher for $225, virtually covering the cost of our mortgage. And then—wouldn't you know it?—I got the call offering me the Astros job. So much for the dream-house plan.

A month later, I rented an apartment in Houston. Soon after, we sold the Alton house, making enough of a profit in the turnaround to have a decent down payment for a new house in Texas.

Our search for a place to settle in Houston coincided with the news that our family was growing. We were overjoyed to learn that Dee was pregnant. She flew down just before I left for spring training and, while I was in Florida, stayed busy house hunting in the greater Houston area. Jean Lillis, the wife of the Astros' third base coach, Bob Lillis, worked in real estate and offered to show Dee homes throughout the area, and their search soon spilled into the regular season.

Finally, Dee found what looked like the perfect place in a charming neighborhood west of Houston. I was on the road in San Francisco when she called to tell me excitedly about it, and I agreed that we should make an offer. Dee immediately notified the owners, only to learn that somebody else had beaten her to the punch by 10 minutes. She was crestfallen, but we both knew another home with everything we wanted was somewhere out there, waiting to be discovered. She and Jean resumed the house hunt and soon found another gem—a ranch home in a pleasant subdivision in the town of Katy, 30 miles to the west on a shaded street called Hockaday Drive.

We bought it right away, moved in during the summer, and in no time learned about the family two doors down—a couple, Nila and Harley Berry, and their four children: Carla in her mid-teens, Mark in his early teens, a toddler named Gayla and year-old Brandon. In fact, Nila and Carla were the first ones to welcome Dee to the neighborhood.

Nila knew all about raising children, which was an immediate comfort to Dee. And it didn't take long for Dee to look upon Nila almost as a surrogate mom and mentor, while also getting to know her four kids. I was constantly on the run with the team, in and out of town, but enjoyed our newfound friendship with the Berry family, and was grateful for the support Nila gave Dee. Given this turn of events, it now felt like a blessing that the first house deal had fallen through—yet never in a million years could

I have imagined the profound twist that life would one day have in store.

By the time the 1978 season arrived, we were fully settled in as Houstonians and ready to welcome our beautiful baby girl, Stephanie Elizabeth, into the world. Her arrival on January 11 coincided with the start of a year that gave me valuable new professional experience. The number of televised games grew to about 100, which added up to more play-by-play work and great exposure.

I also became good friends with the team's new traveling secretary, Gerry Hunsicker. Gerry had come from a college baseball background, having served as an assistant baseball coach at Florida International University in Miami, where he also earned his Master's in education. He was a sharp guy and I had a feeling he was going to go places in the game—and boy, did he ever prove me right.

Dee and Gerry's wife, Irene, became friends right away—both new moms with plenty to talk about, from babies to baseball husbands. Soon enough, Gerry and I became good pals, and the four of us enjoyed catching a meal together whenever schedules permitted and talking about parenthood, life and the game that had brought us all together.

The only negative in 1978 was the season itself. The Astros took a step back from their 81-81 campaign of '77 and finished with a lackluster record of 74-88—fifth place in the NL West. A big part of the problem was financial. Judge Hofheinz experienced increasing money woes and lost ownership of the franchise. It was being run by Ford Motor Company Credit and General Electric Credit when I had arrived—hardly an ideal situation for building a team.

By '78, the tenuous ownership situation took a greater toll as the Astros failed to cash in on baseball's newly created free agent market. One of the few bright spots was the performance of big J.R. Richard, who won 18 games and stuck out 303 batters, becoming the first righthander in National League history to surpass 300. If there was a glimmer of hope for the future, it lay with the pitching staff—Niekro had won 14, Forsch 10, and Joe Sambito was shaping up as a reliable closer.

That core of pitchers helped lead a long-awaited Astros resurgence in 1979. In fact, in the second game of the season, Forsch fired a no-hitter against the Braves in a 6-0 win, facing only two batters over the minimum 27. Calling my first no-hitter from the booth was obviously a thrill, but so was watching this team begin to gel—at one point winning 14 of 16 games and giving Cincinnati's Big Red Machine a run for the money in the final month of play. The rotation had been spectacular: Richard finished 18-13, Niekro emerged as a 20-game winner at 21-11, Joaquin Andujar posted a 12-12 mark and Forsch was more than solid at 11-6, while Sambito saved 22 games.

By this point, because we were broadcasting 100 games on television, Gene and I had a new system in place. He'd do one full game on TV by himself, while I handled that whole contest by myself on radio—and then we'd flip-flop. This set-up not only gave listeners variety but also was a catalyst in my growth as a play-by-play man, since I was going the distance on TV or radio all the time. I loved the arrangement and the Astros made it even more entertaining, finishing just one-and-a-half games behind the first-place Reds with their best record in franchise history, 89-73.

The pieces for another pennant drive seemed to be in place, including a *Sporting News* Rookie of the Year performance by rightfielder Jeffrey Leonard, excellent defense and plenty of speed in the lineup—with four players stealing 30 or more bases. But the biggest development in 1979 was the arrival one month into the season of new owner Dr. John McMullen, a New Jersey resident who had been a limited partner of the Yankees under George Steinbrenner.

Many Astros fans voiced their skepticism over McMullen's emergence as the new owner, viewing him with suspicion—a northerner, swooping in to buy a club he knew nothing about to turn a profit. They didn't care that the man behind the move was actually well respected and popular Tal Smith, who put his past experience as a Yankees executive to good use and—in a move that would later be tinged with irony—helped persuade McMullen to leave New York and buy the Astros.

The truth is, nobody locally, or from anywhere else, had stepped forward to buy the Astros. But McMullen had a few surprises in store for all the doubters. First on the list was a move that shook the baseball world, coming in the form of a blockbuster free-agent signing, when McMullen enticed the pride of nearby Alvin, Texas—superstar righthander Nolan Ryan—to come back home and join the Astros' pitching staff. Word was that Ryan would probably have agreed to a deal in the range of $700,000, a figure that general manager Tal Smith would have preferred—leaving more money available for other signings. But McMullen truly wanted to make an epic splash. That he did, turning the man who had thrown a record-tying four no-hitters for the California Angels—equaling the mark of Dodgers' Hall of Fame lefty Sandy Koufax—into baseball's first $1-million free-agent signee.

Things were about to get very interesting.

CHAPTER SIX

# Heat Wave

The impending arrival of the most feared pitcher in baseball—along with rampant speculation of how Nolan Ryan's incomparable heat might elevate an already sterling pitching staff—wasn't the only noteworthy change in the landscape. The previous season, former Astros pitching star Larry Dierker had retired after his one year with the Cardinals, and joined our broadcast team. Having Larry on the crew altered the format and, in my view, the overall chemistry for the better.

While Gene and I continued to work solo on radio, we both paired up with Larry on TV. I enjoyed the interplay with him, especially the insightful color commentary he provided from a players' perspective. This was the start of a new broadcast experience for me, creating an ongoing repartee with an analyst—the give-and-take approach many baseball announcers used and that I'd follow going forward in my career.

In addition to his expert commentary, Larry was just fun to have around. His recollection of how we first met at the start of the '79 season still makes me smile.

"Dewayne was a young guy, just getting started, but he was all over it. Very organized, bright and knowledgeable. He was living his dream. I used to follow him around and do everything he did to get prepared until I figured out that I had to have my own material. Kenny Hand, Dewayne and I hit most of the high spots on the road. I had a lot to learn about journalism—and they were only amateur drinkers."

The truth is, Larry was very sharp and a quick study, and truly added to the broadcasts—and it's no surprise that he would one day end up as a highly successful manager of the Astros, with a National League Manager of the Year Award to boot. During down-time, Kenny and I always enjoyed comparing notes with Larry about players and teams. He was a fountain of knowledge—having pitched 14 major-league seasons, including from 1964-1976 with the Colt .45s-turned Astros and a 20-win showing in 1969.

We also kidded him over his occasionally less-than-graceful ways.

"Dewayne and Kenny started calling me Sluggo after the character on *Saturday Night Live*—always smashing Mr. Bill," he recalls. "I could be clumsy even though I was a professional athlete. Seems like I was always stepping on their feet or knocking their beer off the bar. More than once I have inadvertently knocked a meal out of a flight attendant's hands while telling a story expressively, hands flying everywhere.

"One night we were all set to do our stand-up open on the broadcast, about five minutes before the first pitch. Dewayne had an elaborately prepared scorecard, which I rendered useless by knocking over a cup of coffee and spilling it all over his carefully organized lineup card. It's hard to write on wet paper with a pencil."

Spilled coffee or not, Larry added extra credibility to our coverage, and his presence on the airwaves as a former pitcher put us in perfect position to discuss the mechanics and exploits of the team's new crown jewel, Nolan Ryan. Kenny was actually the writer who broke the story for the *Post*, detailing Ryan's $4.4-million four-year deal. Given the team's impressive showing in 1979, the notion of making a World Series bid was not far-fetched, and anticipation grew exponentially as the 1980 season approached. From a personal perspective, I couldn't wait for the chance to see the sure-fire Hall of Famer go to work on a regular basis.

At that point, I remember, I had decided to seek a small raise, having established myself as a reliable presence on the airwaves in my first three seasons. By now, the relationship with McMullen and Tal Smith had become strained as two strong-willed personalities clashed on the best way to build the roster. The immediate result was that McMullen took away one of Tal's two titles—that of club president—and hired an executive from the Meadowlands in New Jersey, Bob Harter, to serve as president of the Houston Sports Association, which owned the Astros.

Bob was a good guy and I was still in my mid-20s, representing myself at the negotiating table. "Well, you know we signed Nolan for a million dollars, so we don't have a lot of money available," he explained to me. I thought to myself, "Well, Nolan would have come for $700,000—you could have signed him for that and given me an extra $5,000."

I received a token increase of some sort, though I'm not sure it would have been any bigger even if Tal had prevailed in signing Ryan for less. He preferred to be frugal and, in fact, wasn't crazy about signing Ryan in the first place. Tal's preference was to cultivate players through the farm system rather than mortgage the farm on free agency. It simply didn't make sense to him that McMullen would pay Ryan a million, more or less for show, if he might have gotten him for 700K.

Tal's budget-conscious approach was widely known, and I gently lampooned his style one night at a birthday party Dee and I held for him at our house, with Astros' front-office folks and friends in attendance. I penned some parody lyrics to the old World War II ditty, *My Gal Sal*, then sat down at the piano and led the group in singing: "They call him penurious Tal, he protests I'm not cheap just practi-cale / in arbitration hearings, management's cheering for our pal Tal / he tabulates wild pitches and errors, toward preventing light-hitting millionaires / the agents are crying 'cause Tal's in there trying, he's our Pal Tal."

Everyone got a laugh out of the ribbing, including Tal. He was a true baseball man who had learned the business well—a front-office protégé of Cincinnati Reds general manager Gabe Paul from 1951-60. He followed Paul to Houston in '60 after the expansion Colt .45s came into being prior to beginning play in 1962. Though Paul quickly moved to Cleveland's front office, Tal stayed on to rise from Houston's farm system director to vice president of player personnel, with a role in the building of "The Eighth Wonder of the World," the Astrodome.

When Paul later became president of the Yankees, he lured Tal away to New York for several seasons as head of baseball operations. In that position, Tal helped restore the winning ways of the storied franchise after a long stretch of mediocrity. But when the chance arose to return to Houston as general manager in 1975, he couldn't pass it up. Now, however, his relationship with the man he prevailed upon to buy the Astros was growing increasingly uneasy. And while the signing of Ryan fueled ticket sales and fan expectations, it also created a widening gap between the old-school GM and the ambitious new owner.

McMullen wasn't finished trying to burnish his reputation or endear himself to previously disdainful fans. He shelled out big bucks to bring home another favorite, All-Star second baseman Joe Morgan, who started his Hall of Fame major league career with the Colt .45s before winning back-to-back Most Valuable Player awards and two World Series rings with the Reds. I was elated to see Morgan return to the Astros, bringing back childhood memories of watching Nellie Fox mentor Little Joe on the finer points of playing second base and chewing tobacco. Nellie always sported a cheek-bloating chaw, but as I recall, Joe was far less interested in the tobacco tutoring than in mastering the position, which he certainly did.

All these years later, with Morgan now in the fold—joining Ryan and his million-dollar right arm—the sky seemed to be the limit for the 1980 Astros.

The anticipatory mood was interrupted with a players strike during spring training, but Morgan's veteran leadership paid instant dividends—he persuaded many of his teammates to continue working out unofficially in Florida rather than disbanding and returning home. When the strike was settled, the Astros entered the season with a sense of camaraderie and momentum.

Their Opening Day lineup was formidable: Terry Puhl in right, Craig Reynolds at short, César Cedeño in center, Joe Morgan at second, Jose Cruz in left, Enos Cabel at third, Art Howe at first, Alan Ashby catching and a dominant J.R. Richard on the mound. Richard started off by shackling division rival Los Angeles on two hits over eight innings, and Sambito earned the save in a 3-2 win. The Astros went on to win 16 of their first 22, and you could detect a distinctive new attitude for a club that had never reached the postseason.

McMullen had been right: Nolan Ryan brought another dimension to the club, a touch of swagger though not overly pronounced. Imagine two pitchers now—Richard and Ryan—who could blaze a fastball past a hitter approaching 100 mph, coupled with the perplexingly slow knuckler thrown by Niekro and the steadiness of Forsch. That was a dazzling rotation by any era's standards. Nolan's toughness was genuine—he was a Texas rancher, born in Refugio near Corpus Christi and raised in Alvin southeast of Houston: a man who could deliver calves as easily as strikes on the mound.

One of the things that made him special, in my book, was his work ethic. He pushed himself as much as anyone I ever saw. Nolan had battled with hamstring injuries in his career until he arrived in Houston, but started working with Astros strength and conditioning coach Dr. Gene Coleman, who helped train astronauts for NASA. Gene took Nolan into the pool for intensive workout sessions, significantly diminishing the hamstring issues.

Although Nolan could throw the ball as hard as anybody alive, control had always been an issue for him. But when he came to Houston, we saw him develop into a pitcher with great command. That was a sight to behold—along with his fierceness. Before the start of a game, he'd finish his warm-ups and take a little stroll in front of the mound, and smooth out part of the infield grass about halfway to home plate. It was his way of sending a message to the hitter that there would be no bunting. If someone dared to try to put a bunt down, then Nolan would make sure the batter would go down, too. That was his game.

The broadcast crew had no shortage of topics to discuss during the '80 season—it was a great time to cover the team. They were a scrappy, tenacious bunch, with a knack for capitalizing on an opponent's mistakes, and I felt like the longer a game went on, the better chance the Astros had of winning. They might get blown out one day 9-1, then come back and win 2-1 and 3-1, beating an opponent with defense, speed, timely hitting from any number of players—along with that sensational pitching staff (not at all unlike a team I would come to know well many years later, the Tampa Bay Rays). The team lacked power hitters, but Cedeño and Cruz would have terrific seasons, hitting .309 and .302 respectively, and plenty of players made key offensive contributions—Howe at .283, Puhl .282, and Cabell .276.

But the Astros also had to deal with a shocking setback. Three days after Richard became the first Houston pitcher to start an All-Star Game—one in which he struck out three batters in two scoreless innings—he complained of weakness in his pitching arm. This was alarming to say the least—Richard was off to the best start of his career at 10-4 and a 1.89 ERA. He was examined and told to rest, and everyone connected with the Astros waited anxiously in hopes that the towering 6-foot-8 ace would soon return to the team. But during his first workout, Richard collapsed and was rushed to the hospital, where doctors discovered that a blood clot moved to his neck, requiring emergency surgery to restore the flow of blood to his brain and save his life.

This was a devastating development—Richard was lost for the season and, in spite of a comeback attempt in the minors, would never pitch again in the big leagues. The players were clearly affected by the loss of their teammate, losing five straight games while he was still in the hospital, and by mid-August falling from the division top spot to third place behind the Dodgers and Reds. But with Richard gone, one of Tal Smith's acquisitions from the Detroit Tigers in 1978, righthander Vern Ruhle, stepped up in a big way.

I'd watched Ruhle pitch for Triple-A Evansville as a top Tiger prospect in 1974 when I called Oklahoma City 89ers games on radio, and now our paths were crossing again. He'd battled injuries in Detroit and never won more than 11 in six previous seasons. But Ruhle pitched magnificently in the stretch run with the Astros. With Richard out, he posted a 7-2 mark and finished 12-4, with a 2.37 ERA in 151 innings of work. As much as any single factor, Ruhle's performance kept Houston's postseason hopes alive.

Meanwhile, Niekro's famous knuckleball was as tricky as ever en route to a 20-12 season, coming on the heels of his 21-win season the year before. Ryan was less spectacular in his vaunted return to his home state, compiling a mark of 11-10 with 3.35 ERA, but he had his moments of greatness. Early on, he pitched a two-hitter against the Padres and combined with Sambito on a one-hitter of St. Louis. And another two-hit effort against the Cubs in late August highlighted a 10-game winning streak that pushed the Astros back into first by three games.

The division lead teetered back-and-forth like a heavyweight prizefight, and for six straight days in early September they remained tied for first with the Dodgers. With three games left in the season, the Astros appeared to be in the driver's seat at 92-67. Nobody took for granted they would prevail, but we all liked their chances. They had built a three-game lead and needed only one victory on the road against archrival Los Angeles to clinch their first playoff spot.

The series at Dodger Stadium, built on a hillside of Chavez Ravine, had all the electricity of a playoff showdown. The Dodgers proceeded to amp up the drama, with Don Sutton outdueling Forsch in a 3-2 Dodger win. Their lead now at two games, the Astros sent Ryan to the mound to secure the division title. He pitched seven strong innings, holding LA to six hits and striking out nine. But Jerry Reuss was even better, going the distance for the Dodgers on seven hits in a nail-biting 3-2 victory. Now the lead was at one game, and a sellout crowd of 52,339 packed Dodger Stadium on a Sunday afternoon to watch Ruhle go against Los Angeles' Burt Hooton, who brought a 14-8 record into the contest.

The Astros jumped on top 2-0 in the second, and both managers—Virdon and the Dodgers' Tommy Lasorda—began turning to their bullpen early. Houston used four pitchers in all, Los Angeles five. And the Dodgers prevailed with two runs in the bottom of the eighth off Frank LaCorte, taking a 4-3 lead that held up when Lasorda sent in starter Sutton for the save.

The seemingly impossible had happened: both teams were dead even on the final day of the regular season at 92-70, forcing a one-game playoff on Monday afternoon in Los Angeles. It would be Niekro, looking for his 20th win, vs. Dave Goltz, who had struggled to a 7-10 mark entering the make-or-break game. The matchup clearly favored Houston—and that's precisely how it unfolded, for a change. Two runs in the first, two in the fourth and three more in the fourth vaulted the Astros to a 7-1 romp and into their first playoff series.

The win was keyed by Howe's huge day at the plate, including a two-run homer in the second, a two-run single in the fourth and a 3-for-5 showing. I'll always remember the sight of Art rounding the bases on his homer with a big grin, an index finger pointed skyward, and how the raucous stadium fell silent.

Moments after the game ended, and Houston's milestone of an achievement was in the books, champagne flowed in the clubhouse. But up in our booth on the press box level, Gene, Larry, Bob Green and I faced a formidable challenge. The ushers had warned us to be careful when the game ended, because, in their words, Dodger fans could be awful. True enough, a large contingent of them were busy living up to that description as the jubilant Astros left the field.

Astros wives were seated by the visitors' dugout, and the usher had told them for their own safety, they should leave their seats immediately upon the game's conclusion and make their way into the dugout. Bob and I packed our things and maneuvered our way to the bench to join them as angry fans expressed their frustrations, some—as Bob recalls—even trying to tear up the field. And when the craziness settled down, I popped into the clubhouse to soak up some of the bottle-spraying, hugging and jubilant sights of an Astros celebration a long time in coming.

But the festive tone faded as we hurried to board a team bus to Los Angeles International Airport, ready for an overnight flight to the City of Brotherly Love. A best-of-five National League Championship Series against the NL East Division winners, the Philadelphia Phillies, was scheduled to start the next night, and there was precious little time to get ready for the challenge. My poor newspaper pal, Kenny Hand, had gotten drenched by champagne and unfortunately had to wear his wet clothes on our charter flight all the way to Philly, where the plane touched down about 5 a.m. We checked into our hotel an hour later, got a few hours of sleep, and after lunch headed to Veterans Stadium for the start of what many—including me—would come to regard as one of the most riveting League Championship Series ever.

Game 1 on Tuesday, Oct. 7, 1980 pitted Forsch against the Phillies' sensational lefty, Steve Carlton, who had just completed one of his best seasons at 24-9, along with 304 strikeouts, a 2.34 ERA and ultimately the Cy Young Award. There was no question the Astros players were physically and emotionally spent from the four games in LA and cross-country trip through the night. Still, they took a 1-0 lead into the sixth when Greg Luzinski's two-run blast put the Phillies and Carlton on top to stay in a 3-1 victory.

The next night, Houston turned to Ryan, giving him a golden opportunity to justify some of that million-dollar salary. Philadelphia countered with Dick Ruthven. Ryan only lasted six innings, scattering eight hits and leaving with a 2-1 deficit. The Astros tagged Ruthven for a run in the seventh, both teams scored in the eighth, and the game went into extra innings tied 3-3. But with a four-run outburst in the top of the 10th, aided by Dave Bergman's two-run triple, Houston evened the series with an eventual 7-4 victory.

The NLCS—in those days there was no division series preceding it—then shifted to friendly territory in the Astrodome. The mood on the team plane to Houston was decidedly upbeat and that carried over into Game 3 on Friday afternoon. This time, though, there were no offensive fireworks. Niekro's knuckler rendered the powerful Phillies' lineup—packed with stars like Pete Rose, Bake McBride, Mike Schmidt, Luzinski and Gary Maddox—virtually helpless. Through nine innings, the score was tied 0-0. All-Star Phillies reliever Tug McGraw had entered in the eighth with a runner on second and one out, but got out of the jam, and was still on the mound in the 10th opposite the indomitable Niekro.

In the 11th, Dave Smith held the Phillies scoreless in the top of the frame. In the bottom, with Tug still pitching, Joe Morgan led off with a triple to right and was replaced by a pinch-runner, Rafael Landestoy. Cruz and Howe were intentionally walked, and Denny Walling finally ended the drama with a sacrifice fly to left—giving Houston a stirring 1-0 win and 2-1 series lead, marred only by the costly loss of Cedeño to an ankle injury.

Game 4 featured a series of bizarre plays for both teams. Carlton had been chased after five innings and the Astros appeared to be closing in on a trip to the World Series, holding a 2-0 lead in the eighth. But the Phillies roughed up Ruhle in the eighth to take a 3-2 lead, only to watch Houston scratch out a run in the bottom of the ninth to send the contest to extra innings for the third straight game. In the top of the 10th, Rose singled to center and, with two outs, scored on a Luzinski smash to the left-field corner, barreling into Astros' catcher Bruce Bochy and jarring the ball loose at the plate. Philly went on to win 5-3, sending the series into a winner-take-all Game 5.

Even with the disheartening loss, you had to like the Astros' chances in this one. It was Ryan vs. a rookie, Marty Bystrom, though the kid had been impressive at 5-0 during the season. The Astros struck with a run in the first, but Philly moved ahead with two off Ryan in the second. It stayed 2-1 until Houston tied the score 2-2 in the sixth, then surged ahead with three in the seventh with the help of Howe's RBI triple. With a 5-2 lead and baseball's hardest-throwing pitcher on the mound, the bellowing sellout crowd had reason to cheer with two innings to go for a World Series berth. What's more, Ryan's winning percentage with a lead after seven innings was something like 97 percent.

The noise was deafening—I could actually feel the Astrodome shake—when he toed the rubber in the eighth. But that's when everything inexplicably unraveled. Larry Bowa, Bob Boone and Greg Gross shook Ryan with consecutive singles, and Rose drew a run-scoring walk, cutting the deficit to 5-3. I couldn't believe what I was seeing. Ryan left the game and the Phillies proceeded to score four more times, taking a 7-5 lead. Yet the way this series had gone, anything was still possible—as the Astros proved by scoring two in the bottom of the eighth with two outs and, amazingly, tying the score.

Neither team scored in the ninth, and the series headed—against all odds—to its fourth extra-inning outing in five games. The Phillies, all but dead two innings earlier, took an 8-7 lead in the top of the 10th on doubles by Del Unser and Maddox off Frank LaCorte—and that was all they needed to end the Astros' dream season. It was heartbreaking to watch. The image I remember most is that of Jose Cruz, who'd batted .400 in the series, sitting alone in the dugout, as the Phillies mobbed each other on the field.

As a broadcaster, you have to do a professional job describing the painful scene unfolding before you. But this one hurt. The Astros were one heckuva team and seemed destined to play in the World Series. It definitely wasn't easy watching Philadelphia go on and defeat the Kansas City Royals in six games, knowing that it could just as easily have been the Astros winning it all.

That's the difference between writers and broadcasters: While we follow many journalistic rules, at the end of the day we are marketing people. Yes, you need to establish credibility and trust to develop a strong relationship with your listeners, and get them to believe in you as a broadcaster. I'm never going to mislead anybody. But did I want the Houston Astros to win the

World Series in 1980? You better believe I did. When it comes to the fickle baseball gods, you simply never know when a team that good might ever get the opportunity again.

It turns out that another chance did come their way the next season, but through the most unusual set of circumstances and after a substantial bump in the road.

The chief architect of the Astros' success and the man who had hired me, Tal Smith, had disagreed with new owner John McMullen over various issues from the start. As mentioned earlier, Smith was particularly unhappy about the extravagant contract the new owner handed Ryan when several-hundred-thousand less would have landed his services. That caused a crack in the foundation of their relationship that could not be repaired. In spite of leading the club to the brink of the World Series, earning General Manager of the Year honors in the process, Smith was dismissed prior to the start of the 1981 season.

Even though I knew McMullen and Smith had butted heads, it was still a jolt to hear the man so entwined with the franchise's history and recent success had been shown the door in such unceremonious fashion. A firestorm of fan protests followed. And I believe an undercurrent of resentment followed McMullen in his remaining 11 years as owner.

He replaced Tal with another former Yankees colleague, Al Rosen: a standout player for the Cleveland Indians in the 1950s, who retired from baseball to become a stock broker, and then returned to serve as President and CEO of the Bronx Bombers in 1978 and 1979. Al quickly went about retooling the roster and putting his own mark on the team, signing one-time Dodgers ace and 15-year veteran Sutton, trading Enos Cabell to San Francisco for southpaw starter Bob Knepper, and dealing Forsch to California for infielder Dickie Thon before the season. Then, when play began, he shipped out Dave Bergman, Joaquin Andujar and Rafael Landestoy in other deals.

But the big story of 1981 was a players' strike that brought the season to a screeching halt on June 12, with the Astros sputtering along with a record of 28-29. Though there were no live games to broadcast, Gene and I still found a way to call the action five days a week. We recreated on air some of the great games in baseball history, like Babe Ruth calling his famous home run shot, or the 1934 World Series when Tiger fans drove Joe "Ducky" Medwick of the Cardinals out of left field by throwing garbage at him in response to a hard-charging slide into third base.

My experience with Frank Marx in Triple-A Oklahoma City came in handy for this stint. We went into the studio to record our play-by-play with Bob Green engineering everything to perfection—adding crowd noise and sound effects and producing a broadcast that sounded like the real deal. We just wanted to give the fans a game to enjoy every day.

When a labor agreement was finally hammered out, play resumed on August 10. Now the challenge for Major League Baseball's front office and Commissioner Bowie Kuhn was how to create a viable post-season, given the two-month interruption. The solution: The league would name a first-half winner prior to the strike, and a second-half winner following it.

Despite their inconsistent performance early on, the Astros looked like a different team now that they had a fresh shot at the playoffs. And Ryan helped lead the charge, posting a 5-0 record in the final two months to finish the strike-shortened season with an 11-5 mark and a 1.69 ERA. But his biggest feat, and one that remains forever etched in my memory, came on Sept. 26 in the Astrodome against the Dodgers.

Ryan was magnificent, striking out 11 and retiring Dusty Baker on a grounder to Art Howe at third for the final out of his fifth career no-hitter—moving ahead of Koufax for the all-time major league lead. In the absolute frenzy that followed, Nolan was mobbed and then lifted on the shoulders of his jubilant teammates. I remember making my way down to the field to interview him for our broadcast and bumping into Tony Kubek, who was doing color commentary for NBC's national "Game of the Week" broadcast. There was no time to talk, but it was one of those moments that you look back upon years later and smile—knowing the circumstances of how our paths would cross again, and even place us side-by-side at another breathtaking no-hitter.

In accordance with broadcast hierarchy, Tony talked to Nolan first for NBC, then I got him—no doubt the biggest interview of my now five-year career. The Astros, perhaps feeding off the emotionally charged outcome, went on to win the second half of the season with a record of 33-20. That set up a best-of-five play-off against—who, else?—the Dodgers.

Unfortunately, the series conjured bitter memories of the championship series with the Phillies. After winning the first two games—aided by Ryan's complete-game two-hitter in Game One—the Astros again found themselves one win away from a spot in the World Series. But the Dodgers won three straight in Los Angeles, propelled by pitching gems from Burt Hooton, Fernando Valenzuela and Jerry Reuss, who collectively shackled Houston's offense and allowed two runs among them. Once more, opportunity had ended in heartache.

By now, I was beginning to think that I had developed the competence to handle any situation on air. I'd learned invaluable lessons from one of the all-time greats in Gene Elston. First, and foremost, he taught me to prepare diligently and always put the game first, rather than make the broadcast about yourself. The game was more important than an announcer's personality, even though I endeavored to inject some personality into the proceedings while working with my lively color man, Larry Dierker.

The next three seasons were hardly illustrious ones for the Astros, a fifth place finish at 77-85 in 1982, third place in 1983 at 85-77 and 80-82 in 1984. The best thing by far about '84 was that Dee gave birth to another adorable baby girl, Alexandra Nicole, two months before spring training on January 11, coincidentally on the same day, six years later, as her sister, Stephanie.

With our growing family, our lives were changing happily on the home front. But more change would soon be in the air—famously windy air at that.

CHAPTER SEVEN

# Northern Exposure

One memorable road trip north during this period did not involve boarding the team plane and jetting off to the next city on the Astros' schedule. But it did involve a player who'd been an intrinsic part of the team's success during my tenure, and a man who had become a good friend as well—Art Howe.

Shortly after the 1983 season, I invited Art to take the 900-mile drive with me from Houston to Nashville, site of the annual Baseball Winter Meetings. I'd made plans to attend with the Astros' contingent. The annual gathering of front-office officials—from owners and general managers on down the ladder—was always an excellent place to hear about impending trades, renew old acquaintances, make new contacts or gain insights that could be helpful in the broadcast booth.

For Art, attending the meetings held a very different goal—the possibility of finding a new opportunity in baseball. He had spent the entire '83 season on the disabled list, and though the team still managed to win 85 games, his absence resulted in a costly loss of veteran leadership. I knew Art's contract with the Astros was up and he likely didn't factor into their plans going forward. Dee and I had become close with Art and his wife, Betty, and we even traded off with the Howes when it came to babysitting for one another's children. I wanted to do anything I could to help Art and it occurred to me that he might benefit from attending the Winter Meetings—reaching out in person to prospective new clubs.

Art thought it was a good idea and off we went, making the most of the 12-hour drive by adding a little history and culture to the trip.

"Dewayne decided to give me an education along the way—I remember stopping at all these old Southern mansions from the Civil War era," Art recalled. "And that's when I really started liking country and western music. By the time we got to Nashville, I think we knew all the words to every big hit that year."

I'm glad to have turned Art into a country music fan, but I'm far more gratified that the trip helped open a new baseball door for him. He drew interest from Tony LaRussa, then managing the Chicago White Sox, and that led to an invitation to spring training. But by the end of camp, he had signed with the Cardinals and skipper Whitey Herzog. Mission accomplished.

Unlike Art, the idea of looking for opportunities in other baseball markets wasn't on my mind at this point—at least not at first. I felt I was just about hitting my stride, working a full nine-inning game with the right pacing, either on TV or radio. I enjoyed my job and both Dee and I had developed roots in the community. But by 1984—my eighth year in the booth, hard as that was to believe—my name began to pop up occasionally in discussions among team or station executives looking to fill a broadcasting vacancy. I took that as confirmation that people in the business at least were aware I existed, even though I knew very well Gene was our drawing card and Larry had name recognition as a former Astros pitcher.

One such opportunity arose in 1981 when the Pirates organization and Westinghouse Broadcasting contacted me. The team was adding another person to the broadcasts on KDKA, a station I had tuned in and listened to at night on my green transistor radio. They flew me to Pittsburgh to talk about the job: I'd be sharing play-by-play duties with Lanny Frattare, the announcer who'd once kidded me about usurping his claim to being the majors' youngest man at the mic. It was the dead of winter when I made the trip, and I stayed in a downtown hotel in the Golden Triangle, right across from the Allegheny and Monongahela Rivers.

When I left the hotel the next morning to walk across the plaza to the studios, the wind was whipping off those rivers and practically blowing me backwards. I thought, "What are you doing here? Pittsburgh in the middle of the winter?" I knew they'd want me to live there in the bone-chilling off-season—and I agreed with that view: If you're going to be a primary broadcaster in a town, you should live there.

But I just couldn't see myself making the move. When I returned to Houston, I called the KDKA program director, Lee Fowler, to express my thanks for the opportunity and pull myself out of consideration. At that point, I figured that we would be staying put in Houston for the long haul. I even got a little bump in pay—it seems that Pittsburgh's interest had given me some leverage I would not otherwise have enjoyed. Meanwhile, I kept busy with off-season work doing play-by-play for Texas A&M's basketball team, and the change of pace was enjoyable.

Two years later, however, another opportunity materialized that genuinely got my attention: a chance to join Jack Buck in the booth calling the games of my hometown team, the St. Louis Cardinals. Jack was the one play-by-play guy, other than Gene, who I felt had a special aura about him when I listened to him as a youngster—and even later, when I became a major league baseball broadcaster. He had a deep, resonant voice and a commanding on-air presence. From 1961-1969, he teamed with No. 1 St. Louis play-by-play man Harry Caray, then took over the top spot when Harry was fired following the '69 season.

Dee and I were at home in Katy, Texas one afternoon when the phone rang—Bob Hyland, the regional vice president of CBS, was on the line. He wanted to talk about the possibility of adding me to the Cardinals' broadcast team, which also featured former St. Louis third baseman Mike Shannon as the analyst.

Hyland was a powerful man in broadcasting in the Midwest, an executive of major stature who ran KMOX radio in St. Louis and oversaw the on-air radio talent of the team, among other things. He instilled both respect and fear, and the fact that he had personally dialed my home number to talk to me made a strong impression. In the middle of the call, he said, "Wait a minute, there's a friend of yours who wants to say hello." It was Jack.

During the past few seasons, he and I had covered some of the same games and had gotten to know one another—a thrill for me. "Come up and visit so we can talk about this," Jack said. But as flattering as it felt to receive such a call, I saw a red flag waving in the distance. I remembered, as a KMOX intern, chatting with a news reporter who worked for Hyland, and who, for some reason, felt comfortable confiding in me, a lowly intern, about how miserable he felt Hyland had made his life. Once he had you on staff, he told me, he owned you.

That gave me some pause, but the lure of working alongside Jack was enough to prompt me to take a side trip from a Big Eight basketball assignment at the University of Missouri to St. Louis to talk about the job. I spent the day there, visiting the Anheuser-Busch Brewery to speak with Cardinal ownership, and then met privately with Hyland, who quipped, "Well, how much are you going to cost me?" I employed my old Dick King strategy, and I didn't give a figure first—especially not to perhaps the shrewdest negotiator of all time. Later, I got together with Jack, and he encouraged me to consider the opportunity. "You now, if you came here, we could really have a lot of fun," he remarked. "It wouldn't be like when I was working with Harry."

I knew there was a story there. "What do you mean by that?" I asked.

"Well, for instance, it would be my innings to do the play-by-play, and the Cardinals would get a rally going, and Harry would 'accidentally' spill his beer on me. I'd have to leave the booth to get cleaned up—and Harry would take over."

That was good for a laugh, but then our conversation turned serious. I leveled with Jack and expressed my concern that Hyland was a broadcast god, and could completely dominate a person's life if he chose to. "I have a little family going and I'd like to have a chance to see them once in a while—but maybe I won't be able to if Mr. Hyland has other ideas about the job."

Jack agreed that I would be better off joining the broadcast team as an employee of the brewery instead of KMOX, which was technically possible. But it became clear that Hyland would not have allowed that to happen—he wanted full control of the hires. I simply didn't feel the necessary level of comfort going to work for him, so—much as I would have loved to work with Jack Buck—I opted to stay in Houston.

Yet the more I thought about it over the coming months, the more I realized that Gene, still only in his mid-50s, wasn't going anywhere as Houston's play-by-play man—except eventually to the National Baseball Hall of Fame. He was more than comfortable right where he was, as the franchise's charter announcer dating back to 1962. He simply wanted to go to the park and do the best broadcast he could—and it wasn't in his nature to seek greener pastures. God bless that mentality. He was in it for the pure love of the game. I respected that. And I still idolized him.

The fact was, I loved my job in many respects. I could stay in the position, be patient and see what happened. But I knew that I could never be paid more than Gene. I was 32 and looking at another 10 or 20 years as junior partner. Dee and I talked frequently about our future and it finally came down to this: I had to be open to making a move if the right situation materialized, which—quite unexpectedly—is precisely what happened in November 1984. I received a call with a 312 area code. It was Dan Fabian, the radio program director for WGN in Chicago, inquiring about my interest in joining the Cubs broadcast team. I called to tell Dee, "I'm giving this some serious consideration."

The only problem was that the Astros paid me year-round. Though we didn't have extravagant contracts, we had letters of agreement that spelled out how much money we'd earn per season. When the 1984 season ended, I had no specific duties to perform for the club, but I was still getting paid until March 1. In accordance with the way the arrangement worked each year, I would be asked to sign a new letter of agreement and begin working again with the start of spring training. As the 1985 season approached—starting with the Grapefruit League stint in Florida—I expected the Astros to extend another letter of agreement, and I'm sure they expected me to sign it. However, the overture from the Cubs coincided with the window of time during which I was, technically, allowed to talk with other ball clubs if I wished to do so. And, after mulling it over with Dee, I decided to speak with Fabian and other members of the Cubs organization and see what their offer held.

From working in the industry, I knew already that discontent had been brewing in the Cubs broadcast booth between two pillars of Chicago's airwaves—baseball broadcasting titans Harry Caray and Milo Hamilton. A little history is in order to fully grasp the depths of their mutual disdain—and also illustrate how Milo's long and winding, and occasionally frustrating, career path ultimately had an impact on my own.

A native of Iowa, he'd begun his career broadcasting college sports at his alma mater, the University of Iowa. In the early 1950s, Milo moved to a minor league play-by-play job in the Quad Cities region of the state and landed his first major league position in 1953 doing the games of the old St. Louis Browns. But when the Browns moved to Baltimore to become the Orioles, Milo opted not to go east and instead, in 1954, got hired working for the St. Louis Cardinals alongside Jack Buck—and, in a first go-round, with Harry. After a year, Milo was more or less pushed out when the Cards decided to bring aboard popular former Cardinals catcher Joe Garagiola, who had just retired from baseball the previous year after stints with the Cubs and Giants.

Milo moved on to the Cubs, working for three seasons with fixture Jack Brickhouse and Vince Lloyd—only to be supplanted by former star shortstop for the Indians and Red Sox, and eventual Hall of Famer, Lou Boudreau. After several years out of the game, Milo spent five seasons with the White Sox in a No. 2 role, and then found a home as the lead play-by-play man for the recently relocated Atlanta Braves on WSB-TV in 1966—eventually calling Hank Aaron's record-breaking 715th home run in the Braves' 1974 home opener. But from that lofty height, Milo abruptly wound up out of job following the 1975 season—fired by ownership for being critical on the air of poor attendance at Braves' games in recent years. As a footnote, the team was subsequently sold to media mogul Ted Turner, who would showcase the Braves to the country on new superstation TBS.

Meanwhile, Milo went in search of a new job and was hired by Pittsburgh in 1976 to take over for Bob Prince, who had gone to work for the Astros alongside Gene Elston. Prince's tenure, as you recall, was short-lived and his departure after the 1976 season opened the door to my career in the majors.

Milo, meanwhile, was never entirely accepted by Pirates fans, who, during the previous 20 years, had grown accustomed to Prince's livelier on-air manner. In 1980, after four seasons, Milo jumped at the chance to return to the Cubs as the heir apparent to Jack Brickhouse, working alongside Lloyd once again and the analyst who'd nudged him out in his first go-round with the Cubs, Boudreau. Milo felt he had been promised the top job—as Brickhouse's successor—for the 1982 season, and Brickhouse had touted him publicly as the future voice of the Cubs.

But all of that changed when the Cubs unexpectedly hired the voice of the White Sox on the South Side of town, Harry Caray. Harry had not been getting along with new White Sox owners Jerry Reinsdorf and Eddie Einhorn. And when the Chicago Tribune Company purchased the Cubs from William Wrigley in 1981, Harry reached out to new Cubs management to see if the club would be interested in his services. The Tribune Company was indeed, adding Harry to an already powerhouse broadcast team.

Nobody was less thrilled about the development than Milo, who now found himself with a reduced role and faced competition from Harry in ascending to the Brickhouse throne. On top of that, he always believed Harry was behind the move to force him out in St. Louis decades earlier and bring in Garagiola. All of sudden, Harry was the big talk of the town on the North Side, and the history of bad blood between them was a recipe for disaster.

Harry transferred his famous tradition of singing *Take Me Out to the Ball Game* during the seventh inning stretch from Comiskey

Park to Wrigley Field. The fans loved it, but Milo would purposely stay seated while Harry crooned his crowd-pleasing, off-key rendition over the stadium PA. When Harry was finished, then Milo stood up and took his own seventh inning stretch. That's how things went.

I remember watching a Cubs telecast at home in Houston, before I left for the Astrodome. The San Diego Chicken, a famed mascot that traveled to sporting events all over the country, was cavorting on the field. Harry and Milo were working together in the TV booth for that one season, prior to former pitcher Steve Stone being hired and paired with Harry. It didn't take long for barbs to come out.

In the early part of the game, the Chicken—a.k.a. Ted Giannoulas—was doing its usual on-field antics and Harry, in his inimitable delivery, was describing the action, saying something along the lines of, "Well, the Chicken is doing this and the Chicken is doing that! Milo, look at that Chicken now!"

Essentially, he was baiting Milo, and Milo wasn't biting. He didn't say a word. Finally, about the seventh or eighth inning, the Cubs got a few guys on base, someone hit a double in the gap, several runners scored—and the Chicken started going crazy to cheer them on. Amid the excitement, Milo interjected, "Well, Harry, just look at that Chicken now!" And Harry, not to be one-upped, replied, "Milo, never mind the Chicken—the game's the thing!"

Silly as it was, the exchange typified the growing ill will between Milo and Harry whenever they worked together. Harry's favorite catchphrase was "Holy Cow!" Milo's was "Holy Toledo!"—and the situation was a holy mess. A popular story circulated that the final straw came over a taping of WGN's hugely popular children's program, *The Bozo Show*. The show was a really big deal in Chicago—so big, that the day your child was born, you'd be sure to get his or her name on the waiting list to eventually be admitted into Bozo's live studio audience. It literally took years to happen, and each time the show taped, excited kids would line up with their parents at WGN studios on Bradley Place for their big moment—a chance to watch the show in person.

On one such morning, Milo had to stop by the station, and the lobby was packed with eager youngsters, and for some reason a child saw him and innocently blurted out, "Mommy, look! It's the guy who says Holy Cow!"

That was the worst thing someone could say to Milo, especially during the height of his on-air feud with Harry. He reportedly burst into a colorfully tinged tirade, and all of these bewildered little kids were going, "Mommy, what's he saying? Why is he so mad?" According to the account, that's what cost Milo his job, and it followed him for years to come. In truth, his departure was only a matter of time, because Cubs ownership clearly regarded Harry as their meal ticket. After the Great Bozo Blowup, Milo was out—and the Cubs had an opening on their broadcast team that needed to be filled before the start of the 1985 season.

I eagerly made my travel arrangements and flew into the town where my big-league career had begun eight years earlier, auditioning at Wrigley Field for the Astros' job. Now, I was hoping to follow my tracks from Houston back to Chicago and a chance to be part of the Cubs' standout broadcast crew on WGN.

I went to the radio station and met with radio program director Dan Fabian, GM Wayne Vreisman, and sports director Chuck Swirsky, who had been the one to recommend me. I liked all three of them and had a good feeling about our discussion. Then we all went to the TV studio, where I met with a group of executives, including Tribune Company broadcasting mogul Jim Dowdle, who had pushed for the purchase of the Cubs and later turned the Tribune into a massive media conglomerate.

Jim asked me some probing questions, such as, "If there were one thing you could change about yourself, what would it be?"

"Well, I'd be 6-foot-3 or 6-foot-4," I said, hoping to break the ice. "If I were 6-4, I might have been pitching instead of talking about pitchers."

Then, he asked a probing question. "Do you have an ego?"

I knew the query was rooted in the ego clashes between Harry and Milo. And I also knew that Dowdle was a big supporter of Harry's, cut from the same cloth. I thought for a moment, not wanting to fall into a trap, and then gave what I felt was an honest reply.

"Yes, absolutely. Everybody in this room has an ego. If you didn't, you wouldn't be in this room. The question is, what do you do with it? Do you control it—or does it control you?"

I could tell they liked the answer, and I seemed to have made a hit. I headed home feeling as if Dee and I had a pretty good shot if we wanted to move the family to Chicago. Nevertheless, several things about the situation bothered me. One was the idea of leaving the warm climate of Houston, a place that had been a terrific home for us, and returning to a part of the country known for its long, brutal winters. But we talked it over and decided that if an offer came, it would be too good of an opportunity to pass up. I even confided in Gene. As always, he proved to be a helpful mentor, assuring me that there were any number of wonderful cities in which to live and broadcast baseball, and Chicago was one of them.

Gil Engler, my longtime friend from the early days at KPLR, now wore several hats. One of them involved trouble-shooting for KPLR; the other was representing talent. I called Gil and asked if he would handle my negotiations if our talks progressed. When the offer came soon after, Gil did a fantastic job working out the details, allowing us to have enough money in the process to buy a house in Highland Park outside of Chicago, where the cost of living was considerably higher than Houston.

We signed the contract and I proceeded to notify my Astros broadcast team—starting with the man who'd motivated me as a child to pursue a play-by-play career, Gene. He couldn't have been more gracious or happy for me, and wished me well in the new adventure.

It was tough to say goodbye to Greenie, my engineer. We'd worked many an inning together and developed a close bond. He'd gone through a tough spell for a stretch, dealing with depression, and during that time I would invite him to my hotel room on the road to talk and just hang out, while I prepared my notes for the game. He told me having the company made a real difference to him, but I was happy to do anything to help out such a good pal.

I hated to part with my broadcast partner, Larry Dierker, who had become a genuine friend and an outstanding analyst—and I think he felt the same way. Nor was it easy for our family to bid farewell to our sensational almost next-door neighbors, Harley and Nila Berry and their children, Carla, Mark, Gayla and Brandon, even though we knew we'd stay in touch.

The only person with a decidedly negative reaction to my move was Astros owner John McMullen. He called me at our home before we left to say, "Don't go anywhere yet, because I think there's been tampering involved here."

I can't even recall how I responded, though I'm fairly certain I was momentarily speechless. By that time, I was determined to leave, no matter what kind of obstacle McMullen intended to place in our path.

"We're going to file tampering charges against the Cubs," he reiterated.

"Well," I replied, flatly, "I think you should do what you think you need to do."

The tension was as pronounced as any pitching duel I'd ever called. I didn't know if McMullen was bluffing, but sure enough, Gil Engler was personally presented with a notice of filing soon after at his office in St. Louis—accusing WGN of illegally negotiating with me while I was under contract with the Astros. I wasn't due to begin work at WGN until March 1, 1985, and WGN instructed me to notify them if my pay was cut off prematurely by the Astros—assuring me that they would begin paying me ahead of schedule. Fortunately, that didn't happen, but it was an unexpectedly awkward conclusion to my years with the Astros to say the least. In the end, new Major League Baseball Commissioner Peter Ueberroth—fresh off his stint as head of the 1984 U.S. Olympic Summer Games in Los Angeles—had to get involved in the case. And he ruled that no tampering had taken place.

There was barely enough time now for me to drive my little Datsun 280Z from Houston to icy Chicago. And as an ironic twist, my departure from the Astros would create an opening next to Gene Elston and Larry Dierker to be filled by a familiar broadcasting name—none other than Milo Hamilton.

Now I was heading to the town—and WGN booth—Milo had only recently left behind. I had to drive through St. Louis, so, on a whim, I called a longtime high school pal, Roger Lewis, and invited him to make the final leg of the trip with me to Chicago. He gladly accepted the offer and we cruised into the city, reminiscing about the old days and talking about my new job. After arriving, I drove us downtown to the Hancock Building, where WGN maintained a corporate apartment on the 72nd floor. I recall looking out the window and saying to Roger, "Can you imagine a couple of guys from Wood River being up here with this view?" I stayed for two days, taking care of loose ends and marveling how fast everything had happened. While Roger caught a ride home, I stored my car in the back of WGN's studio, and then jetted off to Phoenix, Arizona—joining my new crew in nearby Mesa for the start of spring training and an unforgettable episode in my life.

CHAPTER EIGHT

# Harry's Town

I quickly learned that there was a fundamental difference between broadcasting with the Astros and my new job with the high-profile and even higher-energy Cubs crew of Harry Caray, Steve Stone and Lou Boudreau. From the moment I began calling games in spring training until the start of the 1985 season at Wrigley Field, one thing became completely clear: Personality was king.

In Houston, I'd tried to be sure that I hit all the key points during a broadcast, that I did a professional job, and had a little fun along the way. Larry Dierker and I had developed a playful rapport, in contrast to Gene Elston's predominantly solitary act. But with the Cubs, showmanship was an essential part of the formula. And fan-favorite Harry—whose wavy white hair, oversized black spectacles and ebullient voice made him instantly recognizable—set the tone.

During that first spring training, the crew wound up at Harry's house in Palm Springs for a backyard party. That was quite a thrill for me, being the new kid in the group. Dallas Green, the Cubs' general manager, and his wife, Sylvia, were also guests—both friendly, up-front folks with big personalities. Dallas, who had signed off on hiring me, introduced me to Sylvia, and she seized the opportunity to have some fun at my expense—well aware of the tampering charges that had been filed by Astros owner John McMullen, a former naval architect. "You know, we're trying to get our son an appointment to the Naval Academy, and we thought John McMullen might have helped us until now—so, you'd better be really good," she said playfully. I laughed, but I knew many people in this baseball-crazy town would be watching and listening to me closely to see how I'd fit in.

None of us tried to compete with the epic Caray charisma, but we each made an effort to convey a distinct personality of our own; without being forced, or the audience would catch on. I embraced this new chance to inject a little humor into the broadcasts, create a conversation with my boothmates and connect with the fans watching or listening. That was how I let my personality shine through, yet my goal was never to overshadow the game—rather, to help enhance people's enjoyment and understanding of what was transpiring on the field.

I derived a great deal of enjoyment myself from our broadcast arrangement. On radio, I was paired with Lou Boudreau as the analyst, while Stone worked the television side with Harry. I'd call the action for the first three innings, then take the middle three on TV with Stone while Harry shifted to radio with Boudreau. Then, we'd swap places again; I'd return to the radio booth for the last three innings and Harry would go back to his TV seat. If the game went extras, we'd continue to switch chairs accordingly until it was all over.

I truly felt honored to be part of this impressive group, and that WGN management had sought me out for the job. One of the guys I got to know quickly and worked with on a daily basis was WGN's venerable sports editor and producer, Jack Rosenberg, a veteran of the station and true ace of the business, who'd worked closely with iconic Cubs announcer Jack Brickhouse for years. Jack's recollection of WGN's decision to add me to the lineup makes me realize how fortunate I was.

"The company saw the intangibles in Dewayne and it turns out the company was right," he says. "He was part of what most people thought through the years was the No. 1 sports department of its kind in the world. We had this broadcast talent, but we were all great friends and we were all proud to be part of such a tremendous operation."

Because I spent most of my time on air with Lou, I got to know him very well and I'll say this: If he'd taken a broadcast performance class, he wouldn't have made it through with a passing grade. His syntax and pronunciation weren't ever going to win any awards, and he wasn't a consummate broadcaster. But Lou was a perfect personality. People loved him as a good guy with a great heart—and more than anything, a baseball man who truly knew the game.

I still have yet to see anybody who anticipated the action better than Lou Boudreau. That's not surprising when you consider that this was the guy who, in 1948, won the Most Valuable Player Award for Cleveland while also managing the Indians to the World Series title; the player voted onto eight All-Star teams; and the man who played a part in history as the shortstop-playing skipper who guided Bill Veeck's Tribe when Larry Doby broke the American League color barrier in 1947.

Lou and I worked together for my first two years in Chicago. I came aboard just after the Cubs' splendid 1984 season, when they finished with one of the best records in club history—96-65—under first-year manager Jim Frey, only to fall to the San Diego Padres in the National League Championship Series. They had won the first two games in the five-game set, but then lost three straight to fall short of their first World Series appearance since 1945.

Their long-suffering fans once again were left to ponder what might have been, but nonetheless approached the 1985 season with optimism and high expectations. With a starting rotation anchored by Rick Sutcliffe, Dennis Eckersley and Steve Trout—and a lineup featuring such standouts as second baseman Ryne Sandburg, shortstop Shawon Dunston, catcher Jody Davis, first baseman Leon Durham, third baseman Ron Cey and outfielders Gary Matthews, Bo Dernier and Keith Moreland—they got off to a great start, sitting atop the NL East in mid-June.

Wrigley Field was filled daily with an air of excitement as the Cubs appeared to be in the midst of an impressive encore performance—with the possibility, this time, of taking the next step into the Series. But suddenly, Chicago's vaunted pitchers began to succumb to injury, and the entire rotation unraveled. The Cubs wound up limping to the finish line, tumbling to fourth place before July arrived and finishing far out of the running at 77-84.

Unfortunately, 1986 was even worse, as the team spent most of the season near the bottom of the six-team division, closing out the dismal campaign 20 games under .500.

Frey wasn't around to see the end of it. Two months into the season, we were in St. Louis for a four-game series—15 games out of first. I remember being high up in the Busch Stadium booth several hours before the game, watching Jim walking forlornly up and down the left field line, like the loneliest man in the world. That was only days before he was fired by general manager Dallas Green and replaced at the helm by John Vukovich. I happened to be at WGN studios when we got word and somebody from the newsroom raced up to me and said, "You've got to go on the air right now, the Cubs just fired Jim Frey!" I wound up breaking the story on WGN TV.

As a point of history, this was also the same day that the club called up two promising rookies from Triple-A, outfielder Davey Martinez and pitcher Jamie Moyer, whose lives would intersect with mine for decades to come. The story of Davey and Jamie's arrival at the clubhouse gives a vivid sense of the team's discordant mood in the wake of Frey's dismissal. When they reached the players' entrance, they discovered they couldn't get in. The team had locked them out and these two skinny newcomers were forced to sit outside, thinking, "Man, these guys must hate us for taking two veteran spots on the roster."

What they didn't know was that the players were engulfed in an uproar over the news of Frey's firing, and they didn't let the pair of rookie call-ups enter until the atmosphere had calmed down. That was the inauspicious introduction to the majors for two players who would make an impact on the game. Davey went on to have a distinguished 16-year career as a .276 hitter and skillful outfielder—and became a constant presence in my life decades later as an original Tampa Bay Devil Ray and bench coach of the Tampa Bay Rays; and Jamie pitched an incredible 25 seasons, compiling a mark of 269-205.

Frey went home, but he wasn't gone for long. When the season ended, my radio partner, Lou, decided to move into semi-retirement. Without missing a beat, WGN decided to hire Jim as his replacement and my new radio wingman. We worked together in 1987, when the Cubs floundered to a last-place finish of 76-85, 18.5 games out of first place under new manager Gene "Stick" Michael, the longtime Yankees infielder and former New York manager.

In the final month of play, Gene got wind that Dallas was going to fire him, but he quit before that fate could befall him—great timing because he'd just guided the Cubs to a .500 record before the bottom fell out. Say this for the Cubs—even amid all the losing, there was never a dull moment. Frank Lucchesi, the former Phillies and Rangers manager (and one-time Oklahoma 89ers skipper during my stint with the team), was brought in on an interim basis and had no better luck in the final 25 games, winning only eight.

Jim was great fun to work with during this forgettable season—his baseball knowledge in general, and of the Cubs specifically, was impressive, and he brought those assets to our radiocasts in a lively manner. In the off-season, Tribune management informed Dallas that he needed to return to managing—he'd won a World Series ring in that capacity with the 1980 Phillies (the team that broke the hearts of the Astros nation in that hotly contested NL championship series). All the managers he'd fired hadn't improved the Cubs in any discernable way, so management wanted to see what he could do in the role.

But Dallas wasn't interested. Perhaps anticipating that more losing awaited, he declined—and was promptly fired himself. Then, to everyone's surprise, Tribune ownership replaced him with one of his "firees"—my partner, Jim Frey. Jim had apparently been so impressive as a Cubs commentator that he had emerged as the No. 1 choice to rebuild the ball club as GM. In the inimitable words of ventriloquist Edgar Bergen's dummy, Mortimer Snerd, "Who'd have thunk it?"

Jim's choice as manager for the 1988 season was quintessential baseball man, Don Zimmer. Zim had managed the Padres, Red Sox and Rangers, and served as Frey's third base coach for the Cubs from 1984-86—and then walked into Dallas Green's office to quit in protest when Jim was fired by Dallas in '86. Now he was back with the Cubs as the fifth manager in three seasons. At the same time, there was a sudden vacancy in the WGN radio booth that needed to be filled as soon as possible. And that's how Dave Nelson—a veteran of nine big-league seasons as an infielder for the Indians, Senators, Rangers and Royals—came to be my new partner.

Dave, I would quickly discover, had a wide-ranging baseball resume and, on top of that, was a first-rate human being. After retiring, he'd become the head baseball coach at Texas Christian University in 1980. Then he went back to the majors as a coach for the White Sox through 1984, before moving to the Oakland A's to serve as director of instruction through the '87 season.

As Dave tells it, he was working with players in the Dominican Republic that December when he received a call from his supervisor, Oakland's director of player development, Karl Kuehl. Karl informed him his name had been mentioned in connection with the Cubs' radio opening. Since he hadn't done any announcing before, Dave was taken completely by surprise by the news. He wasn't sure he wanted to pursue it, knowing he was on a track to succeed Karl whenever he retired. But his boss urged him to consider the opportunity, pointing out that the employer, superstation WGN, was a top-flight operation in a great baseball town.

"The next thing I knew, I was getting a call from WGN's sports director, Chuck Swirsky, saying they wanted to bring me to Chicago for an audition," Dave recalls. "Chuck had interviewed me several times when I coached for the White Sox, and thought I had a pretty good sense of humor, knew the game and would be a good analyst. Even though I'd never been one, I was interested now. So they flew me to town and took me to WGN studios. And that's where I was introduced to Dewayne Staats for the first time. I didn't know Dewayne from Adam. I was a little nervous. But from Day 1, he made me feel very comfortable and welcome."

Dave was a natural and fell into the analyst job with impressive ease. He later told me he felt a little nervous whenever it was Harry's turn to take over for me as announcer in the fourth, fifth and sixth innings.

"I felt a lot more comfortable doing the games with Dewayne, because Harry could be a little intimidating," he reflects. "But Dewayne and I just had a great chemistry. And here's this accomplished broadcaster, with this great voice, but he never put himself above anyone or above the game. And we enjoyed bantering and debating. I remember we really went at it over the designated hitter rule—I took up the pro case from the American League side, and Dewayne took the con side as an NL guy. We really got spirited on the air—when Dewayne feels strongly about something, he's going to let you know about it. And you won't win that debate."

I appreciate Dave's assessment of our work together—and the way we did our best to liven up the broadcast, especially since things were a bit rocky on the field during Zim's first season. One noteworthy event during this time was the first night game played by the Cubs at Wrigley Field, which had finally installed stadium lighting in its 73rd season. The game was scheduled for August 8, 1988 against the Phillies in the fabled park. All the broadcast crew dressed up in tuxedos for the landmark occasion, only to see the game scrubbed by rain. But the weather was fine the next day when the Mets arrived, and Dave and I welcomed night lights at Wrigley on August 9, with a 6-4 Cubs victory before a boisterous sellout crowd of 36,399 on hand to witness history.

The season ended with the Cubs in fourth place at a disappointing 77-84, but there were signs of hope for the next year—such as rookie first baseman Mark Grace, who hit .296, young righthander Greg Maddux, who posted an 18-8 record in spite of the Cubs' troubles, and the uplifting presence of rightfielder Andre Dawson.

Andre had signed with the Cubs in 1987 after 11 sterling seasons with the Montreal Expos, and to this day I'd rate him as one of the hardest-working players I've ever seen. He was unbelievable, and desperately wanted to get away from the hard, unforgiving turf of Montreal's Stade Olympique to save his ailing knees. But his desire for a change came amidst the controversial collusion issue in baseball. In the mid-1980s, Commissioner Peter Ueberroth had urged owners not to compete against one another for free agents—and that adversely affected Dawson.

Nobody was making him any offers, in spite of the fact that he'd hit 20 or more homers in seven of his previous nine seasons. It got to the point when he felt he had no choice—and directed his agent, Dick Moss, to basically offer the Tribune Company a blank check for his services. Moss told front-office officials to fill in the amount they wanted to pay Andre—and he'd sign.

The owners promptly offered the modest amount of $500,000. True to his word, Andre jumped at the opportunity, and proceeded to tear it up in his first year, hitting 49 homers, driving in 137 runs and batting .287. He was tough. I recall how he'd have both knees wrapped to take batting practice, get treatment on the knees after he was done, and then re-wrap them for the game. He was an incredibly positive influence on the team and the fans adored him.

They definitely loved Harry, and I fell into that camp, too. Chicago was and is such a major market, and there was plenty of room for Harry and Milo—if they could have gotten along. In Chicago, fans tend to look at broadcast personalities the way people in Los Angeles look at movie stars, and Harry was king of the Windy City throughout his Cub years, as he entered the home stretch of his Hall of Fame career. During his heyday with St. Louis, he'd also been somewhat controversial due to his outspoken ways, and he had a habit of occasionally embellishing the action—at all of his stops—for dramatic effect. But Harry could break down a game like nobody else. And, as you probably gather by now, he knew how to make the broadcasts fun.

He shared several things during our time together that resonated with me. When he was a kid growing up in St. Louis, during an era in which pioneering St. Louis broadcaster Franz Laux was the Cardinals play-by-play man, Harry was a bit of a street urchin and would sneak into the stadium to catch games. "I realized that when I listened to the games on radio, they were so dull," he told me. "But when I watched at the ball park, they were so exciting." What Harry did—as an extension of his larger-than-life personality—was to carry that child's excitement into his broadcasts. He wanted to have a good time, and wanted everyone else to have one, too.

I'd gotten to know him during my years with the Astros—since Houston and Chicago played each other regularly, we crossed paths fairly often. Those were the days that broadcasters might stay in the press room after a game, kick back and enjoy a few adult beverages. And if Harry was going to be sitting there, having a beer and telling stories with his fellow broadcasters, I made sure I was there, too—with a front row seat. You could learn a lot, listening to some of the game's great announcers and just soaking up the colorful atmosphere. On several occasions, I drove Harry back to his hotel room and had a chance to talk more baseball. Those were rides I enjoyed immensely.

During this period, it also turned out that other people in the industry were listening to me—thanks to the vast WGN signal that carried our voices to markets across the country. I began to get inquiries about possible new opportunities—first from the San Diego Padres. The idea of working in the booth with lead announcer Jerry Coleman was intriguing. He'd been nothing but kind and supportive to me as a young broadcaster and it felt good to be asked about joining the Padres' crew. But I explained that I had a multi-year contract with WGN.

Then came an offer that definitely got my attention.

ESPN was on its way to becoming a worldwide broadcast conglomerate and had just secured its national TV rights deal with Major League Baseball. Naturally, I was surprised and delighted when an ESPN executive, Steve Anderson, called me one day and asked if I'd be interested in becoming one of three principle baseball commentators—along with Jon Miller and Gary Thorne—doing a Wednesday night Game of the Week. The idea sounded extremely appealing, and I'd only have to take off one night a week at WGN to make it work. Steve flew to Chicago and took me out to a nice little Italian restaurant so we could talk it over. I told him that I would definitely like to be part of the venture, and explained that the only hurdle would be working out the logistics with WGN, which had me under contract through the 1989 season.

I had no desire to leave WGN, only to work an arrangement allowing me to fly to wherever ESPN had scheduled a Wednesday telecast—and then return home to Chicago by Thursday in time for the next Cubs broadcast. The plan would require a crazy and tiring whirlwind of travel, but I was young and really eager to make this work. In my mind, it was a win-win: a chance for me to get some national exposure and additional income, and a feather in the cap for WGN to have one of their own showcased on the splashy new ESPN offering.

Unfortunately, the powers at WGN did not see it that way. The problem was this: The station was such a force in the market back then that it virtually "owned" the on-air talent. WGN was so big that it had a waiting list for sponsors, with station officials charging a hefty amount to the advertisers. One of the ways the company justified this was to make its broadcasters exclusive to the sponsors. As a result, we didn't get to do commercials for any business that hadn't signed a sponsorship deal with WGN. That wasn't a big sticking point for me, because I didn't want to do commercials—I just wanted to broadcast baseball games.

But when ESPN came knocking with a new and exciting baseball opportunity, and a chance to advance my career, my WGN bosses had no interest in playing ball. My services were exclusive to them and their advertisers. I pushed back, pointing out the exposure benefits of having a WGN broadcaster included on

ESPN's new national telecast. At one point, they actually considered letting me do the weekly game, but only on the condition that I personally pay the one-night salary of whomever replaced me in the booth on Wednesdays. That was unfeasible for me—which I'm sure they knew—and I didn't try to hide my disappointment.

"Oh, so you want me to pay the ESPN penalty tax," I said with an edge in my voice.

I lost the battle, and the opportunity passed. And the previously smooth relationship I had with my WGN superiors was never quite the same. We were still friendly with one another, but I felt some disappointment over the way the situation was handled. Then, before the 1989 season began, an opportunity arose on another big playing field.

Gulf & Western, which owned the Madison Square Garden Network, had made a bid to buy the Yankees from George Steinbrenner in the late 1980s. That bid failed, but Gulf & Western still shelled out a record $486-million for the rights to televise Yankees games—a fee that was completely unheard of in that era. People, including me, thought it was crazy to pay that amount. I never pictured myself as a player in that story, but fate intervened with a phone call from the executive who ran the MSG Network, Bob Gutkowski. He was aware of my work with the Cubs and wanted to know if I was interested in doing play-by-play. Later, when Bob told me how the idea of recruiting me had dawned on him, I learned that we shared a childhood passion for tuning in distant games on our little plastic radios.

"I was sitting in the hotel room with my family in St. Thomas on a vacation," he recollected. "And I was thinking of what we wanted in a play-by-play man. I wanted to find somebody who was not well-known in our market—and somebody who had the kind of voice I would hear as a kid, listening to ballgames at night on my Vanguard 88 transistor radio. Those great voices seemed to jump through the radio right through the covers of my bed. I wanted a voice like that—a strong play-by-play voice that would go well with the analyst we had in mind, Tony Kubek. I wanted a person who took the game seriously, and was knowledgeable about it.

"So here I was on vacation in the Virgin Islands, watching a game on WGN in my hotel room and I heard Dewayne talking. I sat up and thought, 'Man, this kid's got a voice.' I listened to the games every day that vacation and when I returned to New York, I told our guys, 'I think I've got our guy.' And then we pursued him."

I have to admit that Bob's call caught me off guard. I had never dreamed—not from the time that I was a child or throughout my entire career as a baseball broadcaster—that I would go to New York and be the voice of the Yankees. As a Midwestern kid with deep National League allegiances, I had no aspirations to work there, and had never even considered the possibility. But Bob wasn't just talking money that represented a bump in pay—he was talking double what I was making in Chicago, maybe more.

That certainly offset my pre-existing ambivalence about living and working in the Big Apple. As tantalizing as the offer was, however, I couldn't accept it. I was still under contract with the WGN through the upcoming 1989 season. I explained the situation to Bob, thanked him for his interest in bringing me into the MSG fold and, with a sense of regret, assumed that yet another ship had sailed on without me. But much to my surprise, Bob replied, "Okay, but we're going to come back when your contract is up."

Hearing those words—especially on the heels of WGN blocking the ESPN opportunity—left me momentarily speechless. I told Bob I'd love to talk again, though I knew I couldn't be sure that he'd circle back for me in a year. Whatever happened, it felt great to get such validation for the job I'd been doing. I knew the offer was a direct result of the national TV platform I'd had on WGN, with my three innings with Steve Stone beamed to the whole country—and, it turns out, the Caribbean.

I gave some thought to what might have caught Bob's attention beyond vocal timbre and delivery. The fact was, Steve and I took a slightly more baseball-centric approach to our three-inning partnership. Let me explain what I mean: Harry's philosophy to a telecast was essentially, "Let's have some fun early in the game, and if it develops into a good contest, then we'll get more serious in our coverage closer to the end." Many viewers liked that, but some fans preferred a little more baseball in the mix than entertainment.

When I was paired with Stone, fans got two guys of similar ages who focused on the game, with the entertainment element playing a supporting role. We gave the audience something a little different from "The Harry Show" for the fourth through the sixth. But to be fair, the Cubs were so bad for so long that Harry had the right idea in creating a lively viewing experience. He was the key to that quality of fun, and fans ate it up as a diversion from the woes of their beloved baseball losers.

I was more understated than Harry, though I still engaged in some lighthearted back and forth with Steve. We managed to show the human side of the game through our interaction, without dominating the game itself. More than anything else in Chicago, that approach shaped my broadcast style. And I believe that's what got the attention first from ESPN, and helped me stand out to MSG.

When the 1989 season finally started, rumors abounded that former Phillies superstar Mike Schmidt had the edge for the MSG analyst position. I took note that Bob had hired two members of the radio crew—Tommy Hutton, a former ballplayer with the Expos and Phillies, and Bobby Murcer, the one-time Yankees star—to handle the telecasts. The fact that he hadn't made any outside hires for his TV positions suggested I might indeed still have a shot in a year.

Meanwhile, with all the distractions, I couldn't wait for the Cubs to start playing again in 1989—and it turned out that Zimmer and his Cubs had a surprise in store. They were good. After a so-so start, the Cubs worked their way into the division lead before Memorial Day, slipped back to third in late July, but regained the lead by the first week of August en route to a 93-69 record and NL East title.

Pitching paved the way, with four starters posting double-digits in wins: Maddux with a record of 19-12, Sutcliffe 16-11, Mike Bielecki 18-7 and Scott Sanderson 11-9. The offense rode the bats of Grace (.314), Sandberg (.290 and 30 home runs), Dunston (.278), Rookie of the Year centerfielder Jerome Walton (.293) and Dawson (.252 with 21 homers)—and the Cubs found themselves in the National League Championship Series against the San Francisco Giants.

Against that backdrop of baseball drama, which had the city of Chicago in an absolute tizzy, my own personal drama was playing out. The MSG deal was still alive. In fact, Bob Gutkowski and former ESPN pioneer and past president of NBC Sports Chet Simmons, now retired and working as an MSG consultant, flew to Chicago during the off-season to take Dee and me out to dinner and lay out their plans for me for the 1990 season. The topic of my possible on-air partner came up, and they mentioned their interest in hiring Tony Kubek, the former hotshot Yankees shortstop from their great teams of the 1960s. Bob, who had also worked at NBC in various executive capacities and later followed Simmons to ESPN, had gotten to know Tony well from his baseball work at the Peacock network. He and Chet both appreciated his honest, pull-no-punches style and intimate knowledge of the game. I couldn't have agreed more, and took the opportunity to express my support: "If we could get Tony, that would be outstanding."

I'd only crossed paths with him occasionally—when NBC broadcast one of our games in Houston or Chicago, such as Nolan Ryan's record-breaking fifth no-hitter for the Astros. But he always made great use of local broadcast talent to get up to speed on teams he was covering, and we got to know one another a bit. I liked him as a person—and respected him as a professional.

Soon after that dinner conversation with Bob and Chet, I telephoned Tony to talk confidentially about the situation, and try to gauge his interest in the MSG job. Tony was hesitant. The problem was that New York's often bombastic owner, George Steinbrenner, had no love for Kubek, who never hesitated to criticize the Boss or Yankees on air. That angered George so much that he went so far as to try to get Tony taken off NBC games involving the Yankees. I understood Tony's reluctance, but still gave him a nudge.

"Look, you may not want to go but I really think this could be a lot of fun," I said. "I'd certainly love to work with you."

By the time the NLCS arrived, the rumor mill already had me leaving to cover the Yankees. I was convinced that my superiors at WGN had heard the rumblings, too, because Dan Fabian made an offer that gave me pause: a lifetime contract on WGN radio. I relayed the news to Dee, saying, "Are you kidding me? If somebody had told me when I was covering high school football games at SIU Edwardsville that 10 or 12 years down the road I'd be offered a lifetime contract by WGN, I'd have said, 'Show me where I sign!' "

But there was a flip side to agreeing to the deal. I knew all too well how the station controlled its talent, and I thought, "If I sign this, they will own me." Being prevented from freelancing for ESPN on their baseball game of the week still bothered me. But there was one thing that could keep me in Chicago: written assurance that I would be in line to replace Harry as lead play-by-play man on TV, whenever he chose to retire.

Harry had suffered a stroke during the 1987 season and missed about two months, recuperating at his home in Palm Springs, California, while celebrity guest announcers—stars like Bill Murray and Dennis Franz—filled in during his absence.

Speculation continued to swirl over who might replace Harry if he had to retire due to health reasons. Even though he'd made a remarkable recovery and regained his strength, people regularly asked me, "Are you going to replace Harry?" I wasn't comfortable at all with that kind of chatter and chose not to talk about it. But the honest answer was, yes, of course I wanted to—who wouldn't want that in my position? Finally, near the end of the 1989 season, I approached the head of WGN's television programming, Dennis FitzSimons. I knew Dennis was a good guy and I felt comfortable laying out my thoughts. "Look, a lot of people are asking me about this," I said. "I don't want to make an issue of it, but I would like to have assurance that whenever Harry retires—whether it's in two years or 10 years—I'll get the job. If you can make that commitment, that changes everything."

After five years, Dee and I were growing weary of the harsh winters. Harry had dealt with that by moving to Southern California and Steve Stone bought a place in Arizona, near the Cubs' spring training base in Mesa. If WGN could put my request in writing, I could move Dee and the girls to Arizona—and perhaps spend the next 30 years covering the Cubs from the TV and radio broadcast booth.

Dennis listened to what I had to say, then explained the problem he faced: When Milo had been promised that he would succeed Jack Brickhouse, it created an enormous problem for the organization after Harry unexpectedly became available and got the job instead. As a company, Dennis explained, WGN wanted to avoid that type of situation again. "Look, I can't put this on paper," he said. "But I really think the things that you want to happen are going to happen."

I paused to think, then replied.

"Dennis, I appreciate that. I trust you and believe you. But if you walk out of this office and get hit by a truck, where does that leave me?"

Without anything in writing, there was nothing to prevent Tribune Company and WGN decision-makers from changing their minds if some network name suddenly became available. That was the moment I made my decision: Much as I loved covering the Cubs, and much as Dee and I and the girls would miss all our Chicago friends, I was going to take the MSG job.

I've looked back on that decision and thought about how vastly different life would have been—and the countless things my family and I would never have experienced in the years and decades ahead—had I decided to take Fabian's offer and remain with WGN radio for the long haul or accepted FitzSimon's verbal assurance that I'd one day replace Harry on TV and stayed in

Chicago. My grandfather, Perry Francis Staats, had an old saying: "Just the crook of a finger can change the air current, and even make a leaf fall from a tree." His point was that the littlest thing you do can have a ripple effect on the world around you. Deep inside, I felt the time was right to change the air current in my life and see where it led me. Perhaps, in hindsight, it was all just part of a master plan from above.

I still had a playoff series to broadcast, and the decibel level was off the charts inside Wrigley Field when it began. The Cubs split the first two games with the Giants—losing 11-3 and then winning 9-5—then headed west for two games, hoping to bring the series back to Chicago for a decisive Game 5.

When I arrived at Candlestick Park, there were still rumors that Mike Schmidt was under consideration for MSG's analyst slot—and Schmidt had been hearing them, too. I ran into the former slugger at Candlestick and, in a quiet moment, he said, "Looks like we might be working together." I still didn't know where things stood with Tony. In any case, I didn't want to talk about it—taking the chance of fueling even more rumors in the midst of a tense playoff series. I smiled and responded, "Who knows?"

Once in San Francisco, the Cubs' fortunes took a sharp turn for the worse. The Giants took Game 3 by a score of 5-4 on a homer by Robby Thompson. Needing to win to survive the next day, Chicago's Mike Bielecki held a 1-0 lead in the seventh but gave up a triple to Jack Clark, who scored the tying run on a sacrifice fly. Then, with two outs in the eighth, Bielecki walked the bases loaded. Zim sent in Mitch Williams to end the threat, but Clark responded with a two-run single. The Giants held on to win 3-2, advancing to the World Series against the Oakland A's in a Fall Classic that would be interrupted by the devastating earthquake that rocked the San Francisco Bay Area.

The Cubs flew home dejected by coming so close yet again. I stepped off the plane with the surreal knowledge that I had broadcast my last game for WGN, and with the partners with whom I enjoyed working so much. I signed the MSG deal soon after the series ended and said my farewells at WGN. One of the people it was particularly tough to say goodbye to was Jack Rosenberg, and the feeling seemed to be mutual.

"I was very sad when Dewayne left," he recalls. "We had a great history of longevity: Jack Brickhouse, Harry Caray, Lou Boudreau and Vince Lloyd. Dewayne clearly could have been one of them. But he had to make a business decision. It was a privilege to work with him, and I can't say enough good things about his work as a professional and as a man."

The reality that life was about to change—that I'd soon be working in Yankee Stadium to broadcast games of the most storied franchise in sports—began to sink in. But I wouldn't be working alongside Mike Schmidt. Tony had put aside his misgivings about George and accepted Bob's offer. The new MSG broadcast team of Kubek and Staats was in place and ready to roll.

CHAPTER NINE

# A New York State of Mind: The Yankee Years

As Dee and I prepared to fly to New York to house-hunt during the offseason, the reality of the major change in our lives began to sink in. We felt a rush of excitement over the opportunity that lay ahead in the world's most famous city—mixed with some lingering misgivings about leaving behind our familiar surroundings near the shore of Lake Michigan.

The truth is, we loved a lot about Chicago. Even though we already had a plan in place to escape the miserable winters by relocating to Arizona—sparing us from the harshest weather from November through March—our connections to the Windy City were strong. I thoroughly enjoyed working with my WGN TV and radio colleagues, and valued their friendships. And, despite my differences with WGN over ESPN's offer, despite my disappointment over their refusal to state in writing that I'd one day replace Harry Caray, the decision to move on was one of the hardest I've ever made.

But if somebody tells you, "We're going to pay you twice as much as you're making now and maybe more," you begin imagining what you can do with that money. You think about how much you can start saving for the future, and how you can provide for your wife and children. And that becomes a powerful motivation.

Doing my best to take care of my family was always a driving force for me, just as it had been for my father and grandfather. My new job with MSG was going to allow me to provide for Dee, Steph and Alexa at a whole new level. That fact, coupled with having been sought out as lead play-by-play man in America's biggest media market, was heady stuff indeed.

 120 

At the same time, the idea of establishing deep roots in New York City didn't feel like a perfect fit for a country kid from East Alton, Illinois. I remember telling Dee at the outset, "This will not be a long-term situation. It's not who I am."

Even in the midst of such conflicting emotions, there was one thing about which I had no doubt: I could not have made it to this point in my career without Dee. Her impeccable skill at keeping the household running—while I jetted all over the country on road swings, or was constantly ensconced at the ballpark for the next home stand—made everything in our marriage and baseball lifestyle possible.

The demands of my career, and my desire to take the steps from Houston to Chicago and now New York, would have been enormously disruptive and detrimental to the family without Dee. I'll go a step further: Making those moves would have been flat-out impossible. She was the rock—with her ever-calming influence, terrific mothering skills with just the right blend of love and discipline, and first-class organizational ability that gave the girls a structured environment. With her smarts, compassion and toughness, she could just as easily have been a successful corporate CEO.

That's not to say I didn't play a role around our home with Stephanie and Alexa. It was just difficult to be present as much as I would have liked. During the baseball season, by necessity, my schedule revolved around the team. When I was in town, I had to leave early in the afternoon for night games and get home late, and I'd often be away for long stretches. But I loved being with the girls whenever I could—and always relished the three-to-four months in the offseason when there was time to spend real quality time with Dee and the kids.

I know the moves weren't easy on Stephanie and Alexa as they started grade school and made new friends. The first move from Houston to the Chicago suburb of Highland Park was particularly hard for 7-year-old Steph, who let us know her feelings in no uncertain terms. "I don't want to go!!" she often proclaimed. She had become close to Nila Berry's youngest daughter, Gayla, and to ease the sting, Dee arranged for Gayla to accompany Steph when we made the move north. But the separation was still hard. When it was time for her best friend to return to Houston, I'll never forget how Steph grabbed onto Gayla's leg at the airport gate, dragging along the floor and screaming, "Don't go!!!" We felt her pain keenly.

Stephanie eventually made the adjustment to our new neighborhood, but a girl next door constantly picked on her. It got so bad I actually had to teach my older daughter how to make a fist in order to physically defend herself.

In time, she made new friends on the block and both girls were doing well, thriving in school and feeling at home in Highland Park. But now, at ages 13 and 7, they were being uprooted again, as their baseball broadcaster dad pursued an exciting new opportunity that meant precious little to them. I just had to trust that their resiliency, and their mother's loving support, would lessen their hurt in time.

Dee and I made several trips to the New York City area, and actually looked at some beautiful homes in North Bergen County in New Jersey and Connecticut. We couldn't find anything that felt just right, and that's when Dee and I came to a comforting realization. We didn't have to live in the New York area to make this work. We could create our own version of what Harry Caray and Steve Stone had with the Cubs, and look for a place in warm and sunny Florida—the state where the Yankees held spring training. The arrangement would require I fly home from New York City to Florida as much as the Yankees' schedule allowed, but Dee and the girls could enjoy living in a temperate climate and join me on occasion during the summer to explore the culture and fun of the Big Apple.

Dee had two aunts who lived on Florida's West Coast, in the Tampa area, and we decided to look there first. In short order, we found a designer home nearby that we loved, but decided we should also explore South Florida, where Dee's sister lived—a stone's throw from the Yankees' winter-spring home in Fort Lauderdale. We were interested in a two-story house in Tequesta, and had we bought it our neighbor would have been Joe Namath. I'd have enjoyed that, talking football and sports with Broadway Joe on any given day. But none of the available houses quite worked for us. The more we looked, the more Dee and I got our hearts set on finding a promising lot on which to build our own house.

Looking for a good school system for the girls, with Steph going into middle school and Alexa into first grade, we visited the lovely village of Wellington, once hailed as the world's largest strawberry patch, in Palm Beach County—a short drive to the Atlantic Ocean and a straight 30-minute shot down I-95 to the Yankees' complex. Almost immediately, a two-acre piece of property at the end of a cul-de-sac caught our attention. It featured some 460-feet across the back of a horse trail, bordered a small canal, and was in close proximity to the 13th hole of an adjacent golf course. The only problem: It wasn't for sale. But on a whim—perhaps channeling the childhood boldness that made me think I could track down Walt Bond—I knocked on the door of the man who owned the land and simply said, "You have some land that we love. Would you consider selling it?"

To our pleasant surprise, he was open to making a deal. It no doubt cost us $5,000-$10,000 more than it would have sold for in a regular transaction, but it was worth every penny to us. We were able sell our place in Highland Park quickly and at a nice profit. In fact, we never even listed it; daughter Alexa had told her kindergartner classmates we were moving and word got around, prompting a buyer to contact us directly.

The sale gave us enough money to build our Florida dream home, and we stayed in temporary housing while the house took shape over the coming months. The experience of moving to our new, subtropical surroundings with swaying palm trees and constant warmth eased the transition for the girls. They were especially happy to learn about our decision to buy the open lot next door—and our plan to build a small barn and stable area for horses.

And now that our family had put down roots, it was time for me to make a transition of my own, moving from the National League to the American League, getting to know a whole new team and front office—and being in the media spotlight at a whole new level.

The Yankees were not a good club at this time in their history. Aside from making a run at the AL East Division title in 1985 and 1986 –winning more combined games than any other major league team in the decade—the team had begun to unravel in the late 1980s due to injuries and the departure of key marquee players.

Electrifying leadoff man Rickey Henderson and power-hitting third baseman Mike Pagliarulo left during the 1989 season. And the Dave Winfield era, marked by frequent feuding with Steinbrenner, was about to come to an ugly and ignominious end.

Winfield had been a Yankees fixture since 1981 but George derided him as "Mr. May"—an unflattering comparison to the heroic "Mr. October" moniker of Reggie Jackson for his postseason heroics in the late 1970s. Steinbrenner eventually tried to trade Winfield, in spite of his strong numbers, consistent power and excellent defense, but Winfield's 10 years of service in the majors and five with the same team meant he had the right to consent to or refuse any trade. He wound up missing the entire 1989 season with a back injury, but the deteriorating relationship with his fiery owner was about to reach a new low.

Steinbrenner had paid a gambler with dubious connections $40,000 to try to dig up damaging information on Winfield. When that came to light, the tactic resulted in Commissioner Faye Vincent banning the Boss in 1990 from day-to-day management, though not ownership, of the Yankees. The ban was first announced as permanent, but reduced in time to two years—meaning that Steinbrenner's presence would be virtually nonexistent during the first two years in my new job.

Winfield wouldn't be around much, either. He'd been dealt to the Angels early in the 1990 season, after suing the Yankees for failing to contribute $300,000 to his foundation as stipulated in his contract. As you can gather, the environment I was moving into was in a state of considerable flux. As their offense deteriorated, the Yankees had finished fifth in 1988 and 1989. The one remaining bright light was All-Star first baseman Don Mattingly, coming off six straight seasons of hitting over .300, including a career high of .352 in 1986. The pitching staff did not contain much depth with a rotation of Tim Leary, Dave LaPoint, Andy Hawkins and Chuck Cary, leaving Yankee prospects dim heading into the 1990 season.

During my first spring training in March of '90, Dee stayed home in Highland Park so the girls could finish up their school year before moving to Florida. Meanwhile, I utilized every bit of available time to get up to speed on my new team. Fortunately for me, the Yankees' new pitching coach was Billy Connors, whom I had come to know well during his stint with the Cubs in the same capacity. Billy was a huge help in furthering my knowledge of the team. He kept meticulous notes on every pitcher's strengths, weaknesses and individual performances, maintaining catalogues and volumes of videos. And his records were not only of his Yankee hurlers but of opposing pitchers around the league. Essentially, he had kept detailed scouting reports on all the other teams, and was gracious enough to share that treasure trove of inside data with me.

Just as Cubs manager Jim Marshall had lent such a valuable helping hand at the start of my career—going out of his way to help me with my Astros audition—Billy was doing the same for me now. After team workouts, I'd take one of his reports on a given team back to my condo and transfer the vital information to my own book that I kept on players and teams. Studying Billy's insights was like taking a master class on baseball, and put me in perfect position for the upcoming season with my new partner, Tony.

Something Tony remembers saying that spring training still gives me a chuckle.

"I told Dewayne, 'If you can work with Harry Caray, you can sure work with me!'"

Recalling his experience with Harry, Tony added: "Broadcasters like Harry and Milo Hamilton had pretty big egos to say the least. I worked one World Series with Harry when he was still with the Cardinals. He was okay—he said what he said and did what he did. Harry was just Harry. He was the kind of big-personality broadcaster who did his own thing, and sometimes it was for self-aggrandizement."

Tony's reflection on working with Harry in the 1968 World Series between St. Louis and Detroit triggers my own recollection of that showdown: I was 16 at the time, camping out with some friends at the Busch Stadium box office before the Series began, hoping to buy a ticket. (For the record, we succeeded in getting into a standing-room-only section for Game 2, watching Mickey Lolich shackle the Cards 8-1, hit the only homer of his career and earn one of his three victories in the Series).

Now, as Tony and I looked ahead to our first season together, we knew that neither of us approached broadcasting in a personality-driven manner: Whatever we said on air, it was always more about the game than about either of us.

I actually had very few dealings with George while I worked in New York, but in that first spring training, prior to his suspension, he'd drop by camp on occasion. I had the chance to sit with him in the dugout early one day and chat—just a quiet little exchange about the team and baseball itself, and I found him to be quite engaging (something I'd heard he could be if he wasn't mad at you).

When the season began, Steinbrenner was out of the picture. Another familiar face from my years in Chicago was on the scene to help the Yankees: new general manager Gene Michael. Gene and I had a good relationship during his short stint managing the

Cubs and he was very helpful to me now—always accommodating and willing to share insights about his players, team and the American League in general.

With the freedom to make decisions without interference from above, Gene began to orchestrate a shift away from the pricey free-agent acquisitions favored by Steinbrenner—in hopes of developing New York's farm system. It's worth noting that Gene's approach gradually produced a new wave of Yankee stars who would eventually become the core of the franchise's future resurgence—players such as outfielder Bernie Williams, shortstop Derek Jeter, catcher Jorge Posada and closer Mariano Rivera.

But in 1990, the picture was bleak. Bucky Dent, the Yankees' former shortstop, started the season as manager. After a dismal start of 18-31, however, he was replaced by Stump Merrill, who fared no better at 49-64 for an overall record of 67-95—good for dead last in the division.

Making matters worse for the '90 Yankees was the back injury plaguing their best hitter, Mattingly. He was forced to go on the disabled list in July and didn't return until season's end, finishing with a career-worst .256 batting average and only five homers.

From a personal perspective, the bright spot of this first year was getting to work for Bob Gutkowski, who changed the paradigm of regional sports networks. Prior to his whopping purchase of the club's broadcast rights, not a single Yankees game was on basic regional cable.

"It was all on pay TV," Bob explained. "When we took the Yankees away from Cablevision, it really changed the industry and that's why it was so important to get a strong broadcast team in place. I remember a few network presidents calling me up and saying, 'Your production is as good as ours,' and that was very gratifying to hear. We all came from the networks and it was very important to us to create that here."

Bob ran a totally first-class operation and treated us extremely well. I regarded him as a true executive, not simply an administrator. He was a leader with vision, someone unafraid to make big moves and decisions. He brought some of the network swagger from NBC to his job as President and CEO of Madison Square Garden. In that capacity, he was responsible for the New York Knicks of the NBA, the New York Rangers of the NHL, and MSG Communications, which included the nation's largest regional cable network—the MSG Network that broadcast the Yankees.

Bob liked center stage, being in the action and making deals. He was a handsome man with thick gray hair and a well-trimmed, salt-and-pepper beard, and was always immaculately dressed—as if he'd just stepped off the cover of *GQ*. The MSG Network had the Knicks telecasts but needed something to broadcast during the dog days of summer. Baseball was the perfect solution, increasing the value of the network by 2,000 percent at the time.

One of the great things Bob did was stand up for his broadcasters any time there was pushback from the Yankees' front office. There were no issues with me as a play-by-play guy, since the nature of my job was basically to convey what was going on, with a little slant and opinion to it. Tony had a different role and style. He was an honest and opinionated man who said what was on his mind and what he believed. Bob was aware of that when he hired him and anticipated the possibility of conflict between Tony and George, given their acrimonious history. If necessary, Bob was always ready to run interference. When it came to protecting his on-air talent from any meddling or attempts to undermine us, he was fabulous.

Of course, that wasn't an issue during those first two seasons—with George essentially out of the picture—though you better believe it would become one down the road.

Right from the start, Bob did everything to make life for Tony and me as comfortable as possible. During the season, when we were in the city for home games, both of us had our own suites at the Regency Hotel at Park Avenue and 61st in midtown Manhattan, right across from Central Park. Our rooms featured little kitchenettes, which were convenient if we wanted to eat in during a home stand. But more often than not we'd unwind after a ball game by going out to eat at any number of enticing restaurants in the Park Avenue neighborhood.

Downstairs at the Regency in those days, the bar was always crowded and the dining room was especially known as the site of the "power broker's breakfast. " Executives from all over the city—and the world, for that matter—would meet over coffee, eggs and toast to make big deals. But the coolest aspect of the Regency was that Yankees Hall of Famer Mickey Mantle had a place there. I became acquainted with Mickey through Tony, who knew him well from years of playing together on so many great Yankees teams—and sharing World Series championships in 1958, 1960 and 1961.

Back in those days, Tony and second baseman Bobby Richardson formed a great double-play combination and were basically the wholesome "milkshake guys" amid plenty of hardcore partiers—chief among them, Mantle. But despite the difference between them, Tony and Mickey had maintained a good friendship through the years. Mickey's liver had worked overtime with all the alcohol he'd consumed. And now, when I met him, his liver wasn't processing normally, which meant he'd feel the effects of only one or two drinks. When we were at a table in the Regency bar, I saw the calm, steadying influence Tony exerted on his old friend—a function of the man Tony was, not the broadcaster or the former ballplayer.

Different memories of those evenings come to mind. Every once in a while, there might be a colorful moment with Mickey yelling off-color song requests to Keith, the Regency's talented piano bar player. And other visitors joined us from time to time, such as Broadway star Robert Goulet, who squeezed into our booth one night to enjoy some libations and share war stories. On other occasions, Bob would take us out on the town, perhaps to dinner at upscale Elaine's with MSG clients. Life was always interesting while we were in town, but Bob also made sure that on our days off, we could get home to spend time with our families.

Whenever our schedule allowed it, Tony would fly back to Wisconsin, where he lived with his wife, Margaret and four children, and I'd fly to Florida to see Dee and the girls in our newly completed home in Palm Beach County. We flew commercial most of the time, and Bob made sure we always booked first-class seats. That's simply how he did business.

Many times, getting from Yankee Stadium to the airport required clockwork precision. Let's say it was a Sunday afternoon following a game, with Monday scheduled as a day off for the team, and no broadcast by Tony and me slated for Tuesday. That gave us an eagerly anticipated two-day break. We'd arrange to have our car service—another Gutkowski perk for every game we worked—waiting for us outside the ballpark.

As soon as the last out was made and our wrapup was complete, we'd ride the elevator down from the press box, step onto the sidewalk and jump in the limo idling at the curb. Our driver would race to LaGuardia International, drop off whichever one of us had the earliest departure, then proceed to the next terminal. Invariably, we'd be in a time crunch. But in those days, flying commercially was infinitely easier than it became after 9/11. We didn't have to wait in a long security line to be x-rayed before boarding, and we often made a mad dash to our respective gates, gripping our briefcases, to catch the plane just before the doors closed.

The 1991 season wasn't much of an improvement over our first one together. With Merrill still managing, the Yankees finished an even 20 games under .500 at 71-91. But they at least placed ahead of the Orioles and last-place Indians, who'd managed to lose 105 games. Mattingly rebounded from his back problems to hit .288, but off-season surgery seemed to have sapped his power and made him more of a slap hitter. Catcher Matt Nokes and leftfielder Mel Hall provided whatever power there was, with 24 and 19 homers, respectively, and second-baseman Steve Sax stepped up to lead the team in hitting at a .304. Other than Scott

Sanderson, who posted a 16-10 record in 208 innings, pitching was problematic.

But a year later, change was in the Bronx air. George Steinbrenner returned from exile and promptly made a managerial move, shaking things up by replacing Merrill with a youthful Buck Showalter, an astute and equally intense baseball man. George had also been saving up some vitriol for one-half of the MSG broadcast team, Tony. But if ever there was someone who could be a match for the Boss, it was Bob Gutkowski. I'll let him tell the story of what happened next.

"Prior to George coming back, I had heard that he was having tapes made of Dewayne and Tony on air—and how they dealt with the Yankees and George being suspended."

Things started heating up at that point, as Bob tells it, with word spreading that George wanted to get rid of Tony when he got back. "I'd heard about this," Bob recalls, "and I said, 'Let's start getting some tapes of Marv Albert,' because Marv was our guy and a great New Yorker—and also very honest and critical of the Knicks and Rangers. We have to be that way in New York. The last thing we ever wanted was a homer. And Dewayne was not even close to that. He was really outstanding in the way he presented the realities and odysseys of the club. Tony certainly was no homer, either—but had that lingering background with George.

"So George got all of his tapes made," Bob's story continues, "and the day after he got back in baseball, he called me and said, 'I'm coming up to the office.' And sure enough, he comes walking down the hall with about 12 tapes under his arm. He came in and sat down and we started flipping tapes into my VCR.

"The screaming and yelling in my office was so bad that my assistant eventually called the head of security, because she was worried that George and I were going to get in a real fight. But when the door finally flew open, he and I were laughing, arm in arm. I told him, 'George, we're not getting rid of Tony.' And he said, 'I understand that.' Then he looked at me and said, 'You know what, I like the other kid, Staats, though.'

"That's what you had to do with George. You had to go back with him and fight him the way he would fight with you. We actually had a very respectful relationship. And he thought Dewayne was terrific."

George's re-emergence ended what seemed like a rudderless period for the Yankees, when they were reluctant to spend the big money on prized free agents. His return, along with the shrewd managing of Showalter, seemed to light a much-needed fire under the Yankees.

They still struggled, but took a step forward with a 76-86 record—good for fourth place. Rightfielder Danny Tartabull provided some additional muscle with 25 homers, Mattingly held his own at .288, leftfielder Hall had another good year at .280 with 15 blasts, speedy centerfielder Roberto Kelly batted .272 with a team-high 28 stolen bases and Bernie Williams also began to come into his own in his second season, hitting .280 in a part-time role.

That set the stage for what turned out to be a successful 1993 campaign, fueled by several key off-season moves. Kelly was sent to Cincinnati in exchange for Paul O'Neill, who contributed superb defense in right along with a .311 batting average and 20 home runs. But the big news was a pair of high-impact free agent signings—the kind that had been missing in Steinbrenner's absence. The club signed All-Star Red Sox third baseman Wade Boggs, after 11 years of being a thorn in the side of the Yankees. Boggs bounced back from a down year in Boston in '92 to hit .302 and provide his usual flawless glove at third. And southpaw Jimmy Key assumed the ace role after nine seasons in Toronto—and lived up to expectations with an All-Star season and 18-6 record.

Their presence helped energize the roster, but many other players made a noteworthy impact in '93: former Rangers catcher Mike Stanley had a sensational year in his second New York season, hitting .305 with 26 jacks; Mattingly continued to be Mattingly, batting .291 with an improved home run output at 17; Tartabull led the team with 31 round-trippers and 102 RBI; and Williams settled into his new spot in center, hitting a respectable .268 on the cusp of longterm stardom in the Bronx.

Finally, the Yankees' pitching was headline material, too—and not just Key, but another lefty acquisition in the off-season, Jim Abbott.

Abbott was—and is to this day—one of the most inspirational individuals with whom I've had the pleasure of crossing paths. He was born without his right hand, but his left hand befuddled hitters with a 95-mph fastball mixed with a mean cutter. His parents raised him never to consider his condition a handicap, and it never was.

He learned to pitch while resting his mitt on the end of his right forearm, and—after his delivery—he would deftly place the mitt on his left hand in order to field any balls in his vicinity. When he fielded a grounder, he would tuck the glove between his right forearm and body, pull his hand out of the mitt and grab the ball—usually in time to make the play. The absolutely amazing aspect of this was how routine he made this all look.

At the University of Michigan, Abbott won the James E. Sullivan Award as the nation's best amateur athlete in 1987 and became a No. 1 draft choice the next year of the California Angels.

In 1989, the Angels added him to their rotation as a rookie before he'd ever seen any action in the minors—something almost unheard of in baseball. He rewarded their confidence with a 12-12 record and 3.92 ERA, earning enough votes to finish fifth in the American League Rookie of the Year voting. Two seasons later, he led the staff and finished third in the AL Cy Young voting with an 18-11 record and a 2.89 ERA on a mediocre Angels club. A year after that, in 1992, Abbott took a beating with a 7-15 record on a California team that finished 18 games under .500, but he still managed to post an excellent ERA of 2.77.

The Yankees wanted to upgrade their pitching as part of the renovation, and traded three promising prospects in December of '92 to obtain Abbott. He got off to a slow start with his new team, losing five of his first six decisions. But then he began to get in the groove, posting an 8-4 record heading into a Saturday afternoon home game against the Cleveland Indians on September 4, 1993. The Yankees were playing great ball at this point, only one game out of the division lead behind Toronto at 77-60. And Abbott was about to add a monumental punctuation mark to their efforts.

Through the first six innings, he held Cleveland hitless, scattering four walks along the way. But two of the runners were wiped out in the early innings by double plays turned by third baseman Boggs and shortstop Randy Velarde, while New York's offense built a 4-0 lead.

In the top of the seventh, Abbott faced the meat of Cleveland's lineup—All-Star second baseman and .300-plus-hitter Carlos Baerga, fearsome slugger Albert Belle, and Randy Milligan, hitting at a plus .400 clip after joining the Tribe midseason from Cincinnati. He retired all three on groundouts, and a wave of nervous excitement swept through the crowd of 27,000-plus fans—not to mention the broadcast booth—with everyone fully aware of the historic possibility unfolding before our eyes.

As the top of the eighth began, Tony turned to me in the booth.

"I just said, 'This is it—I'm not going to say another word,' " he recollected. "Dewayne looked at me kind of funny, like, 'What?' But I knew Dewayne, as a play-by-play man, could call the game with some pauses and let the drama that was building come through. If you have two guys trying to make this more dramatic than it already is, you can detract from what's happening on the field."

I've always respected baseball's tradition of not actually explicitly saying what is going on in this particular pitching situation—not out of superstition, but simply because it's part of the game's history. I've always tried to say it without saying it—perhaps with a comment like, "You may want to call your friends, folks—something very special is happening right now." I honestly don't remember what I said on this day, especially after Tony decided to let me do all the talking.

In the top of the eighth, the crowd bellowed as Abbott struck out the sixth hitter, dangerous Manny Ramirez, to start the inning, then retired Candy Maldonado on a groundout to short. But hearts pounded throughout the stands—and among countless MSG viewers—as Abbott worked the count to 3-2 on future Hall of Famer Jim Thome and then lost him on his fifth walk of the game.

Coming to the plate was Sandy Alomar Jr., a potent right-handed bat to pinch hit in the nine hole for Junior Ortiz. On a 2-1 pitch, he coaxed a grounder to Boggs, who fired to Mattingly for the third out, as the crowd let out a collective sigh of relief.

In the ninth, the Indians had the top of the lineup ready. Fans were on their feet and screaming as centerfielder Kenny Lofton grounded out to second baseman Mike Gallego for the first out. The next batter, shortstop Felix Fermin, hit a deep shot to left-center, but it was snagged for the second out by Bernie Williams. I remember the deafening roar inside Yankee Stadium as Baerga stepped to the plate. He fell behind 0-1, then made contact—a playable groundball to short. This was it! Verlarde snagged the ball and fired to first for the final out of what remains one of the more thrilling moments of my broadcast career—Jim Abbott's no-hitter. Pandemonium reigned in the stands and on the field below as the Yankees mobbed the man who had just authored the 4-0 victory and astonishing baseball event.

Tony was right. At this point, it was best to say as little as possible and let the drama on-screen do all the talking.

I can't think of a better partner to have shared the Yankees experience with—and our chemistry in that game typified the friendship we had in and out of the ballpark. During our frequent dinners together, we obviously talked baseball, but we also covered topics that ranged from politics, to what was going on with our families, to events around the world. At Yankee Stadium, we stuck to our own pregame routines, often arriving at different times to begin our mental preparation. Here's Tony's description:

"I always thought it was important that we go our own ways. Too often, you see guys who work together standing around together near the batting cages. We never did that. Dewayne might be behind the cage, talking to Buck Showalter, and I'd be on the other side of the field talking to somebody completely different. That approach is important because the variety of information you pick up makes for a more stimulating broadcast.

"But we never felt compelled to work something we learned into the broadcast—it had to fit in naturally because otherwise you can take away from the flow of the game. Dewayne and I shared the philosophy that what's happening on the field is the most important thing."

I feel highly honored by Tony's assessment of the work I did with him:

"Many times," he said, "guys who've done a lot of radio as a baseball broadcaster come into the TV booth and try to do the game as if it's radio—but television is a visual medium, and Dewayne never had any trouble making that adjustment. He didn't talk too much and try to paint a picture like you have to do on radio. He just told the story and did a TV broadcast the way it was supposed to be done. I also consider accuracy the biggest thing in any broadcast—and that was something Dewayne excelled at as much as or more than any other guy I worked with."

I always placed a heavy premium on accuracy—even when it came to an impression I was occasionally coaxed into doing of my former partner Harry Caray. For some reason, the breathy enthusiasm of Harry's voice was easy for me to master. The Yankee beat writers and others in the organization had heard me replicate it from time to time. And one day at County Stadium in Milwaukee, the writers prevailed upon me to use it to play a prank on the stoic Showalter. Apparently, Harry and Steve Stone had made a mildly critical comment during a WGN telecast about one of Buck's moves in a game. That got back to him and he bristled that Harry had questioned his tactics.

The plan called for me to dial the clubhouse when Showalter was addressing all the Yankee writers, pretending to be Harry.

When the moment arrived, I placed the call to the manager's office and one of the PR guys—aware of the flak he might catch if his role in the ruse was discovered—reluctantly handed the phone to Showalter. On cue, I went, "BUCK! This is Harry Caray in Chicago, and I just want to tell you I think you're doing a great job up there! I also want you to know we heard you're a little upset about something we said the other day."

The whole time I was talking, continuing to shower Showalter with compliments, he sounded increasingly peeved, mustering only a periodic, bristly "Yeah." I felt it was time to push the envelope a bit after talking up his team's potential, and how fortunate he was to have former Cubs pitching coach Billy Connors on his staff. "And you've also got that fine young broadcaster, Dewayne Staats—he used to be with us, you know?"

Around the room, writers were snickering, trying to keep straight faces and Buck, growing impatient with my faux Harry banter, suddenly picked up on the reaction. "Wait a minute, who is this?"

I replied, as earnestly as possible, "Why, it's Harry!"

But Buck didn't buy it. "Hey," he blurted out. "Is this you Dewayne?"

I'd been found out, and owned up with a nod to Harry's home run call. "It might be. It could be. It is!" To his credit, Showalter never held it against me—and we always got along well in the seasons that followed.

The final year of my MSG contract was 1994, and that happened to be a season abbreviated by a players' strike that began August 12. In an attempt to offset baseball's financial struggles at the time, major league owners had proposed a players' salary cap, as well as a plan for franchises to agree to share local broadcast revenues to help smaller-market clubs. The Players Union was vehemently opposed to a salary cap, triggering a strike that would wipe out a combined 948 regular-season games and the entire postseason.

What a shame it was, because Showalter's fine managing in 1994—and the money Steinbrenner had begun to spend on free agents after his return in 1992—had resulted in an impressive turnaround. At the time of the strike, the Yankees were running away with the AL East, leading the second-place Orioles by 6.5 games with a sensational record of 70-43. Mattingly was swinging a hot bat at .304 and was possibly looking at the first World Series appearance of his remarkable career. O'Neill was on a blistering pace, hitting .359 with 21 homeruns, and Key was lights out, dominating opponents with a 17-4 record, while free-agent closer Steve Howe, in spite of his previous off-field troubles, was perfect at 3-0 with a 1.80 ERA.

But it all came screeching to a premature conclusion in early August. Tony had one more year left on his contract with MSG, and he could easily have worked for many more. But after 40 years of travel as a player and broadcaster, including 13 as a Blue Jays analyst in addition to NBC, he had seen enough. When the strike began after a Yankees' road game, he called his wife, Margaret, and said, "I'm getting out." He flew back to New York to tell Bob and thank him for the opportunity—and all the support fending off Steinbrenner—and then returned home to Wisconsin to enjoy retirement.

As I think back on his decision, I realize that Tony seemed to grasp something more quickly than a lot of people. While many of us spend so much time thinking about and planning for tomorrow, he seemed to understand that what we really have is today. By going home when he did, he picked up more than twenty years of "todays" with his wife and family. It was pure Tony, a man with integrity in abundance and, next to my dad, the most straightforward, honest man I've known.

For me, the time seemed to have come for a departure as well—and not just because my good pal and colleague had gone, or my contract was up. As I said earlier. I'd never envisioned defining my career as a Yankee broadcaster and this felt like a logical moment to make a break.

Working for Bob Gutkowski, covering the team and living in New York, had been a terrific experience. Dee and the girls had been able come up for long visits during the summer and enjoy the many great cultural and entertainment assets the city has to offer. My wife loved the theater and she would take Steph and Alexa out to Broadway shows, in addition to catching games at Yankee Stadium. But it had been five years, and things were beginning to fall apart on the MSG side as well. There had been a corporate takeover and a period of austerity was kicking in. Bob decided it was the right time to leave, too.

"We had created such a culture at the Madison Square Garden Network," he reflected. "I just think everybody felt we'd had an incredible run in the market and it was time to move on. The band was breaking up. But for those five years, we were very proud at the network of the way Dewayne and Tony presented the product. They were a great tandem—and I'd put them up against anybody."

In addition to Tony, Bob and me, other people in the operation began leaving right and left—and it quickly began to feel as if nobody at the MSG Network was even home. Meanwhile, I hadn't renewed—and they hadn't renewed me. If I'd wanted to negotiate a new contract, my business manager and longtime friend Gil Engler wasn't even sure who he was supposed to talk to.

To make things even weirder, the new ownership at MSG kept sending me my paychecks—even though technically I wasn't working for them. I didn't cash any, though, and eventually wound up sending them back. It was very strange period indeed, made worse by the fact that baseball was on strike, meaning daily business and communication was essentially shut down. Clearly, the time was right for a change.

But if I was going to leave, I needed to have an idea of where to land next. One place held a tremendous amount of appeal, in part because it would allow me to stay in Florida: ESPN. It had only been five years since the network had tried to hire me for one game a week while I worked at WGN. I talked it over with Bob and Chet, both of whom had great perspective and history at ESPN, and they thought it was a good idea to see if any opportunities existed for me at the network. Gil made the initial contact on my behalf. I was far more experienced and marketable now—and this time, there was nothing to get in the way.

CHAPTER TEN

# A Changing Life in the Spotlight

I'm a firm believer that things happen for a reason, although I had no way of knowing what the reason was when I signed on with ESPN in 1995. Money was not the motivating factor. Contrary to what people assume, the pay was considerably less than what I had earned with the Madison Square Garden Network. The truth is, the worldwide broadcasting behemoth based in Bristol, Connecticut was a professional lifeline for me—offering exposure on the national stage beyond anything I'd experienced before, and a perfectly timed transition away from the rapidly unraveling MSG platform with the Yankees. And as far as I was concerned, that was a very appealing combination.

My work was much more familiar now to the ESPN powers who had offered me a spot on their baseball broadcast team while I was at WGN. And the timing happened to be perfect—the network wanted to hire new talent for the Wednesday Night Game of the Week, which featured contests on both the East and West Coast.

Soon after ESPN became aware of my interest and availability, I received a new offer and jumped at it: a chance to be part of the network's Wednesday baseball crew, as well as doing play-by-play in college football and college basketball. But best of all, I would be able to base out of our home in the Wellington-West Palm Beach area. And that meant spending more time with Dee and the girls—now growing up fast at 17 and 11—than any other period of my career with the Astros, Cubs or Yankees.

In recent years, at the end of the baseball season, Dee and I had started a tradition of flying to Greece to visit members of her extended family. These were wonderful trips—both celebratory and relaxing, as we fully immersed ourselves in Greek culture and cuisine for several weeks. During my time in New York, we even bought and renovated a small home in Rhodes that had been in Dee's family for several generations, giving us a comfortable place to stay during our visits. With all the flying I did during the course of a season, I had accumulated more airline travel miles than I knew what to do with—and this was a particularly meaningful way to put them to use. Dee took the girls with her to Greece during the summer, giving them a chance to connect with their heritage and relatives, and then she and I would take our own vacation there during the fall.

The baseball strike, meanwhile, stretched through the offseason, with the league's executive council making plans to play with replacement players in spring training and, if necessary, the regular season. That idea created an uproar among already disenchanted fans, and even angered some baseball insiders. Detroit manager Sparky Anderson, for one, refused to work with replacements and was placed on an involuntary leave of absence.

Finally, on April 2, 1995—a day before the season was scheduled to begin with replacements—the strike was settled when the Court of Appeals for New York's Second Circuit upheld a preliminary injunction against the owners (issued by future U.S. Supreme Court Justice Sonia Sotamayor). After a 232-day work stoppage—the longest in Major League Baseball history—the owners had lost. The upshot: The players and owners had to adhere to the terms of the previous collective bargaining agreement until a new one could be agreed upon, and the '95 season started three weeks late, shortened from 162 games to 144.

Against such a divisive backdrop, my tenure as an ESPN baseball play-by-play talent began. The structure of my workweek had a distinct upside, in spite of the heavy weekly cross-country travel involved. I only had to cover one baseball game per week when I wasn't assigned to a college contest. Realistically, a coast-to-coast trip still required a total of three travel days when you factored in flying to and from destinations like Los Angeles, San Francisco, Oakland or Seattle. That often left me four full days with the family and a chance to experience a whole new rhythm on the home front. Indeed, that first year on the job was marked by a tangible change of pace. I was able to attend school functions for the girls I'd previously had to miss, be home during the week to go shopping or out to eat with Dee, or help around the house when I would otherwise have been at the ballpark.

I truly savored this new-found family time, giving me more opportunities to be there for the girls. That was especially important for Alexa, being six years younger than Steph. "It was great when dad would come home, whether it was in Chicago or our new place in Wellington," she recollects. "After school, he'd pick up me up and that was really exciting. When he was gone, my mom was really good about keeping us busy growing up. I played basketball on a boys' team and Steph took more to the piano and dance. But we always loved it when dad could be there with us."

Being together was special for all of us, though the next trip was always right around the corner—and the logistics of my ESPN assignments occasionally made my head spin. Because the baseball season overlapped with college football, my schedule could get crazy during the weeks I was scheduled for both baseball and football. For instance, I once found myself flying out of West Palm Beach to LAX on a Tuesday, doing a Dodgers broadcast on Wednesday night, then, on Thursday morning, catching a flight to Honolulu so I could cover the University of Texas opening its football season at the University of Hawaii on Saturday. I arrived home in West Palm on Monday—only to turn around and fly back to the West Coast to catch a Mariners game two days later in Seattle. Fortunately, that kind of itinerary was the exception to the rule.

ESPN was beginning to blanket the country with its Major League Baseball coverage, employing multiple crews to cover different games five nights a week. Early on, I crossed paths with Buck Martinez, who played 17 seasons with the Kansas City Royals, Milwaukee Brewers and Toronto Blue Jays, and who'd joined ESPN in the early 1990s as a color analyst. I was delighted to get to know him better now as a fellow broadcaster, sharing various assignments with him as part of ESPN's ever-growing talent pool. Buck and I were both fortunate to be part of what truly was a golden era of expanding baseball coverage at the network, and we enjoyed the times we shared a booth.

"ESPN did such a great job with baseball and hiring baseball purists to broadcast the games, like Dewayne—people who just loved the game and wanted to do as many games as possible," Buck recalls. "Dewayne always understood the role of a play-by-play broadcaster. He understood that every game has a story—and he knew how to find the storyline and convey it with the analyst in an engaging way.

"We both learned a lot, I think, from Tony Kubek. Tony and I were both analysts with the Blue Jays, and he was a great mentor to me—helping me become a better analyst. And I think Dewayne benefitted from Tony's presence in New York as much as I did in Toronto.

"I think what Dewayne and I had in common was that we were both baseball fans, first and foremost. And when you make a living doing what you love, it's a perfect situation. Dewayne was much more advanced in his experience than I was at the time, so I learned from him as well."

Somehow, even amid the ESPN whirlwind, Dee and I managed to go to Greece that fall for two weeks in 1995—and I still wound up covering eight or nine college football games. There was no longer an off-season in my work schedule, with college basketball soon leading into 1996 spring training and the start of a new baseball season. Then, barely a month into the season, life took an abrupt and frightening turn.

One day, Dee told me she was starting to experience a strange and unsettling sensation—having trouble understanding what people were saying during her phone conversations.

"People's voices sound distorted, almost like cartoon characters," she said.

At first, we thought the problem might have been caused by a virus or infection and would just pass on its own. When the difficulty persisted, Dee made an appointment with an ear, nose and throat specialist. But the doctor could find no clue as to what was causing the problem. Feeling heightened anxiety yet still hoping there was a simple explanation, we decided to see a Sarasota neurologist who had a good reputation. He performed a CAT scan, then sat us down in his office to show us the results. We could tell from his serious manner that the news was not good, and our hearts sank as he pointed to the dark image on screen—a small tumor in Dee's brain. It was pressing against the auditory nerve, explaining why she'd been having so much difficulty processing voices on the phone.

Dee and I felt numb as we tried our best to focus on what the doctor was telling us. And then, as if we were on some surreal rollercoaster ride, we suddenly experienced a sharp emotional swing. Apparently there was some good news to latch onto amid the bad. The tumor appeared to be an acoustic neuroma, an uncommon yet benign and slow-growing mass—one that develops on the primary nerve leading from the inner ear to the brain. We instantly felt a weight lift from our shoulders upon hearing that the tumor wasn't malignant, though the doctor glumly underscored that this specific tumor can cause hearing loss or persistent ringing in the ear—a condition called tinnitus.

The more he talked, the clearer it became he had a terrible bedside manner. The doctor may have been an expert in his field, but his entire tone seemed to be one of doom and gloom. He matter-of-factly explained that the surgery to remove the tumor would leave Dee without hearing in the affected ear, and severing the nerve—as he would need to do—would leave her with some degree of paralysis, causing one side of her face to droop. You can imagine what it was like to hear such a blunt, unsympathetic prognosis. Dee was shaken, and so was I. We left his office—making the long drive back across the state to Wellington—absolutely sure that we would never return.

As we pondered other options for treatment, I remembered that my younger sister's husband worked with various medical practices in St. Louis. When we returned home, I called him and he recommended a neurologist he knew and respected there, Dr. James Benecke. We made a call and learned that Dr. Benecke was skilled at doing this type of delicate surgery. Talking with him by phone, everything about his manner and experience struck us as positive—diametrically opposite from our first doctor. Dr. Benecke explained to us that he was always extremely gentle with the involved nerve, and though Dee might suffer some paralysis in her face, there was a good chance she would regain function. His pleasant manner—straightforward yet upbeat—was exactly what we needed under the difficult circumstances.

We made arrangements to travel to St. Louis, where Dr. Benecke performed the surgery. Dee was incredibly brave. In essence, she had to have her skull broken for the tumor to be removed, but she never complained, though I know how excruciating the ordeal had to have been. I took time off from work to be by her side and, within several weeks, she was well enough to go back to Florida, and to continue her recuperation at home. When I returned to the road for ESPN, it was extremely hard knowing Dee was on her own without me, living her new reality—loss of hearing in her ear, as she had been warned, along with the array of meds required to keep the pain manageable.

Needless to say, this was a very emotionally trying time for Steph and Alexa. They rose to the challenge like troupers and did all they could to help their mom through her deeply traumatic ordeal. In a way, pouring myself into my weekly assignments became therapeutic for me. I could go to a ballpark somewhere out West and compartmentalize my feelings—focusing totally on the broadcast and doing my job, then catching a flight home to Florida, anxious to be with Dee and the girls. I didn't share what was going on with my colleagues, but guys like Buck knew what was happening, and I felt their support implicitly.

"Baseball announcers are basically the same as baseball players in one key way," Buck says. "Especially from our generation, we knew we had a job to do and when you were at the ballpark, you did it. That's how we were brought up. For those hours he was at the game, he focused fully on that—and then he focused on what was such a difficult situation at home with his wife."

As the months passed, Dee gradually recovered and the partial paralysis in her face healed as Dr. Benecke had thought might happen. Miraculously, she was back to being her old self, full of life. Her inner strength and determination were truly remarkable, and once again, she was captain of our ship, keeping the family on course. What a blessing for us after such a frightening experience. The journey had deeply affected all of us—and we moved forward with a greater appreciation of the value of little things in life, the daily interactions that had meaning for us all.

My ESPN work regimen kept me busier than ever over the next 18 months, though the constant cross-county flights each week were beginning to wear on me. One bright spot, however, was working with a new member of ESPN's West Coast broadcast crew. Starting in 1997, I began doing many of the Wednesday Night Baseball telecasts with a newcomer to the network — and a veteran of baseball's managerial ranks—Kevin Kennedy.

Kevin had just come off two strong seasons at the helm of the Red Sox: an 85-77 record and third-place finish in 1996 and an 86-58 mark, after taking over early in the year and leading the Sox into the post-season. He'd also managed the Texas Rangers for the two seasons prior to that, finishing 86-76 in 1993, and 52-62 in the strike-shortened campaign of 1994. Kevin brought a sharp eye for the nuances of the game into the booth, drawing on his experience in the trenches. It was enjoyable to hear his insights from the perspective of a former skipper, just as it was when I worked alongside Jim Frey in the Cubs' radio booth.

We hit it off from the start and got along well on and off the job. All these years later, his kind words mean a lot to me.

"I knew of Dewayne's vast experience as a broadcaster going into the job and learned a lot working with him," Kevin says. "I always had respect for the play-by-play guys because I was just learning the fine points of being an analyst. I was green those first few years at ESPN, and Dewayne was so professional. He was great. I worked with other guys who had a way of talking down to you. But Dewayne never did that. I recall being a little nervous at first, but he treated me as an equal and made me feel very comfortable from the start.

"The thing with Dewayne was he would let you talk. My bosses at ESPN had told me that my job was to explain 'how' and 'why'—and Dewayne gave me the space to do that. With some guys, you had to really fight your way in to make a point. But he knew when he wanted to make a point—and also knew when to lay off and let the analyst get in there. That trait is so important, and really helped me develop a flow with him.

"But there was something else I observed about what made Dewayne special and made an impact on me—his incredible preparation. We once were assigned to cover the Little League Western Regional World Series in Riverside, California. We had been in Los Angeles doing a game the night before, and I remember that Dewayne drove to Riverside to attend the kickoff luncheon for the Series. I had a prior commitment and arrived a little late, but there he was—jotting down all the players' names and stats, preparing for the Little League World Series like it was the actual World Series. That was impressive—and typical of how he always worked."

One of the residual effects of working at ESPN mirrored my experience at the WGN superstation: People in different parts of the country recognized me on the street. They called my name, or approached me—wanting to ask me questions about this game or that event—and I always had fun with it. But in my heart of hearts, I knew that what I was most comfortable doing—what truly made me happy—was covering a major league baseball game every day in a local or regional market.

I had done that for five years in New York with the Yankees, and by 1997 was nearing three years on national television covering a variety of sports. I was incredibly grateful for both experiences, but neither represented my true career aspiration. Each assignment had served an important purpose. MSG had given me enough of a financial bump to be able to put some money in the bank, while working alongside such high-caliber professionals as Tony Kubek and Bob Gutkowski. ESPN had elevated my profile—and, more important than anything, given me the priceless gift of time to spend with my family at such a crucial period of our lives.

The two professional experiences gave major league clubs and broadcast networks a clear picture of my work, heightening my chances should any openings arise. While I wasn't actively looking to leave ESPN at this stage, I had grown a bit weary of being pulled all over the country week after week. Dee and I agreed if the right opportunity came along, I would consider it.

One night, after covering a Mariners game in Seattle with Kevin, we'd gone out for a beer and the conversation, at some point, turned to the expansion Tampa Bay Devil Rays. "You know, we ought to put in for that—that would be a great gig for us," I said. We never got around to that. But then, in the late summer of 1997, I received a phone call from Dean Jordan, the president of SportsChannel Florida, the state network that broadcast the National League's Florida Marlins.

The network had just made a deal to carry the games of the expansion Devil Rays, and was in the process of assembling a television crew for the inaugural season in 1998. Dean wanted to know if I had any interest in the job—and I most definitely did. The idea of getting in on the ground floor of a franchise, in an area that had been hungering for major league baseball, held instant appeal—as did the geographical proximity of St. Petersburg to our home across the state.

The SportsChannel Florida guys were aware of my work, and seemed as eager to speak with me as I was to them. Within a matter of days, they flew me to Tampa for a meeting that included Dean, SportsChannel Florida vice president Rod Mickler and Devil Rays owner Vince Naimoli. We actually met at Tropicana Field, even with construction crews busily refurbishing the 10-year-old facility and hurriedly getting it baseball-ready. Amid drywall and plastic sheets, we worked out the basics of a deal that would make me the Devil Rays' first play-by-play man—and bring me back to the baseball broadcast booth on a regular basis.

We finalized the contract in the fall, though the SportsChannel folks held off announcing the news for about two months. I continued to do work for ESPN during that period, and then—in December 1997—was introduced as the voice of the team. It was an exciting moment for me, even knowing that it would likely take a few years for the franchise to become competitive. I knew how hard business leaders in the Tampa Bay area had worked to land a franchise since the 1970s, and now—beneath the slanted domed roof and catwalks of the Trop—the dream was about to take shape. I couldn't have been happier to be a part of it.

Once I was on board, attention focused on hiring an analyst to work alongside me in the booth. I instantly thought of Kevin, called him up to suggest he go for the job, and talked him up to my new bosses. They had interest, but Kevin was already negotiating with Fox Sports about a studio analyst position, which would allow him to stay in his hometown of Los Angeles. On top of that, he was newly married and had just bought a house in the LA area. The timing just wasn't right for him to pursue the opportunity.

Dean, Rod and others at SportsChannel Florida consulted with me about possible color commentators and reached out to various potential candidates, including Bob Montgomery, a former catcher who worked as the Red Sox color commentator. During the process, I received a call from Joe Magrane. I had occasionally covered Joe during his pitching career with the St. Louis Cardinals and later the California Angels, and had then worked with him from time to time at ESPN, including a stint at the College World Series. Joe was highly interested in the job, and I encouraged him to go for it. He had a live-wire personality and we kidded around a lot with each other. On top of that, he was bright and well-spoken, and there was no question he knew baseball. It didn't take long for him to emerge as the top contender.

Still, the position remained unfilled with the season fast approaching. In fact, Devil Rays pitchers and catchers had already reported for spring training at the northwest St. Petersburg site previously used by the Mets and Cardinals—eventually renamed the Raymond A. Naimoli Baseball Complex. I had gone to watch workouts and remember sitting inside a trailer with Vince and Rod just as Magrane showed up to be interviewed. We exchanged friendly greetings as I got up to leave and give them some privacy. But as I headed to the door, I took the opportunity to give him a friendly jab—typical of the kind of shots we'd exchange with each other. I said to Vince and Rod, tongue placed firmly in cheek, "Look, the only thing I can tell you about Magrane is if you hire him you should probably strike the morals clause in these contracts." In the final analysis, I was excited about the prospect of Joe joining our crew, with his multi-faceted tool box that would surely be needed in the early years of an expansion team.

Shortly after the interview, Joe got the job and our partnership was official. The question now was what kind of team would these baby Devil Rays put on the field, and how long it might take to become competitive. Given some of the names on the roster, we even thought there was a chance they might win sooner rather than later.

CHAPTER ELEVEN

# Growing Pains

There are two reasons that the date February 27, 1998 holds particular meaning for me.

For starters, that day on the calendar marked the inaugural Devil Rays telecast for SportsChannel Florida. Our coverage of the club's very first spring training game at newly christened Florida Power Park went off remarkably well. Joe and I welcomed viewers for the first time and established a comfortable on-air rapport. The only thing that would have made the broadcast better was a Tampa Bay victory, but the cross-state Florida Marlins undermined that possibility with a 2-1 victory before a nonetheless upbeat crowd at Al Lang Field.

The second reason is tinged with regret. Though I certainly had to be in St. Petersburg for our big launch, I wished that somehow—on this very same day—I could have been 1,000 miles to the north. With mourners packing Chicago's Holy Name Cathedral to pay their final respects, my friend and former colleague, Harry Caray, was being eulogized in a funeral service fittingly filled with humor and all things baseball. He had died just two weeks shy of his 84th birthday, and his family was joined by a throng of celebrities and athletes—from Cubs slugger Sammy Sosa to former Bears head coach Mike Ditka—as well as many grateful fans.

I got a good picture of the event from my friends in attendance and widespread media coverage, including a detailed account in the *Chicago Tribune*. Pete Vonachen, the owner of the minor league Peoria Chiefs, provided a tribute that had everyone in the pews laughing at memories and quips about his dear, longtime friend. When the reverend asked the gathering to applaud Harry,

Pete, standing by Harry's casket, interjected, "Please father, don't resurrect him. We couldn't go through this again."

At one point, Pete recalled Harry's fondness for friendly imbibing, describing it second only to his predilection for socializing—an impulse which often led the two of them to leave their drinks at the bar completely untouched, while going in search of a livelier nightlife scene.

"If I gave everyone in here one of the drinks we left behind," he said, "not one of you could pass a Breathalyzer test."

But speakers also underlined Harry's generosity to Maryville Academy, an institution for abused and neglected children, and his perpetual kindness to anyone who approached him for an autograph. And Pete closed on a note of seriousness, talking about the lessons to learn from Harry's life: Players should be good to the fans, and friends should take time to reaffirm their love for one another.

When the service ended and the crowd began filing out, the organist—rather than playing a solemn hymn—performed a lively rendition of *Take Me Out to the Ball Game*.

The old ball game was what Harry was all about. And in St. Petersburg that spirit had finally come to life after decades of tireless—and often acrimonious—civic efforts around the region to land a major league franchise. It was exciting to be riding the first wave of big-league baseball in Tampa Bay, and—from a personal standpoint—to be back in the booth calling baseball games again in a local market.

Spring training wasn't just a time for the Devil Rays ball players to work themselves into form. It was a time for the broadcast crew to develop a rhythm and chemistry in the booth, become more acquainted with each other's styles and learn to play off one another. That process was made easier for Joe and me from having worked together at ESPN—and simply by the natural way our personalities clicked. I'd covered Joe when he pitched for the Cardinals, often in big games against some of the best pitchers in baseball—John Smoltz, Tom Glavine, Greg Maddux, Orel Hershiser and many other No. 1 starters of the day. I loved those games because Joe always set a fast tempo, similar to the quick, energetic manner he displayed in the booth.

He was outspoken and off-the-cuff in his analyst style, while I tended to project more of a steady tone as play-by-play man. But we enjoyed kidding around and doing what we could to liven up the proceedings. Or, as Joe says: "Dewayne had to be the traffic cop and provide a certain sense of organization. I just thought it was a very good mix, because at times I'd go off the reservation and he was right there to bring the focus back, or to play the role of straight man to something I'd say."

I knew from experience that sometimes egos can pose problems in the booth, and I shared my observations with Joe. I told him the underlying strength of a crew comes from the confidence the broadcasters have in each other, and the loyalty they feel for one another. With such a solid foundation, reinforced by good preparation for each broadcast and the interplay of our respective personalities, I believed that all the baseball talk would just flow naturally.

Though our personalities were like night and day, we shared Midwestern roots—he was born in Iowa—and a similar philosophy about the game that fortified our budding partnership and friendship. Again, I defer to my old boothmate for elaboration.

"We would talk everything from politics to teams to baseball history, and I'd always refer to Dewayne—as well as other folks from the part of America we refer to as 'flyover country'—as a Central Time Zone type guy. It was a way of describing that person as a Steady Eddie. In other words, we'll be there for you to help you plow the Back 30 or change your tires, or do whatever you need. That's how I viewed Dewayne—he was ready for work every single day. He was completely prepared, completely loyal—and it got to where we could finish each other's sentences, and knew the direction we were going with something.

"In addition, both Dewayne and I have a great appreciation for the history of baseball. Not every play-by-play and analyst have that in common, and we were definitely connected from that standpoint. All I ever wanted was to be a major league pitcher—and I used to listen to Jack Buck call Cardinals games on my little transistor radio, just as Dewayne had listened to his, and dreamed of becoming a broadcaster. I had great admiration for Tony Kubek as a Yankees analyst, because he had that reverence for the game, and he and Dewayne had been such a great combination. So many aspects of our partnership intertwined, and that made a difference."

There was another key position to fill for our telecasts—the job of roving reporter to provide player interviews and color from the stands, the field and the clubhouse. I knew just the guy for the role—a young, television broadcaster with an affable manner and a strong baseball background: Todd Kalas.

I was well-acquainted with his father, the acclaimed play-by-play man Harry Kalas. Harry had left the Astros announcing team before I arrived to broadcast for the Phillies, but our paths had intersected frequently over the years. Along the way, I had come to know of Todd and his terrific background—he'd graduated from Syracuse University's top-notch broadcast journalism program, did radio work for the New York Mets for two seasons, and, for the past three years, worked on the Phillies' television crew. What's more, I knew he'd served as sports director of Clearwater's Vision Cable earlier in his career and lived locally in the off-season.

One afternoon during spring training at Al Lang Field, I said to my boss at SportsChannel Florida, Rod Mickler, "You know, Todd Kalas has a home in the area. He'd do a great job for us." Mickler was interested, but there was one problem: Todd had just signed a contract to do the Devil Rays' pre-game and post-game show for WFLA-AM 970 radio. He tried to work out an arrangement that would allow him to do the radio job and also work fulltime as the Devil Rays reporter for SportsChannel Florida, but logistically it wasn't possible.

Fortunately, the two stations worked out a deal that allowed Todd to do about 40-50 home games on the telecast the first few seasons, while working 162 pre- and post-game shows for WFLA. After that, he joined us fulltime on TV. Todd's personable, incisive and humorous reports—plus his consistently smooth interaction with us—became an integral part of the show over the course of the entire season.

"I would see Dewayne through my work with the Mets and Phillies, but I didn't really get to know him until I worked for the Devil Rays," Todd recalls. "Dewayne, Joe and I hit it off right from the start. And when I finally started to travel with the team, we'd see each other a lot more—going out to dinner and just hanging together. There were five of us: Dewayne, Joe, our director Thom Hastings, and our graphics coordinator and associate producer Tom Barberi. That's really where our camaraderie and on-air style developed. Joe had his crazy sense of humor, and he and Dewayne always worked incredibly well together."

We were well aware that there would be a fair amount of losing in that first season of '98, typical of any team just coming into existence. Nonetheless, as the season neared, Joe and I looked at the roster that General Manager Chuck LaMar had assembled, and thought the team had some real potential—if key players flourished or were given an opportunity that they hadn't previously enjoyed elsewhere.

There was a nice mixture of veterans and youngsters on the squad—managed by Larry Rothschild, a former big-league reliever who became a pitching instructor with the Reds, Braves and Marlins. The infield looked surprisingly promising, with John Flaherty and Mike DiFelice catching; hometown hero Fred "Crime Dog" McGriff, the longtime power-hitter for the Jays and Braves, at first base; solid defenders in Miguel Cairo at second and Kevin Stocker at short; and the gem of the whole bunch—third baseman Wade Boggs, who had signed with the Devil Rays to finish out his Hall of Fame career across the bay from his hometown of Tampa.

I liked the outfield versatility with such names as Quinton McCracken, Randy Winn, Davey Martinez and former first-round and second overall pick of the 1991 draft, Mike Kelly.

Paul Sorrento had some left-handed pop as a designated hitter. And the pitching featured some veteran arms in Wilson Avarez, who had been a standout with the White Sox; Rolando Arrojo, a former Cuban National Team star making his big-league debut; and experienced closer Roberto Hernandez, who had been a mainstay of the Chisox bullpen.

As expansion teams go, there was reason to think this one might at least buck the trend and be somewhat respectable—even in the talent-heavy American League East, alongside the Yankees, Red Sox, Orioles and Blue Jays. But such optimistic thinking was confronted with harsh reality in the season opener at Tropicana Field on March 31, 1998.

After all the hoopla and pre-game festivities faded, along with the smoke from a fireworks display, Alvarez took the mound to face the Detroit Tigers—and that's when the tone of the season was set. He was a major disappointment. Nobody expected he would win 20 games, but there was reason to think his won-loss mark might be .500 or even a bit above. Richie Garcia was the plate umpire for the opener, and I later reminded him that he'd called Alvarez' first pitch in Devil Rays history—to Detroit center-fielder Brian Hunter—a ball. I said, "Richie, I've often wondered, 'What would have happened if you had called that pitch a strike? Would it all have been different?' "

Alvarez lasted 2.1 innings, yielding nine hits and six runs, as the Tigers built an 11-0 lead en route to an 11-6 victory, dampening the celebratory mood of the sellout crowd. The only notable occurrence was the first home run in team history, a sixth-inning shot by Boggs. From the start, LaMar admitted he'd overspent for Alvarez, but felt that was the amount he had to pay—and the pricetag raised expectations for his projected ace. In spite of the season-opening pratfall, the Devil Rays took the next two from Detroit and, after 19 games, surprisingly stood at 11-8. But that's when the bottom began to fall out.

In spite of some solid pitching from Arrojo—who emerged as the staff leader with a 14-12 record—the team had difficulty getting quality innings out of its starters, and didn't score runs like we thought they might have. A long season has a way of equalizing things, making players look like who they really are. And soon enough, the Devil Rays looked like a first-year expansion team, finishing dead last in the division at 63-99.

During the inaugural season and for the team's early years, I worked several innings on radio—joining Charlie Slowes in the booth, while Paul Olden handled those innings with Joe on TV. I enjoyed having the chance to reconnect with my radio roots. But my primary role was on TV with Joe as we did our best to make the telecasts fun and informative, and build an audience.

Devil Rays owner Vince Naimoli, who had doggedly fought to get the franchise for Tampa Bay, was a constant presence. Though he was well known for his bluster and feistiness, I never had any issues with Vince—not one. In terms of his putting the hammer on you, I simply never experienced any of that. To his credit, he'd enlist opinions of people around him—including occasionally asking me for my thoughts about the team and ways it could gel. I remember stressing the need to develop players through the system, saying, "You know, at some point, you're going to have to start playing a lot of kids to make long-term strides." But he wanted to compete immediately—and that, as it became increasingly evident, just wasn't in the cards.

Away from the ballpark, life in the Tampa Bay area was wonderful. After I took the job, Dee and I had come over to the West Coast two or three times and scouted out the whole region. She wanted to live on the water, so initially we looked at property to the south of the Sunshine Skyway Bridge in Bradenton and Sarasota.

Those are great areas, but I felt that the daily drive to the ballpark would have been too long. One day, we found ourselves standing on Clearwater Beach, and I looked into the distance and saw the stretch of land—connected by a bridge—called Sand Key. New condominiums were springing up along the Gulf of Mexico beachfront, and we discovered one under construction that had everything we wanted: reasonable proximity to the Trop—and surroundings that felt to us like paradise.

Dee had wanted a place on the sixth floor, picturing herself leaning over the balcony, calling to our girls at the pool down below when she needed to tell them it was time for dinner. But that one had been sold, so we bought the unfinished unit on the 16th floor—inheriting a stunning view of the Gulf and the evening sunset on the horizon. While our unit was being built, and the inaugural season approached, I stayed in a small condo down the road. Dee remained home in South Florida with Alexa, who was finishing up the eighth grade. And Steph, who'd been attending Florida Atlantic University on the East Coast, transferred to the University of South Florida in St. Petersburg, and stayed with me.

When the '98 season was over, we were all able to move into our dream home. I couldn't believe our good fortune. Our family was together again in simply one of the most beautiful areas of the world I'd ever seen—a long way from my smalltown East Alton childhood. I still did a little work for ESPN, covering basketball in the offseason. And in no time, it seemed, Year Two of the franchise was upon us.

The significant addition for the 1999 season was brash slugger Jose Canseco, now in the final stages of his colorful and, at times, controversial 15-year career with Oakland, Texas, Boston and Toronto. Jose didn't disappoint while he was in the lineup. He hammered 34 home runs and earned a spot on the All-Star team, but then suffered a back injury and missed most of July and early August. McGriff also contributed his share of dingers with 32.

But the homer that had everyone in baseball talking was delivered on August 7, 1999. Boggs came into a home game against the Cleveland Indians, needing three hits to reach 3,000 for his career. After a first-inning groundout, he singled to right in the third for No. 2,998 and singled again to right in the fourth for 2,999. When he stepped to the plate in the sixth, with the Indians leading 11-7, the near sellout crowd showered Boggs with a huge ovation. And he responded by making history, hitting a shot deep to right that cleared the wall—making him the first major leaguer ever to homer for his 3,000th hit.

I happened to still be in the radio booth for that groundbreaking event, calling it alongside my partner, Charlie Slowes. Everyone knew it was gone the instant the ball left his bat. I'll never forget the sight of Boggs pointing skyward as he rounded first base, then kneeling down and kissing home plate. That home run instantly became the signature moment of the franchise and would remain so for years to come. It ranked as the clear-cut highlight of the second season, which saw some minor improvement with a 69-93 record, though the Devil Rays were still entrenched in the division cellar.

There was another highlight that year—on a more personal playing field. Steph had been doing some part-time work at Tropicana Field, working as a statistician for visiting telecasts and a stage manager in the booth during broadcasts. It was a great way to earn some extra money while attending USF, and she'd always loved baseball—from the time she was a little girl, learning how to keep score from her mom.

Being at the park frequently, Steph was aware that the Rays had called up a 21-year-old righthanded reliever named Dan Wheeler, a 6-foot-3, 220-pound draft pick who had come up through the team's farm system. I'd gotten a scouting report on him, hearing that he had a great slider and threw the ball in the low 90s. But when he made his early September debut in Baltimore, the radar gun registered him at 93 and 94 mph. I was impressed—but apparently not as impressed as Steph.

Shortly after the season, I attended a team-related function in the Bradenton-Sarasota area, planning to go straight from there to Tampa International Airport and catch a flight for an ESPN basketball assignment. Steph wanted to be able to borrow my car while I was gone, so she came to the function with me, planning to drop me off at the airport afterwards, and drive herself home. She joined me at a table designated for the Devil Rays, a spot where Dan Wheeler also happened to be seated. He and Steph talked and seemed to hit it off. Steph wasn't star-struck by baseball players—the game had been part of her life ever since she was a baby flying with her mom and dad on a Houston Astros charter. She'd never dated players; both Dee and I would have discouraged that. Let's just say many young, single ballplayers don't always have the best of intentions.

That afternoon, I could see that Steph and Dan were enjoying each other's company. But with Dan soon moving up and down between Triple-A Durham and the Devil Rays, there was no reason to think their friendly conversation would lead to anything serious.

The 2000 season was Tampa Bay's first year without Wade Boggs, and he would certainly be missed. After his momentous year in 1999, Wade had suffered a knee injury and decided to retire—with a lifetime .328 batting average, and a likely first-ballot election to the Hall of Fame.

This was also the year of the highly touted, and equally ill-fated "Hit Show."

With attendance slipping in a worrisome way at the Trop, Vince Naimoli and Chuck LaMar opted to do something splashy to lure more fans to the games. Vince was also getting pressure from the franchise's limited partners to make the product more appealing to the public. That gave rise to the idea of assembling a lineup heavy with power, on the theory that fans would flock to the park to see offensive fireworks. To make it happen, LaMar pinpointed and signed two free-agent sluggers, 32-year-old third baseman Vinny Castilla and 34-year-old outfielder Greg Vaughn, who would be paired with McGriff, 36, and Canseco, 35. "Hit Show" billboards and other marketing efforts popped up all over the area, but the actual Hit Show players—a little long in the tooth—had less pop than fizzle.

You could argue that Vaughn and McGriff did their parts with 28 and 27 homeruns, respectively. But Castilla, who had enjoyed consecutive seasons of 40, 40, 46 and 33 homers before joining

Tampa Bay, finished with a mere six long balls. Canseco, in the DH role, managed just nine as he continued to unravel physically, and after spending June on the disabled list, he was waived and claimed by the Yankees in August. As big a bust as the Hit Show was, the acquisition of veteran, oft-injured pitcher Juan Guzman was equally disappointing. LaMar settled on the long-time Toronto hurler late in the free agent process after better options had already been scooped up, threw as much money as he could afford at Guzman (a cool $12-million over two years)—and hoped for the best.

Instead, what he got could hardly have been worse. The right-handed Guzman logged an inning and two-thirds for the Devil Rays in the fifth game of the season, gave up seven hits and eight runs for a 43.20 ERA—and was done for the year. He underwent arthroscopic surgery on his right shoulder, and never pitched in the majors again. That summed up the sorry state of affairs as much as anything.

When it was all over, the third season under Larry Rothschild wasn't much better than the first two: 66-92. Dan actually put the finishing touches on the campaign on October 1, 2000, getting his first big-league win on the last day of the regular season—a 3-2 decision over Boston at the Trop. It was a Sunday afternoon contest, and I remember that day for a particular reason. After the game, Dee, Alexa and I went out to dinner at a favorite Italian restaurant of ours, Villa Gallace, on Indian Rocks Beach to mark the end of another long season—and we waited at our table for two guests, Steph and her now-boyfriend, Dan.

They'd stayed in touch while he was in Durham, and gone on a few dates after he'd been called up by the Devil Rays in September. I already had a good feeling about Dan as a person, based on all my own scouting reports and my limited dealings with him. He was a tall, good-looking kid from Rhode Island who struck me as friendly and genuine. But it didn't matter what I thought. Dee had her own opinions about baseball players and Dan would need to bring his A-game if he had any hope of making a positive impression on her. Here's how Steph remembers it:

"Dan and I drove to the restaurant separately from Tropicana Field, and when we arrived, Dan was a little nervous. And I kind of had some fun with him, saying, 'Oh, don't worry. Meeting my mom is like facing Nomar Garciaparra in the bottom of the ninth with the game on the line.' We walked in and it was like a scene out of a movie. My whole family was sitting there around a table, and my mom was just sitting at the end, looking pleasant with her hands folded. Dan greeted my dad, whom he knew, and then he turned to my mom and said, 'Hello Mrs. Staats, it's really nice to meet you.' "

Dee looked up at him from her seat and responded, "Let me tell you something, I don't like baseball players. They're philanderers and only care about themselves. They don't save their money. They can't be trusted." She continued to tick off other criticisms from a list in her head, then summed it up with a simple phrase:

"So what makes you different?"

I'm thinking, "If he can convince her, he can get big-league hitters out."

And Steph was clearly hoping Dan would say something, anything, to put her skeptical mother at ease. Looking back at that moment, she remembers how much her boyfriend was caught off guard by the icy reception. "He was stumbling over his words at first," she says.

But under the circumstances, I was pretty darn impressed. Like a good reliever, he regained his composure under fire and replied, "I know what you're saying, but I'd like to think I'm different."

"Well," Dee answered, "then sit down."

He did. We had a wonderful dinner, and a special relationship between Steph and Dan continued to flourish. Dee quickly grew to like him as much as I did, and we were pleased to see he had such strong determination to succeed in tough circumstances.

The 2001 season began with disarray for the Devil Rays—and only got worse. After a 4-10 start, LaMar had seen enough to know things weren't likely to improve and dismissed his beleaguered charter manager. Larry was a great pitching coach, and the benefit of hindsight has shown us he was better suited for that role than as a skipper. His strict, meticulous approach—insisting that every minute had to be accounted for—had worn his players out over time, leading to Larry wearing out his welcome.

In fairness, a manager is really only as good as the players he can put on the field and Larry didn't have much to work with—many of the players had experienced their share of failure elsewhere, which is why they were on an expansion team to begin with. You're not going to build a strong building unless you have enough bricks. For that reason, I've always felt it's hard to evaluate an expansion manager. The one legitimate way I think you can do that is to ask, "Did any of the players that he had at the outset get better?" But after an avalanche of losing, with no clear end in sight, the only real question was when Larry would be shown the door.

LaMar's choice of a replacement was first-year Tampa Bay bench coach Hal McRae—a heck of a hitter during his career with the Kansas City Royals who'd gone on to manage the club for four seasons in the 1990s. But Hal had no better luck after taking over 24 games into the season, as the team sputtered to another disappointing finish, 61-101.

Dan only pitched 17.2 innings with the Devil Rays during that dreary campaign, spending most of the season in the minors again, frustrated by a lack of work—with Guzman and other Rays' pitchers getting most of the innings in their rehabilitation stints.

After the season, Dan decided to take matters into his own hands, and arranged to play winter ball in Venezuela. By now, he and Steph had decided to get married and she was thinking about visiting him in Venezuela. But before that could happen, he called her with an urgent message: "There's no way you're coming down here," he said. It turns out he had been awakened the night before by the sound of a violent disturbance on the street. A military action by the country's new strong-armed government, run by President Hugo Chavez, was in progress. That was the end of winter ball for Dan, who left the country as quickly as he could.

But things didn't go as planned upon his return. At the Baseball Winter Meetings in early December, Chuck LaMar—needing to create a roster spot for a new reliever claimed in the Rule Five draft from Atlanta—announced Dan's release from the team. Not long after that disappointing turn of events, Dee and I attended the annual Devil Rays' Christmas party, and LaMar suspected Dee would give him an earful. Hoping to be proactive, he sought us out in the crowd and said, "I know you're looking for me."

"You bet I'm looking for you," she shot back. "You fired the groom!"

That was quintessential Dee for you. In the end, Dan made the point moot by signing with the team that had triggered his release, the Braves, while the Devil Rays began a 2002 season that would soon deteriorate into a new low.

Hal McRae was a good man, with a great baseball background. Now, given a full season to show what he could do, there was hope he would be a welcome change from his serious-minded predecessor and take the team in a new direction.

Hal had said he didn't want to manage again until the time was right, and when LaMar offered him the job, I'm sure he realized it wasn't the greatest opportunity. Still, it was a chance to make his own mark on the ball club as the architect of a dramatic and long-awaited turnaround. For a while, his presence raised hopes that the young team would improve, but the air of hope and heightened expectations didn't last long.

Hal had no choice but to play the hand he was dealt—and there were definitely no aces to be found, of either the figurative or literal variety. Despite winning their first three games, the Devil Rays experienced a new level of futility at 55-106 record—with No. 1 starter Tanyan Sturtze's 4-18 record summing up the dismal situation. McRae was dismissed when the season ended, but in recognition of the fact his hands had been tied by a subpar roster, LaMar simultaneously hired him as assistant to the general manager. The cold truth was that nobody could have come close to a winning record with this team.

From a broadcast perspective, it was definitely a challenge to keep the viewers engaged amid such consistently colossal losing. Our approach was simply to play it game-by-game and inning-by-inning. It was what it was, and we couldn't change that. We chronicled what was happening and kept things as entertaining and insightful as possible. Whenever possible, we'd look for the silver lining—like young left-handed pitcher Joe Kennedy, who showed promise with an 8-11 record and 4.53 ERA, or Paul Wilson, who, despite his 6-12 mark, was a hard worker attempting a comeback. Joe remembers the challenges of those early days in the same way.

"Dewayne and I hung out together on the road, and Todd was with us a lot, along with the guys from the production truck, and we'd talk about how frustrating it was. There were 25 guys on the roster but, in those early years with the Rays, it seemed like 75 guys—it was a merry-go-round of players coming and going. I just wanted to go for the fun factor in the broadcasts, to distract from the horrible baseball. It wasn't the players' fault—many of them just didn't have the ability. There weren't a lot of first-division type guys.

"As an analyst you could easily jump on five mistakes in an inning, but then all of a sudden Dewayne and I would wind up sounding like the two old grumpy guys in the gallery of *The Muppet Show*, complaining how bad everything was, and nobody wanted to hear that. So we just made a concerted effort to be as entertaining as possible. When you're doing so many games, you can't be annoying—and you can't be dull.

"Many times what was fun and kept us occupied and focused was having two-to-three different layers for a telecast. People who watched carefully would get some inside references and buried punch lines. Or people watching casually might go make themselves a sandwich and mow the lawn, then come back and check out what was happening. We kept our eye on the ball and did the game in a way that hopefully made it enjoyable for any type of viewer."

Once again, the bright side from the Staats' perspective was on the home front. One month into the offseason, on November 10, 2002, Steph and Dan were married at the Greek Orthodox church we attended in Clearwater, Holy Trinity.

I remember the heart-to-heart talk I had with Steph when she and Dan decided to tie the knot. I told her about the importance of recognizing the unique situation she would be in—how when her husband failed, he would do so in public. He'd be all alone in the middle of a baseball diamond, in front of a live audience numbering in the thousands, with even more watching on television. And then he'd wake up the next morning only to see his failure chronicled in black-and-white in the morning paper and on the Internet. Steph understood and was prepared for whatever challenges might lie ahead tied to her husband's profession. The truth was, Dee and I couldn't have been happier for them—or more pleased to welcome Dan into the family.

The joyous day was not unlike Dee's and my wedding almost 30 years earlier—just a larger and more modern sequel of sorts to the hit 2002 movie, *My Big Fat Greek Wedding*.

The whole Berry family came from Houston. The Magranes and various members of the Devil Rays organization were in attendance, with a memorable reception at the Belleview Biltmore Hotel. Dee and I couldn't have been more delighted or proud of our little girl and the wonderful young woman she'd become—or her choice of a husband, despite Dee's admitted initial skepticism.

Dan went on to sign with the New York Mets in advance of the 2003 season, working his way up from Norfolk to the big-league roster. He was a member of a bullpen led by the gifted likes of John Franco, Mike Stanton and David Weathers, soaking up all the pitching tips and knowledge that he could. He became a better pitcher because of it, setting the stage for good things in his future.

But in other ways, in spite of big changes on the horizon, life was about to take some unexpectedly difficult turns.

CHAPTER TWELVE

# A Reflection on Lou—and Loss

With the epic 2002 season mercifully in the rear-view mirror, and attendance continuing to nosedive, Naimoli and LaMar were highly motivated by a desire to stem the mounting tide of losing seasons.

That led them to make a play for one of the top managers in the game—and a popular Tampa native to boot. On October 28, 2002, they traded All-Star centerfielder Randy Winn to Seattle for the right to negotiate with—and immediately hire—the Mariners' fiery, charismatic and toweringly successful skipper, Lou Piniella.

Lou had a year left on his contract, but he'd told the Mariners he wanted to be closer to his Tampa home, paving the way for a deal that had the local media working overtime. Needless to say, this was monumental news for the downtrodden Devil Rays and their fans. An excellent ballplayer for the Royals and Yankees, Lou had managed New York, Cincinnati and Seattle over the past 16 seasons, enjoying four first-place finishes and the once-in-a-lifetime 2001 season with a mark of 116-46, tying the 1906 Cubs for most wins in a season.

What better man for the job of turning around a franchise mired in mounting losses? Lou's homecoming was a daily topic in the press and trumpeted by the club throughout the offseason. Dee and I spent part of that winter in Greece, immersed in our own ongoing renovation project –fixing up the house we'd purchased from Dee's aunt in the Rhodes village of Paradisi. We cherished this time together and marveled at the many ways we'd been so blessed—with a wonderful marriage, awesome children, a part-time place in Paradisi and a full-time home in our beachfront, Sand Key paradise.

That put the perpetual losing ways of the Devil Rays in perspective. The way I saw it, I made my living doing what I loved at the ballpark—and somebody sent me a check for doing that. Would I have liked to have seen the team win more games? You bet. But I was taking care of my growing family and, in the big picture, had no complaints whatsoever.

During this time, Dee also devoted herself to giving support, in any way she could, to Irene Hunsicker, her dear friend from our first years with the Astros—and the wife of my good pal, Gerry Hunsicker. Gerry was now Houston's general manager, and Irene—who had been a nurse and hospital administrator in Philadelphia—was battling uterine cancer. Dee was constantly in touch with Irene, visiting her in Houston whenever she could. Irene was a fighter and, even when she was ill, became a patient advocate at M.D. Anderson Cancer Center. We were overjoyed when she rallied and regained her health, and the bond Irene and Dee shared grew even deeper.

As always, it only seemed to take a blink of an eye for pitchers and catchers to report for spring training—this time, in 2003, with a new sense of purpose and optimism. But no matter how good the manager is, it's still up to the players to get the job done—and the Devil Rays weren't capable of that. They finished spring training at 8-19, the worst record in the Grapefruit League. And things didn't get much better when the games began to count. I loved being around Lou, and his career as both a player and manager spoke for themselves. But managing the Devil Rays became immensely frustrating for him from the outset. I believe he came here thinking he could raise the level of play and make the consistently underwhelming team competitive—with the added satisfaction of achieving that goal in his hometown area.

But he quickly realized he wasn't going to have the tools to pull it off. Without question, the Devil Rays had some promising parts of the puzzle. The young outfield tandem of second-year player Carl Crawford in left field and rookie Rocco Baldelli in center made a splash, both with their superb defensive ability, speed and bats—C.C. hitting .281 and stealing 55 bases, Rocco hitting .289 with 29 swipes. Rightfielder Aubrey Huff had come into his own, hitting .311 and belting 34 homers with 107 RBI. But there just wasn't enough quality pitching to keep the Devil Rays in games. After ace Victor Zambrano's 12-10 record, no other starter had a winning mark.

Lou's famous temper flared at times, but even when he was frustrated and angry, he could be humorous. Some of his tirades were actually quite entertaining. I loved that quality about him—his pure, unfettered honesty and willingness to wear his emotions on his sleeve. We got to know each other well on a day-to-day basis and he was—and still is—one of my favorite people to be around. But the final 2003 results, while better than the year before at 63-99, still left much to be desired.

I have to admit the persistent travails of the team became a distant concern to me during that season.

I was on the road with the Devil Rays when I received a call from Dee. She had awakened that morning feeling terribly sick. Almost overnight, she had developed a deep cough and what seemed like a respiratory virus of some kind. She went to our doctor, who immediately referred us to a specialist for X-rays. I returned home right away to be with Dee for the appointment, and Alexa insisted on coming along as well. We were hoping it was just a really bad cough and cold, but Dee had an inkling it was something else, as did I. The results confirmed her fears: She had pneumonia—caused by a tumor in one of her lungs.

Nothing can prepare you for a moment like this and the blur of emotions that ensue. We'd been through it all six years earlier, with Dee's brain tumor and the trauma of major surgery, and prayed she would never have to experience anything like it again. But now, like a shadowy intruder, the specter of cancer had re-entered her life—and the life we shared and cherished.

Dee had never smoked a day in her life, but the out-of-the-blue diagnosis left us stunned and scared: lung cancer, completely unrelated to the brain tumor. My mind raced with questions to pose to the doctor. How big was it? What kind of treatment did he propose? His initial response was that the pneumonia may have saved Dee's life, by alerting us to the presence of cancer. He explained that the next step was to have a biopsy done on the tumor. We were told that it would be a good sign if there was not a lot of bleeding. When the results arrived two days later, we were informed that there had been quite a bit of bleeding—and our hearts sank. We knew now we were in for a battle.

We also knew there was no better place in the world for Dee than M.D. Anderson. When we'd called the Hunsickers to tell them about the shocking news, their response was instantaneous, and so typical of them. They told us, in effect: "You get over here now—we'll get you right in at M.D. Anderson." What a caring gesture from two great friends. We made arrangements and headed for Houston, and the Hunsickers insisted we stay at their house. In days, Dee was undergoing extensive testing and evaluation to determine the best course of treatment. Doctors didn't want to do surgery initially, opting instead to put Dee on a regimen of chemotherapy, in an attempt to shrink the tumor.

Chemo lasted three months, which Dee was able to receive back home in Tampa Bay. Then, after the three months of treatment, we all returned to M.D. Anderson for the surgery. Alexa and I were there, but Steph was pregnant and couldn't make the trip. Soon after we arrived, Dee's sister, Eirene, flew in, and my old newspaper friend from Houston, Kenny Hand, came to provide support. The surgery took a long time, longer than we thought it would. I thought to myself, "This probably isn't good."

Finally, the surgeon came out with news. We thought, going into the operation, they were going to remove the tumor and take a portion of the lung around it. But he explained that he had decided to remove the entire lung, which took us all aback. His reasoning: The lung was filled with small tumors, making it essential that it all be removed.

I knew people could survive with one lung. But he also said something that sounded disturbing—in cases with multiple tumors in one lung, there's a chance the other lung is similarly afflicted. Furthermore, if they had known how extensive the cancer was, the doctor said, they wouldn't have put her through surgery. I never shared that information with Dee. Privately, while standing there in a state of semi-shock, I suspected this was going to be a tough one to beat, and wondered whether a lung transplant might be a possibility, and if Dee would be eligible for that surgery.

In the meantime, we waited for Dee to be wheeled into the recovery room. Bless her heart—when Alexa, Eirene and I walked in to find her, we heard a voice from the back corner. Dee had just had her lung taken out, and she was still drowsy from anesthesia and painkillers, but she saw that we were looking for her and called out softly, "Here I am. Here I am." I thought, "Oh my gosh—what strength and spirit she has."

For all intents and purposes, the surgery was a success, but now came a difficult and painful period of recovery—and a new normal in our lives filled with tanks of supplemental oxygen. After eventually leaving the hospital, we stayed with the Hunsickers again, then returned home to our lovely place on the beach, which now seemed like a sanctuary from all Dee had endured.

Gradually, over the coming months, Dee displayed enormous fortitude and slowly returned to her active ways—completely involved with the daily details of our lives. Alexa lived with us in our condo, while Steph and Dan lived just down the street. Being in close proximity at this time made such a difference, as did our proximity to the water. The beach by our condo, with the gentle Gulf surf washing over our feet, was a perfect place for Dee and me to take slow, sunset walks and count our blessings, in spite of the hardships.

Returning to work was my own sanctuary from all that was going on. As I had done with Dee's brain tumor, I was able to delve into work and compartmentalize my professional and personal life. My boothmate, Joe, was fully aware, and I knew from him that many of my broadcast colleagues we crossed paths with were concerned—but everyone was considerate to give me space and deal with my feelings privately.

"Dewayne never brought it to the ballpark with him," Joe recollects of that difficult time. "You don't want to pry every day for updates, especially when there might not be a good prognosis. It's the elephant in the room that you don't want to talk about, so it was like, 'Okay, let's do a game.' That's what we did. And I was amazed by how strong and dignified he was to be able to get through that during the season—it really was awe-inspiring. Announcers from other teams would come through and ask how he was doing, and I'd just answer, 'Central Time Zone Guy. Steady Eddie and always ready.' I wasn't trying to be pithy—there was just no other way to say it, other than say, 'Geez, I just don't know how he's doing it.' I just sensed he wanted to come to the park and I decided we'd just keep things completely normal. I'd goof off as usual and we'd do our regular thing."

Joe was right. I preferred to focus on the job at hand and not talk about what was going on with Dee. But I'll give Lou credit. I remember sitting in his office one day and he broached the topic, and was so kind and sympathetic. I've never forgotten that.

Lou had plenty of other things on his mind—like how to push his young group of players to the next level in 2004.

Once again. Crawford and Baldelli continued to emerge as a sensational young tandem in left and center. Carl hit .296 and raised his stolen base total to 59, with Rocco finishing a solid .280 with 16 homers. Huff was once again a powerhouse, adding 29 homers with 104 RBI and hitting .297.

In addition, former Yankees' stalwart and Tampa native, first baseman Tino Martinez, had signed with the Devil Rays for the 2004 season and provided veteran leadership—along with 23 homers and .262 batting average. He displayed his clubhouse influence on one occasion after the Devil Rays surged to even their record at 35-35 in late June, following a rocky start of 16-31. When a young player jumped around the clubhouse jubilantly after the game, Tino stopped him in his tracks, saying, "We don't celebrate being .500 here, pal." I loved that.

Unfortunately, Tino's sentiment was well-founded, because the celebration turned out to be highly premature. With pitching once again sub-par (only Zambrano had a winning record, 9-7), the second year under Lou was step a forward with the most wins in franchise history, but still a last-place 70-91.

On the home front, Dee continued her brave fight, staying involved in our daily lives and never complaining about the discomfort or pain she endured. During a September trip to M.D. Anderson for additional treatment, we learned that our dear friend and former neighbor, Nila Berry, had passed away suddenly from an aneurysm. Dee, even in a weakened state, insisted that she accompany me to the evening visitation outside of Houston—she would never have missed it. Early the next morning, she was back in treatment again, powering through as always.

Meanwhile, Lou's discontent over what he viewed as a lack of sufficient commitment to build the team continued to grow. That coincided with big news at the top of the franchise's pecking order—Vince Naimoli, who had been looking to sell the club he had fought so hard to obtain, made a deal with a new group headed by Wall Street wiz Stuart Sternberg. Stu, a New Yorker and avid New York Mets fan, wanted to own a team—and, given his druthers, the Mets probably would have been his first choice. But he had done wonders at Goldman Sachs and liked the challenge of helping a troubled ball club, which was struggling not only on the field but at the turnstiles.

The transition to Sternberg's takeover for the 2006 season actually began in 2005, as two key members of his administrative team began work in the Devil Rays' front office: Andrew Friedman, learning the player personnel operation, and Matt Silverman, acquainting himself with the administrative workings of the club. I liked them both. They were obviously sharp—having distinguished themselves for Sternberg on Wall Street—and each shared a general geographical connection with me: Andrew came from Houston and Matt from Dallas, which gave us plenty to talk about beyond the team. I think we all felt an increasing curiosity about how the impending change of ownership would impact the club.

But Lou was losing his patience. Instead of building on the strides of the previous season, the Devil Rays began backsliding. At one point, the opening-day starter, Dewon Brazelton, completely lost it en route to a 1-8 record. Lou pulled him out of a game when he couldn't throw a strike and Dewon headed—in full uniform—directly to the parking lot, having decided on the spot to quit baseball. Pitching coach Chuck Hernandez chased Dewon down at his car and attempted to calm him down, while reliever Rob Bell warmed up in the bullpen. Adding to the general state of chaos, several of Bell's pitches sailed high out of the pen area and down toward first base, causing Lou to shake his head with his touch of humorous exasperation.

"I'm looking for my pitching coach but he's in the parking lot trying to talk my starting pitcher out of quitting," he told me later. "And there's a guy in the bullpen who's throwing at the first base coach."

That was bad enough. But the low point came in Pittsburgh on June 11, when the stumbling Devil Rays were battered by the Pirates, 18-2, falling to a record of 20-42. It marked the sixth time that the team had allowed 10 or more runs in a loss over the previous 13 days. Soon after the game, Lou ripped into franchise ownership old and new, asserting that it did not care enough about winning, saying, "They're not interested in the present. They're interested in the future. And that's their right. But when other teams are getting better presently, you are going to get your butts beat and that's exactly what's happening."

"I'm not going to take responsibility for this," he fumed. "...If you want answers about what's going on here, you call the new ownership group and let them give them to you."

If Lou harbored any thoughts about staying with the club for the final year of his contract in 2006, it's fair to say that his commentary closed that door tightly. And yet, amid the often glum atmosphere, there were still moments of levity. One such instance occurred on Greek Heritage Day, when I was asked to throw out the ceremonial first pitch. Just prior to gametime, I left the booth, took the elevator down to field level, and prepared to take the mound. Of course, that left Joe all alone upstairs and he decided to have a little fun, as he recalls.

"Being alone at the mic, the word 'unsupervised' comes to mind. My job was to introduce Dewayne throwing out the first pitch on air after we came out of our commercial break. That's when the thought popped in my head ——how we used to tease him that he had a similar look to Jeopardy host Alex Trebek—with the moustache, and similar hair and coloring. So when the break ended, I said, 'Now let's go down to the field for the first-pitch ceremony—and, oh look, hey, it's Alex Trebek throwing out the pitch!' The centerfield camera picked up Dewayne from behind, throwing the ball to the catcher, whereupon I said, "And we'll be right back with the starting lineups.' "

"Well, Dewayne came back up and had no idea what I'd said and we went ahead and did the game. But when I was home that night, I flipped on ESPN and they cut to the beginning of a Devil Rays highlight, and said 'Alex Trebek throws out the first pitch before a Tampa Bay game.' That went through their SportsCenter show at 11 p.m., and through the shift change at 2:30 a.m. or so and a whole new crew repeats the same shot and report of Alex Trebek throwing the pitch. I was still up and saw it and thought, 'Oh my goodness, you're doing it again?' The next day, the morning SportsCenter repeated the highlight *again*.

"Dewayne was a bit irritated, not so much at me, because he knew that's what I did from time to time. But he was more miffed at ESPN. We were sitting inside the Trop's food room, and ESPN's *Pardon the Interruption*, with Tony Kornheiser and Michael Wilbon, came on one of the mounted TVs across from us. In the rundown of the show's upcoming stories on the right of the screen, I could see a reference to Alex Trebek. And when the story finally came up, Wilbon—to his credit—said, 'That's not Alex Trebek, that's Dewayne Staats.' "

I actually got a kick out of it, especially a line Joe was quoted on in the press coverage about the case of mistaken identity:

"Apparently they didn't get it in Bristol. I'm hoping for a retraction, I'm working with somebody smarter than Alex."

As the season wound toward a conclusion, the Devil Rays managed to start playing better baseball, going 39-34 after the All-Star Break to finish 67-95. But even with the improved play, Lou had clearly had enough. He reached a mutual agreement with new ownership to release him from his obligations, reportedly accepting a $2.2-million buyout on the remaining $4.4-million on his contract. And on the final day of the season—ending with a 6-2 loss to Baltimore—he said his farewells on the field to fans who had lined up to shake his hand, wish him well and thank him for his efforts, in spite of the disappointing outcome.

Sadly, there was another goodbye that had to be said that season.

After a courageous fight, never wavering in her remarkable spirit or deep faith, my beloved wife Dee—and amazing mother of Steph and Alexa—passed away from lung cancer midway through the season. It was absolutely devastating for me, and for the girls. We leaned on each other for support more than ever, keenly feeling Dee's presence, love and strength—and that gave us strength to carry on the way she would have wanted.

I remember birthdays and important dates in baseball and history, but—maybe as a coping mechanism—I honestly don't recall the date Dee died. All I know is that she wasn't just a terrific wife, but she was a great baseball wife. She took her last breath right before the All-Star break—almost as if she was looking out for me until the very end, so I'd have more time to grieve and make arrangements without having to miss work.

The funeral service was scheduled at Holy Trinity, the church where we'd celebrated Steph and Dan's wedding only three years earlier. And now they had an adorable baby boy, Gabe—a grandson Dee thankfully got to dote on before she passed. The Wheelers lived in Houston, following a trade Gerry Hunsicker had worked with the Mets prior to the 2005 season, adding Dan to the Astros' bullpen—a move both Dee and I had been very excited about. I remember her saying to Dan before he left, in the playfully tough manner she often liked to adopt, "I know you'll do well. You have to—you can't embarrass me in front of my friends."

Now, our friends from Houston—the Berrys—were driving through a tropical rainstorm in the South, spurred by Hurricane Dennis, to make it to Clearwater for the funeral—torrential weather that mirrored the raw emotions I felt.

The night before the service, I had cautioned Steph and Alexa, "You know, tomorrow could be very difficult, so prepare yourselves." But when the time arrived, the visitation and service were anything but somber. Family, friends and members of the Devil Rays organization packed the church in a celebration of Dee's joy of life and her love of the people in it. It was such an outpouring of positive emotion, I know she had to be looking down and smiling.

I took a few more days off after the All-Star break, then returned to the booth. In times like this, it helps to have something to come back to. And at the top of the show that night, I started off by acknowledging how profoundly meaningful the support had been for our family—and that I knew Dee's memory would be eternal.

Something Irene Hunsicker had told me at the service was a lasting gift. "You know, you were the love of her life," she said. What a powerful sentiment that was, and it buoyed me in the days and months to come, as the painful 2005 season wore on. I coped in my own private way, missing Dee terribly every day that went by.

After the season was finally over, Steph and I decided to attend the World Series, which pitted the Astros against the White Sox. It was good to enjoy a change of scenery, and see old friends from each of the cities I had worked in. But I'd be lying if I didn't say that I felt Dee's presence all around us the entire time. When we returned home after Chicago's sweep, Lou was by now long gone, and attention turned to the new, incoming ownership of Team Sternberg. A big afternoon event was held in October inside the ornate ballroom of the Renaissance Vinoy Resort in downtown St. Petersburg, where Stu, Matt, Andrew and limited partners—as well as various Devil Rays players—met with the local media and local dignitaries. I was there as well, and was impressed by the entire introductory event, including the myriad yellow and black "Under Construction" symbols throughout the room. That was a nice touch.

Stu stated his commitment to putting an entertaining, winning product on the field for fans. He talked to reporters about his passion for the music of Bruce Springsteen and made an all-around excellent impression with his "can-do" attitude. I looked forward to seeing the new management team implement its plans, but was also still adjusting to my life without Dee, still quietly mourning her loss.

That winter, I flew to Houston to attend another funeral—an untimely death in the Berry family, Carla's husband, Halloway. I'd last seen them in 2003 when Dee was first diagnosed with her lung cancer. Carla and Halloway had planned a trip to Clearwater Beach, unaware of Dee's diagnosis, but their presence turned out to be very helpful to us.

Much of my trip to Houston for Halloway's funeral remains a hazy memory, but I remember driving Carla to the service, paying my respects and then flying home later that day. Alexa and I did our best in the coming weeks to get used to life in the condo without Dee. It was hard to do, with so many things wherever we turned to remind us of the hole in our lives.

Alexa remembers that difficult period vividly. "My dad has always been the cool, calm, collected type, but this was the first time I ever saw him vulnerable, and that was so hard to watch," she says. "We were living in the same home but moving in our own worlds. We grieved in completely different ways, maybe because dad and Steph are the analytical ones, and I was like my mom—more bold and emotional. He wanted to be by himself, and I just ran from that—I wanted to go out and be with friends."

When I did go out, I spent a fair amount of time down the street visiting Steph, Dan and grandson Gabe. But unbeknownst to me, Steph and Alexa had information from their mom that she hadn't shared with me: "Your father should remarry after I'm gone—he's too young not to."

Once again, it was classic Dee, always planning, always taking charge and caring for the people she loved. Steph had gotten tired of me sitting around in a daze, she later told me, closing myself off from the world.

"It was really tough afterwards," Steph says now. "He would come over, because Gabriel was a baby, and it was kind of like therapy for all of us. Dad would just sit on the couch and kind of stare at the ceiling. Or he would go in the bedroom, close the door and listen to music. My mom had always said to me, 'If anything happens to me before your father goes, you have to get him remarried. He cannot be by himself.' And when she got sick, we'd have a lot of conversations and she would emphasize that.

"After some time had passed, Alexa and I encouraged Dad to get out there. Reluctantly, he might meet somebody for coffee but nothing ever transpired. In March of 2006, Dan and I and the baby were going to be in spring training with the Astros, and my good friend from childhood, Gayla Berry, Carla's younger sister, happened to be in town for a conference. We met for dinner and talked about how Carla was coping with the death of her husband. I asked her, 'Do you think Carla will ever get married again?' And Gayla went, 'Yes. She can't be by herself. She's way too young.' And I answered, 'Well, you know my dad can't either. Why don't we see if we can get them together, and see what happens."

Together, they nudged along a plan for Carla to come to Clearwater for a visit. In the past, I'd invited her and Halloway for spring training, but I didn't imagine that Carla would want to come by her herself now. Steph and Gayla, however, urged her to visit, relax on the beach—and give herself a chance to have some fun after so much sadness.

Carla liked the idea and made the trip, and I was glad to see her when she arrived, though I had no more inkling of what was going on behind the scenes than she did. Since the Wheelers were 90 minutes away in Kissimmee, where Dan was training with the

Astros, I suggested we drive over to see them during her stay and catch a baseball game while we were at it. Seeing Steph, Dan and baby Gabe was a wonderful way to spend time together in a relaxed atmosphere, and we enjoyed each other's company.

But the best part of the visit occurred when Carla came by to visit Alexa and me at our condo. After a while, Carla and I decided to go out on the terrace overlooking the sand 16 stories below, where we could hear the rhythmic sound of the surf washing up on the beach. We talked and talked—about our deep sorrows, about so many different thoughts and events in our lives—until we realized it was about 3 or 4 in the morning.

We knew it was time to call it a night. But I definitely had enjoyed her company and we seemed to feel a special connection, born of our losses and the deep bond uniting our families.

I planned to call her when she returned to Houston. And as I thought about it in the wee hours of the morning, I'd have sworn that Dee was up there trying to take care of things—as always.

CHAPTER THIRTEEN

# Not Your Average Joe

The wayward course of the franchise—marked by seven last-place finishes in eight years of existence—changed on November 15, 2005. That was the day Joe Maddon was introduced as the next manager of the Devil Rays, after an exhaustive six-week search that included higher-profile candidates such as Bobby Valentine, Joe Girardi, Alan Trammel and John McLaren, who had served as Lou's right-hand man. It makes you wonder how different the history of the team might have been if they hadn't picked the man with the distinctive black-rimmed glasses and innovative—at times, quirkily unconventional—approach to the game.

As a longtime Angels bench coach and manager in their farm system, Joe didn't have the kind of instant name recognition that would energize the beleaguered Devil Rays fan base. But he had everything Tampa Bay's new front office was looking for—and, as it turns out, considerably more.

Joe had made quite an impression on new principal owner Stu Sternberg, Vice President of Baseball Operations Andrew Friedman and President Matt Silverman, wowing them with his intensive preparation and thorough analysis of the young team's strengths and weaknesses, and bringing along to the interview a thick folder of data assessing the players. Joe was one of the first baseball guys to embrace the use of computers in evaluating talent and trends—and was a perfect fit for the statistic-oriented sabermetrics approach favored by the new crew.

But that was only part of how he won over club management. Joe had gained extensive experience in the minors developing and motivating young players—an ideal asset for a Devil Rays roster desperately in need of guidance. His entire being projected optimism, enthusiasm and energy, traits that could surely help offset the malaise born from such relentless losing. It was instantly clear to anyone who talked—or listened—to the 51-year-old rookie big-league skipper that he was a gifted communicator with a pleasantly unconventional outlook on what it takes to succeed.

He was the antithesis to the club's first manager, Larry Rothschild, with his heavy reliance on rules in relating to his players and insistence on controlling every possible detail. Joe expected accountability and a full effort, but he couldn't have cared less about enforcing a dress code for his players on the road—as it would become famously clear in the seasons to come—or managing every minute of the players' pre-game schedule. Joe was different from anyone I'd seen at the helm in my career, no question about that. And you couldn't help but enjoy that difference. After eight seasons of severe losing, with managers who were more traditional, hiring somebody with a new approach made complete sense.

Very quickly, you saw the atmosphere in the clubhouse start to change. Joe would not acknowledge a negative side of a given situation. In the midst of prolonged losing, it's extremely easy for a manager to be pulled into the negativity, singling out players for blame or complaining about bad luck. But there was none of that with Joe. He always looked for the positive, and saw the losing atmosphere simply as an opportunity to move forward. They'd been so bad for so long, and he embraced the challenge of creating a fresh start for the franchise.

His first season on the job produced a won-loss mark that looked strikingly similar to the ones that had preceded it: 61-101. But even then, there was a different feeling surrounding the team. Everybody realized it would take some time to turn things around, and the atmosphere changed from overly somber, critical and concerned to one that was constantly upbeat. I love Lou—his great sense of humor, his bright baseball mind. But he had grown very frustrated, and frustration saps your energy. Joe came into the job knowing that nobody expected him to turn the team into an instant winner. Ownership, the front office and the field manager were all on the same page in this regime—a crucial element of successful ball clubs.

I give Joe immense credit for sticking to who he was at his core, remaining relentlessly, unabashedly optimistic from the outset about prospects for success. Baseball is filled with failure—it's part of the very nature of a game in which a great hitter only succeeds in three of every 10 at bats. Failure is a reality, and it's how you deal with it that separates people. Joe was in a situation where he could be as positive as he wanted to be and focus on the bright spots, knowing he also had time to address the team's deficiencies. The team's personnel budget was only about $40-million, so Andrew wasn't in a position to throw money around blindly to build the roster, as so many bigger payroll teams can afford to do. Instead, they combined their penchant for analytics with a positive approach and the team slowly began to come together.

I was delighted my old friend, former Astros general manager Gerry Hunsicker, had been hired in late 2005 to help advise 29-year-old Friedman in revamping the roster. Having Gerry and Irene around was wonderful from a personal point of view, especially given the deep connection we shared with Dee. But Gerry's savvy, knowledgeable touch as a personnel executive—working in the background—provided a valuable extra layer of support in assessing trades and roster moves.

One of Andrew's key deals that first season came in July, when he sent hard-hitting rightfielder Aubrey Huff to Houston for a pair of minor league prospects—a 22-year-old righthanded pitcher they coveted named Mitch Talbot and a 25-year-old switch-hitting shortstop, Ben Zobrist. Interestingly enough, they viewed Talbot as the key to the trade, but he never made any impact, spending most of his time with Triple-A Durham. Who knew acquiring Zobrist would become an essential step in the team's turnaround?

While Ben worked on his game in Durham, and made only a negligible impact in limited duty with the parent club that season, other players provided glimmers of hope for better things to come. Crawford continued his emergence as one of the more exciting outfielders in the game, hitting .305 with 58 stolen bases, 18 homers and 16 triples. Baldelli, coming back from knee and elbow surgery in 2005, still hit .302 with 16 homers after returning to the lineup in June, and two players showed glimpses of potential after being promoted from Triple-A: B.J. Upton, then a 21-year-old infielder, and outfielder Delmon Young, just 20. Switch-hitting catcher Dioner Navarro, 22, joined the club from the Dodgers, acquired in a deal that sent pitcher Mark Hendrickson and catcher Toby Hall to Los Angeles.

At the same time, the pitching staff was starting to come together with 22-year-old lefthanded ace Scott Kazmir, acquired a year earlier from the Mets, leading the staff with a 10-8 mark and 3.24 ERA. And 2006 marked the arrival of 24-year-old right-handed pitcher James Shields, who'd worked his way up through the Devil Rays' farm system and posted a 6-8 record with a 4.84 ERA.

You'll notice I pointed out the ages of these new players. Part of the transformation was the increased youth of the players, both on the pitching staff and with the position players. The formula was becoming clear: a move toward young players mixed with a handful of veterans.

In addition, versatility was an important component of the building process. You never were aware of whose idea it was—or whether it was a combination of Maddon and Friedman—but they knew that with a limited payroll, having depth on the roster was essential. Unlike many other teams with more money to burn, they couldn't afford to pursue many players who could just play one position or fill one role on the roster. Their idea was to build depth through versatility. As simple as that sounds, there weren't a lot of other teams doing that at the time. The new vision was to have every non-pitcher on the team play as many positions as they could, resulting in great maneuverability. That's what Joe's approach quickly became: creating favorable match-ups against opponents through heightened versatility—and that laid the groundwork for a reversal of fortune.

In many respects, that first season together was all about Friedman and Maddon each settling in, trying to establish their own identity, and establish a new way of doing things and a new culture. They were under construction, in keeping with their theme before the season, and Joe was a big part of the construction crew.

While a new foundation formed with the Devil Rays in 2006, my budding friendship with Carla began to take shape as well. The late-night conversation she and I had on the terrace of my condo turned out to be a pivotal experience. It was entirely spontaneous, but we shared so much about the pain of losing our spouses that each of us felt a connection. Here were two people in similar situations—Carla's husband had passed away the year before, and Dee had died only a few months before that. We knew each other, had been at family functions, weddings and funerals and events in between. And the Berry family had been part of the early family life Dee and I had in Houston in the mid-1970s, the friendly next-door neighbors who had greeted us so warmly when we first moved into our new house.

But our lives were on entirely separate paths. Carla was the oldest child in that family, so she was first to leave for college—only three or four years after we arrived—and quickly set her own career path. As our conversation progressed, we realized, sitting out there, that we had a lot in common. We continued to stay in touch by phone and our feelings for one another began to deepen. But Carla didn't want to rush into anything. "I don't know if I'm really ready for a relationship like this or not," she told me. She felt the need to work through the loss of Halloway, and I completely understood—I was still working through my own feelings of life without Dee. I told her, "Look, take as much time as you need and let me know how you're doing."

A month went by in which we didn't communicate much. We both agreed it was good not to proceed too quickly—that we should take some time and think about what we wanted to do.

We put the brakes on because we both felt that something might be brewing. There's an old saying I've always ascribed to, and the gist of it is this: If you catch something and let it go—and it comes back to you—you know it's for you. The truth is, we both individually needed time to clear the deck and make sure it felt right to move forward with a relationship.

That included doing the right thing with our respective families—and in the memories of Dee and Hal. Our families knew each other, just as Carla and I did, and a tremendous bond existed. But I wanted to be sure Steph and Alexa felt comfortable with my dating Carla. And Carla's approach, because she knew and loved Dee, was never that she intended to try and replace Dee. This wasn't about replacing people—you can't do that. Their memories stand on their own; the lives they led stand on their own. We wanted to be absolutely certain the people who needed to know realized this is how we felt.

On top of all this, Carla was extremely busy after returning to Houston in her job as an addiction counselor, while trying to finish earning her master's degree in counseling. She lived in Montgomery, Texas, drove an hour south to Houston for her job, and attended classes at Sam Houston State University—40 minutes north of Montgomery in Huntsville. As a result, we did most of our talking when Carla was driving, heading from one stop to the next amid her hectic schedule. We got to know where all the cellphone towers worked and where the dead spots were, when we'd lose our signal.

Carla told me that, for the first time in any relationship she'd had, she checked ahead of time with her family—her two brothers, Mark and Brandon, sister Gayla, and her dad, Harley—about how they felt. When she told Brandon she was thinking about getting more serious with me, she said, "Dewayne and I are thinking about dating. You know what that would mean, right?" Brandon wasn't sure, so Carla continued, "Well, when the baseball season begins, I would maybe fly in to where Dewayne is covering a game and join him on the road in different cities where the Devil Rays are playing."

Brandon had only one question: "Can I date Dewayne, too?"

He was on board, as was everyone else, including her paternal grandmother, whose only question was: "What does he believe?" It was important to the matriarch of the family that faith be at the center of our relationship, which it definitely was.

Carla did fly in for some road trips during the 2006 season, but it was like a whirlwind. She'd finish the work week, fly out on a Friday, join me for a day or two, and then jet back to Houston for her job and classes. In only a matter of months, we realized we had something very special going. On a day off during a road trip in Boston later in the season, we went out to dinner at an Italian restaurant in the North End. We had a great seat, a picturesque view of the quaint neighborhood through the restaurant's ornate wrought iron railings, and we were swept up in conversation. It just seemed natural for me to tell her she was the kind of girl I wanted to spend the rest of my life with. I popped the question—and to my relief and joy, she said yes.

My main concern for my daughters was for them to feel good about my moving forward with Carla, even though they had shared with me their mother's wish that I remarry. And I did tell them, once we decided to get married, that Carla made me happy. I said to them, "You know I love your mother, and all three of us have great respect for her memory. But that's a completely separate entity from what is happening with Carla and me." I told both girls, "You will see me be very happy with Carla"—and that's what they wanted to see. They held no resentment whatsoever.

We set a date to be married on February 3, 2007. There are no rules for these situations—when each person has lost a spouse—but we simply felt the right amount of time had elapsed since saying farewell to Hal and Dee, and it made sense to take the next step. Carla had finished her master's during the fall, and to celebrate, I drove to Houston after the Devil Rays' 2006 season ended, picked her up and headed back with her to Tampa Bay. There was a torrential rainstorm as we left Houston that lasted all the way to Natchez, Mississippi—so I wrote a little country song for Carla to commemorate the momentous occasion. I still remember some of the lyrics that came to me behind the wheel: "We're drivin' hard out of Texas in a cherry red Mustang/ headin' for the state line, starin' down a heavy rain / leaving' all the clouds behind us, searchin' for the bright sunshine / lookin' for a distant rainbow and racin' against time."

I'm not sure the tune would have made the Country Top 40, but it was a hit with Carla. Pushing through the storm was like a cleansing rain—after all we had been through—as we set out to begin a new life together.

We arrived back in Tampa Bay with just enough time for me to get prepared for the Devil Rays' 2007 spring training. Hopes ran high that the team could take a tangible step forward, fueled by their manager's irrepressibly upbeat attitude. Carla, a similarly positive and optimistic person by nature, predicted the team would finally break out in a big way. I tried to temper her expectations, saying the Devil Rays still had a way to go before becoming a good ball club. We were discussing this at Al Lang Stadium during a Grapefruit League game and my prognostication for Tampa Bay's final record was there'd be a minor improvement over 2006: 66-96. I claim no special powers to foretell that future, but that's precisely how the team finished.

Yet within that homely won-loss mark lay some clear signs of a better-looking future. One of the big stories at the end of spring training—and an even bigger one throughout the season—involved first baseman Carlos Peña.

Carlos had been a major leaguer for six seasons, a fine defensive first baseman with power potential, who nevertheless had bounced from Texas to Oakland to Detroit to the New York Yankees to Boston. He enjoyed two strong seasons with the Tigers in 2003 and 2004, hitting 18 and 27 homers, but was eventually released after an up-and-down season in '05 and a dismal spring training in '06. After a stint at Triple-A Columbus for the Yankees, he saw limited action with the Red Sox and opted for free agency, hoping to find a team to give him a chance as a starter.

Friedman saw an upside to inviting Carlos to camp on a minor-league contract—he was a smart, upbeat veteran presence, and the kind of player whose natural leadership skills might be a steadying force on a young squad. But at the end of the exhibition season, there just weren't enough spots on the roster and Peña was cut.

As he prepared to head home to Orlando, however, his great attitude shined through, stating he would be back as the team's starting first baseman in 2007. Then, on the final day of spring training, first baseman Greg Norton injured his knee—creating a roster opening and a chance for Carlos to re-sign with the team immediately. Nobody could have imagined the outcome. Though the Devil Rays struggled for much of the season, he emerged as a major bright spot hitting 46 home runs—19 more than his previous best—driving in 121 runs (39 more than his prior high) and batting a career-high .282.

More than anything, Carlos became a cornerstone of the infield and an upbeat personality in the clubhouse on a team gradually beginning to take shape. Friedman put in a high bid of $4.55-million for Japanese star third baseman Akinori Iwamura of the Tokyo Yakult Swallows, and he proved an instant asset for the Devil Rays. After a torrid first month, hitting .339, Aki finished the season with a .285 batting average with 10 triples and 82 runs scored.

Jonny Gomes, in his fifth season with the club, continued to add some pop at the plate with 17 homers and a lively, gung-ho style that helped keep the mood loose and fun. Second baseman Ty Wigginton contributed effectively with a .275 batting average and 16 homers. And Carl Crawford continued to establish himself as an elite player, both defensively and as a multiple offensive threat, hitting .315, with 57 extra base hits, 80 RBI, 93 runs scored and 50 stolen bases.

One serious area of concern revolved around centerfielder Baldelli—once a shining light of the franchise, likened to a future Joe DiMaggio by Vince Naimoli. After battling back from Tommy John surgery and knee reconstruction that caused him to miss 2005 and the first half of 2006, Rocco was now suffering from a mysterious medical condition that drained his stamina and strength. The initial diagnosis was mitochondrial disease—a debilitating condition that can cause muscle weakness—but he wasn't responding well to treatments and was only a shadow of himself, in limited action.

In need of help in center, Maddon turned to B.J. Upton, who had proven overly error-prone at shortstop. In his new position, Upton's speed and athleticism made him an excellent fit. And at the plate, B.J. enjoyed a breakout season, hitting a career-best 24 home runs to go with 82 RBI and a .300 batting average. Meanwhile, the defining trait of the team's emerging personality—pitching—continued to evolve in encouraging fashion.

In his second season, Shields moved to the top of the rotation with a 12-8 record and 3.85 ERA, followed by Kazmir at 13-9 and a 3.48 ERA. That solid one-two punch was rounded out by other promising young pitching arms. Edwin Jackson's wildness contributed to a 5-15 record, but he threw hard and was a great kid at 23. Andy Sonnanstine was a great contrast to Edwin because of his changing speed and deception, and Jason Hammel, at 6-feet-6, and 225 pounds, had a terrific pitcher's build and good arm. Both showed off their potential, in spite of their 6-10 and 3-5 records.

Another bright spot, I'm proud to say, was provided by a reliever who'd come up through Tampa Bay's system—a pitcher who was suddenly re-acquired from Houston for Ty Wigginton on July 29, 2007, just before the trade deadline: my son-in-law, Dan Wheeler. Carla was in an airport when she got a text from Steph: "Dan was just traded to Tampa Bay!" I'd been talking to them prior to that, and Dan had a feeling he'd be traded somewhere, but none of us guessed this. After sending the text, Steph called me with the happy news: "We're Devil Rays!"

Dan had spent the previous three seasons with the Astros, building on the knowledge he gained in the Mets' bullpen. He'd gone to the World Series in 2005 with Houston, and become a great setup man to closer Brad Lidge, with consecutive season

ERAs of 2.21 and 2.52. I picked him up at Tampa International when he arrived in town. And, as we drove across the Courtney Campbell Causeway, I brought up the question of how we'd deal with this unusual situation: a father-in-law calling games in which his son-in-law was pitching. It took about a minute. Basically, I said, "Here's how we should handle it: You do your job, I'll do mine—and it'll be okay."

That probably worked to Dan's detriment. Obviously, I wanted the Rays to win—I was broadcasting their games, and it's a lot more fun when things are going well. There was a little lift in my delivery when they won, but I was very conscious about not wanting to appear I was favoring Dan Wheeler because of our family connection. I wound up being more reserved about him on air than any other player who's ever come through this team. More than anything, I think I undersold him, because there was a lot to sell. But it was always very gratifying to hear Maddon say—on more than one occasion—that Dan was the first guy the Rays acquired who started the turnaround. It wasn't because he was vocal, but because of the way he went about his business as a pro, and the way he helped change the culture in the bullpen.

The standings didn't reflect these varied signs of hope, as the Rays at several points fell 31 games under .500. But in a 15-game stretch from August 22 to September 5, they won 11 games, including a 17-2 victory over Baltimore featuring 22 hits, including two homers by Carlos Peña. Maddon kept telling the players—and the media—things were getting better and major change wasn't going to happen overnight.

I thoroughly enjoyed talking with him about the Devil Rays and baseball in general. Joe had grown up as a fan of the St. Louis Cardinals and the two of us had many discussions about the great teams we watched as kids in the 1960s—like the 1963 squad that won 93 games but still finished six games behind the Dodgers; and the '64 Cards who won eight straight games in late September, barely edging out the Phillies and Reds for the pennant on the last day of the season.

St. Louis had gone into the final weekend of the season playing the lowly Mets, needing only one victory to clinch it. But the great Bob Gibson lost the first game in a 1-0 decision to Al Jackson. The Cardinals got blown out 15-5 in the second to fall into a tie for first, and had to summon Gibson from the bullpen in the final game after falling behind 3-2 in the fifth inning. Gibson pitched the final four frames to get the win, sending St. Louis to the World Series, where they beat the Yankees in seven games, with Gibson going the distance in Game Seven in a 7-5 win.

Those were all stories Joe and I loved dissecting. He was always willing to make time to sit in the dugout or at his desk and talk, whether to me specifically or to the media as a whole. I could never have done that, because I would have been so concerned about all the other things I had to get done before the game. But Joe embraced that part of his job and fully enjoyed his relationship with the press. He made plenty of time for scribes and broadcasters before and after games, building a reputation as a guy with plenty to say about many topics. And soon enough, there would be a lot more to talk about.

CHAPTER FOURTEEN

# Making Magic

The first visible change in the franchise's identity was unveiled to the public on November 8, 2007, in a festive late-afternoon event by the downtown St. Petersburg waterfront. A huge crowd gathered in front of a stage in shaded Straub Park for the official announcement that the name of the club had been changed from the Tampa Bay Devil Rays to the Tampa Bay Rays. The color scheme would now shift from purple and green to Columbia blue and Navy blue—with a distinctive gold sunburst.

Fans already knew the changes were coming, since word had leaked out in the press a month-and-a-half earlier, but that didn't dampen the air of excitement.

The team moniker no longer had the connotation of a bottom-feeding fish—a nickname that had initially drawn protests from some parts of the community for its inclusion of "devil." Now, the devil had been designated for assignment. The new burst of light on the jerseys referenced the sunny landscape of West Florida, and the alliterative name rolled easily off tongues—the Tampa Bay Rays.

It was a natural, and the more traditional style of the uniforms were on display this day—modeled by various Tampa Bay players—and they looked sharp. Stu Sternberg, a New York native with an affinity for the old Brooklyn Dodgers, wanted to come up with a uniform that had both a modern feel and a classic style. Being a uniform guy myself, and one who favored the dignified appearance of the Cardinals' uniform, I was an instant fan of the new look. As a rebranding effort went, the front office and talented marketing staff hit this one right on the barrelhead.

I helped serve as emcee at the event and the genuine enthusiasm of the crowd was impressive. The evening ended with a concert by Modern Wild, the rock band whose front man was actor Kevin Costner, forever associated with hit baseball movies *Field of Dreams* and *For the Love of the Game*. Carla and Joe Magrane's wife, Renee, were sufficiently excited about the appearance of Costner, and joined a throng of fans across the street at the Renaissance Vinoy, where he was staying—hoping to get an autograph or snapshot with him prior to the show.

From a public relations perspective, the tone for the upcoming season couldn't have been set any more successfully. From a baseball perspective, Friedman made an excellent move three weeks later that would significantly strengthen the team. He sent troubled slugger Delmon Young to Minnesota in a six-player deal that netted the Rays fiery, right-handed starting pitcher Matt Garza and front-line shortstop Jason Bartlett. A day later, Friedman signed former Angels closer Troy Percival—a bulldog of a reliever with 324 career saves, and a player well-known to Maddon from his years as an Angels coach.

And another piece of the puzzle fell into place in mid-December as the Rays' young personnel wiz signed 35-year-old long ball threat Cliff Floyd—coming off a .284 season with the Cubs and boasting 222 career homers—to a one-year deal.

Now the question was how the newly named and outfitted Rays would follow up three months later, when they took the field in spring training. I fully expected the team would be better in 2008, based on the improvements I'd seen in 2007. But little things began to happen starting in camp that played a role in propelling the team forward. One was an exhibition game dustup with perennial power New York, when utility infield prospect Elliot Johnson, an undrafted free agent, crashed into Yankees catcher Francisco Cervelli at home plate at Al Lang Stadium. Johnson was tagged out while Cervelli suffered a broken wrist. New York manager Joe Girardi fumed over what he called an unnecessarily aggressive play, but the Rays seemed to be making a statement: They were not going to allow themselves to be pushed around any more.

The team had its No. 1 pick from 2006 in camp, third baseman Evan Longoria, who looked more than ready for prime-time. With Evan at third, Aki Iwamura graciously and effortlessly made the switch to second base. And that's where he was later in camp, when Yankees' outfielder Shelley Duncan slid into him, spikes aimed high in an apparent payback move for Johnson's perceived transgression. Lingering tensions spilled over as Jonny Gomes—who graduated from the school of hard knocks—got in a fight with Duncan and benches cleared. Once again, Rays players were out to show they had a new attitude. Joe wasn't there leading the charge, inciting his players. But I believe he imbued in them a level of expectation for gaining the respect of other teams, in order to reach the next level.

This certainly wasn't the first time a Tampa Bay team had run-ins with an opponent. One on occasion, Devil Rays pitchers had thrown at a few Red Sox batters in retribution for some offense, but their pitchers didn't have enough command to actually hit them. They missed their mark entirely in an utter display of futility. Now they were starting to act like a team that had to be dealt with.

Before camp ended, Friedman had made another move of note, signing burly left-handed power-hitter Eric Hinske, formerly of the Blue Jays and Red Sox, to a minor-league contract. Hinske made the team and, along with Floyd, gave the Rays another deep threat from the left side, and one more key veteran to balance the team's youth. It was definitely an encouraging sign that, for the first time, the Rays finished spring training with the best mark in the Grapefruit League, 18-8.

There was only one surprise. Longoria, who hit .262 with three homers and displayed an excellent glove at third, was sent to Durham for the start of the season. The speculation was that the move allowed the front office to delay Evan's eligibility for free agency until after 2014, but Friedman denied letting business considerations influence the decision. Whatever the case, Evan would be back up in early April, signing a six-year, $17.5-million contract, worth up to $44-million over nine seasons, and become the face of change on this revised edition of the Rays.

Everything felt different as the season progressed. The Rays closed the first month of the season at 14-12, their first winning record in April ever. Along the way, Friedman sent a pitching prospect to Milwaukee for left-handed-hitting outfielder Gabe Gross, who would fill a part-time role in right field and become another moveable piece in Maddon's matchup strategy. With a 7-3 win over Texas on Memorial Day, the Rays achieved something remarkable: They sported the best record in the American League at 31-20, making them the first team in more than a century to own the best record in baseball at that stage of the season—after posting the worst mark the season before. Having been in the booth to witness the banner seasons of the 1980 Astros and the 1989 Cubs, I'd seen little things happen that make you realize something special might be transpiring. And those events—tangible and intangible—kept occurring for the Rays.

In early June, they were in Fenway Park, the site of much Tampa Bay misery over the years. Emotions ran high on June 4, when Boston centerfielder Coco Crisp stole second base and—at the end of his slide—jammed a thumb on shortstop Jason Bartlett's knee. He claimed that Bartlett had knelt down in a conscious attempt to hurt him. Later in the game, Crisp stole second again—this time sliding feet-first at Aki in a move that could easily have caused an injury. Joe jawed at Crisp moments later, and criticized him after the game for trying to hurt a Rays' player.

That set the stage for the next night, when Shields hit Crisp with a pitch on his first at-bat of the night. Coco charged Shields on the mound, fists flew and players from both benches poured onto the field. Naturally, Gomes—never one to miss a chance to have his teammates' back—was right in the middle of the brawl. When the dust settled, he was ejected along with Shields and Crisp. Multiple suspensions followed—Shields, Edwin Jackson, Crawford and Gomes for the Rays; Crisp, pitcher Jon Lester and first baseman Sean Casey for the Red Sox. But the key point amid the chaos was that, once again, the Rays had stood their ground rather than be bullied around by another division heavyweight.

That offset the sting of having lost all three games at Fenway, falling to second place behind Boston by a game-and-half. Red Sox closer Jonathan Papelbon derided the Rays behavior as cheap, and declared that the matter was not settled—words that would prove prophetic, and ironic, as the season wore on.

The race was far from over, and the Rays regained the division lead three weeks later on the strength of seven straight victories. By July 6, they were in uncharted territory, holding a 55-32 record with a five-game lead in the division. Nobody could have imagined that—I know I didn't, given the long, losing history of the franchise. But as quickly as success had come, it looked like the magic ride might finally have come to an end.

Cruising toward the All-Star Break with seven games to go, the Rays inexplicably lost all seven of those games, including dropping the last four contests at Cleveland. After the final loss to the Indians, I remember sharing a cab with Floyd to the airport from Jacobs Field and telling him, "You know, everybody's going to say that this is it for you guys."

He looked at me calmly and replied, "Nah, this isn't it. We're going to be fine."

Cliff sounded convincing, and it turns out he was right.

The Rays badly needed to snap out of their funk when play resumed after the break, but found themselves trailing 1-0 to Toronto at the Trop. And, from a psychological viewpoint, the last thing they needed was to drop their eighth straight. That's when another one of those little moments made such a big difference—a two-run homer by relative newcomer Ben Zobrist in the bottom of the seventh, helping the Rays regain their winning ways. It was the first of many major contributions to come from the player who'd earn the nickname "Zorilla." The win put Tampa Bay back on top in the division, and back in the groove with a 63-44 record to close out July.

In August, the Rays acquired Baltimore submariner Chad Bradford. The playoff-tested vet with experience on four different teams—and a 0.00 ERA in 17 postseason games to show for it—added an extra dimension to the bullpen. But at the same time, a wave of injuries threatened to derail the Rays. First, Bartlett missed 12 days after injuring a finger attempting a bunt on August 3. Then came potentially crushing blows. News broke that Crawford had a tendon injury on the middle finger of his right hand, and would need surgery that might cause him to miss the rest of the season. He was placed on the disabled list on August 10, and the next day Longoria joined him after being struck in the hand by a pitch, causing a fracture. Then, in a serious blow to the bullpen, Percival suffered a knee injury fielding a ball off the mound and headed for the DL.

But the Rays refused to cave. With a roster stocked by design with versatile players, the team kept rolling. Willy Aybar filled in admirably for Longo. And Rocco Baldelli, gone but not forgotten, returned in Crawford's absence—having now been diagnosed with channelopathy, enabling him to receive more effective treatments. He still didn't have the strength to play for long stretches, sometimes kneeling in right field during breaks in the action. But he showed flashes of the old, healthy Rocco—hitting .263 with four homers in 28 games down the stretch, another phenomenal twist to a rare season in the making.

Amid the spate of injuries, Maddon's easygoing style helped keep the clubhouse relaxed—a hallmark of his managerial approach. Incredibly, the Rays won 21 of their 28 games in August and headed into September with a very real chance of achieving a surreal outcome: winning the pennant.

If there was one game on which everything hinged, it was September 9, 2008 in Fenway Park. Tampa Bay had dropped six of seven games—including being blanked 3-0 by Lester the night before to start the critical three-game series, and seeing their division lead shrink tenuously to one-half game over the Red Sox.

The Rays jumped ahead 3-2 in the fourth, but watched their lead slip away as Boston scored twice in the bottom of the eighth for a 4-3 edge. But in the top of the ninth, up stepped Dan Johnson. He had been claimed off waivers in early April, then sent to

Durham, biding his time for what turned into a date with destiny. His chance came that day when the Rays called him up to provide an extra left-handed bat. He might have started the game, but was late in arriving to the park due to the long trip from North Carolina. Now, with his team down to its final three outs—and about to fall into second place, Maddon sent in Johnson to face Boston's dominant closer, Papelbon, who had a golden opportunity to settle the matter with the Rays, as he'd proclaimed in June.

Statistics weren't reassuring at this moment. D.J. was a lifetime 0-15 pinch-hitter in the majors, and Tampa Bay was in hostile territory at Fenway that night. But oblivious to the odds, he drilled a 3-2 Papelbon pitch deep into the rightfield seats to tie the game at 4-4, as the Rays erupted over the dramatic shot that revived their hopes.

Back-to-back doubles followed later in the inning by Fernando Perez, the poetry-writing outfielder from Columbia University, and Navarro, for a sudden 5-4 lead. And Percival closed the door in the bottom of the ninth—fittingly retiring the pugilistic Crisp on a popup, with the tying run on second, to preserve the biggest win of the season.

The Rays were by no means home free, falling into a tie with Boston a week later. But two big wins at Tropicana Field over the Red Sox followed—with Dan Wheeler earning the decision in a 2-1 walk-off win. Three days later, they officially clinched their first post-season birth, beating Minnesota 7-2 as the home crowd celebrated joyously over a moment long in coming.

With three games to play, the Rays fell 6-4 in Detroit and had to watch on TV as Boston, two games back and still alive for the division title, hosted the Yankees. But after a lengthy rain delay, New York won in a 19-8 rout, mathematically handing the Rays the AL East crown. Meanwhile, in Detroit's visiting clubhouse, the champagne flowed late into the night as the Rays basked in their first division title. Despite dropping three of their last four games, they finished with a record beyond all reasonable expectations: 97-65.

I'd seen a lot wild occurrences in my 32 years. But this season topped them all—and things were just getting interesting.

A general state of euphoria settled into the Tampa Bay region in the days to come. The Rays, the longest of long shots only eight months earlier when they unveiled their new look and name, were actually playing in the post-season—having won 97 games a year after losing 96. It was an incredible achievement.

But now came the serious business at hand: the American League Divisional Series against a talented Chicago White Sox team that had won the AL Central Division with an 89-74 mark. The showdown created an unusual situation for Joe Magrane and me, since the networks took over the telecasts for the post-season. When the Astros reached the post-season in 1980, Gene Elston, Larry Dierker and I broadcast all the playoff games, in addition to the network's playoff coverage. But now only the Rays' radio guys, Andy Freed and Dave Wills, were working the games.

Instead, Magrane and I did a pregame and postgame show in a makeshift set outside the Trop. Would it have been nice to call the action on television, after watching so many losses over the previous 10 years? Absolutely. But that's not how the system worked. And doing the before-and-after shows in such an electric atmosphere was still fun, with exhilarated Rays fans crowding around us to soak up the pinch-me-I-must-be-dreaming experience.

The Trop was rocking in a raucous sellout as the Rays took the field in their first playoff game, meeting the White Sox and buoyed by the return of star left fielder Carl Crawford. But the game had barely begun before a new concern arose. Peña abruptly departed in the second inning, with a report he was suffering from blurry vision due to a fluke eye injury at home the night before. Losing their Gold Glove first baseman and home run leader was a terrible, unexpected blow. But injuries hadn't undermined the Rays in August and didn't now. They prevailed in a 6-4 decision, with

Shields getting the win, Wheeler the save and Longoria bashing a pair of homers.

The next night, in Game 2, Kazmir got in an early hole, giving up a pair of White Sox runs in the top of the first, but the Rays roared back to win 6-2. And after losing in Game 3 at U.S. Cellular Field 5-3, they once again celebrated a franchise first on the road, advancing to the American League Championship Series with a 6-2 victory—this time powered by a pair of Upton homers and a solid outing by Sonnanstine.

But anybody who cared the slightest bit about the Rays was also keenly aware of the other ALDS. On the same day Tampa Bay dispatched the White Sox, the Wild Card Red Sox took care of business against the 100-game-winning Los Angeles Angels of Anaheim, taking three of four as well. As Papelbon had suggested amid the contentious atmosphere in June, there was, indeed, a matter left to be settled.

The two American League teams that held one another in complete and utter contempt—the Rays and Red Sox—were about to meet again with a trip to the World Series on the line. It didn't get any more dramatic than this.

If ever a League Championship Series had the feel of a World Series, this was it. The testiness and tightness of the race fueled the stakes of the seven-game series, beyond the sheer historic aspect for the Rays and their fans. Many Tampa Bay players had shaved their hair into Mohawks, promptly dubbed Ray-hawks, and legions of fans followed suit in a show of solidarity.

The Rays had won the regular-season series against Boston 10-8, but now it was a clean slate as the teams squared off before another bellowing, cowbell-crazy crowd in the Trop. But perhaps it was inevitable the home team would come out a little flat after riding such an emotional high. Boston took the opener 2-0, with starter Daisuke Matsuzaka pitching a no-hitter into the sixth and getting the win.

Game 2, on the other hand, was through the roof in white-knuckle intensity. With the decibel level deafening for the Saturday night showdown inside the dome, Boston scored twice in the first, but the Rays answered with two in the bottom of the frame on Longoria's two-run jack. When Boston moved ahead in the third on a Dustin Pedroia homer, Tampa Bay added two in the bottom of the third with the help of an Upton shot.

This was starting to look like two boxers punching and counter-punching in a prizefight.

The Rays then extended their lead to 5-3 on Floyd's homer, only to watch the Sox jump ahead 6-5 in the fifth on solo shots by Pedroia, Kevin Youkilis and Jason Bay. Not to be outdone, the Rays struck for three when their turn arrived, taking an 8-6 lead. Finally, it seemed as if the home team was taking charge in its desperate quest to even the series.

At some point during the wild proceedings, the crowd roared when former *Saturday Night Live* prime-time player, Rob Schneider—drawn to the Rays' underdog story line—appeared in a humorous taped spot on the scoreboard to deliver a motivational pep-talk. Perhaps it fired up the Red Sox because they soon scraped back into a tie with runs in the sixth and eighth. As frantic as the pace had been, the bats now fell silent, and the game remained tied through nine innings, through 10, and into the 11th.

In the top of that inning, Boston threatened with two walks before rookie phenom David Price, the team's No. 1 pick from 2008, got the final two outs. In the bottom of the 11th, finally, the Rays stirred back to life.

Navarro walked and the fleet Perez pinch-ran, moving to second on a Zobrist walk and advancing to third on a groundout. An intentional walk to Aki loaded the bases to create a double-play chance, while the boisterous home crowd stood and bellowed with Upton stepping into the batter's box. B.J. fell behind in the count 0-2, then lofted a fly ball to shallow right. The moment J.D. Drew caught it, Perez tagged up and broke for home, even though Drew had an easy throw from close range. But Drew's hurried release was slightly off line, and Perez slid into home safely behind a catcher the Rays would come to know better one day, Kevin Cash—giving his team a heart-pounding and crucial 9-8 win.

Losing a chance to go up 2-0 in the series seemed to take a psychological toll on Boston, while simultaneously energizing the Rays. In Game 3 at Fenway, Tampa Bay body-slammed Boston 9-1 and starter Lester—with homers yet again from Longo and B.J., along with Baldelli and Peña this time, and a fine pitching effort by Garza. Unbelievably, Game 4 was more of the same: the Rays scored three in the first and never looked back in a 13-4 demolition of Boston, powered by homers from Peña, Longoria and Aybar and seven strong innings from Sonnanstine. Could it really be this easy after all the suspenseful action between these teams?

For all intents and purposes, it looked as if the Rays had the ALCS title wrapped up when they turned Game Five into a similar romp. The Rays' very own Bash Brothers—Longoria, Upton and Peña—all homered again to help create a 7-0 lead by the top of the seventh in eerily silent Fenway.

But somehow, someway, the Red Sox climbed out of the hole.

Tampa Bay's animated Aussie reliever Grant Balfour came on in relief of Kazmir to face the bottom of the order, but was greeted by Jed Lowrie's leadoff double. Two routine fly outs followed, but then Crisp singled in Lowrie and Pedroia kept the inning alive with a base hit. That brought up the ever-dangerous David "Big Papi" Ortiz, who crushed an 0-1 pitch into the right field stands for a three-run homer to shake his teammates out of their three-game trance.

Now within striking distance, trailing 7-4, the revved-up Red Sox jumped on Wheeler with three in the eighth to tie it, aided by a two-run homer from Drew, then stunned the Rays in the bottom of the ninth. J.P. Howell got the first two outs, before eventually giving up the game-winning single to Drew, atoning for his less-than-stellar throw in Game Two.

Boston was back—and Tampa Bay back-pedaling, heading home to St. Pete with a 3-2 series lead that suddenly felt extremely precarious. The pressure shifted in a big way to the Rays, and they played like it in Game 6 at the Trop, losing 4-2 and managing only four hits while Shields was unexpectedly shaky. All the momentum resided with the Red Sox heading into the seventh and deciding game, featuring a duel between Boston ace Lester and Tampa Bay's tightly wound standout Garza, who needed to keep his emotions in check for his team to have any chance.

Boston scored in the top of the first on a homer by the increasingly annoying Pedroia. But Garza stayed cool, settling into a rhythm. That allowed the Rays to tie it in the fourth, when Longoria doubled home Peña, and take the lead in the fifth after Baldelli—continually rising to the occasion to remind us of his one-time greatness—singled in Aybar. Garza was brilliant as the game progressed, and the Rays gave him some welcome breathing room in the seventh on Aybar's solo homer, extending the lead to a much more comfortable margin of 3-1.

But this was vintage Red Sox-Rays, which meant only one thing: the outcome was far from decided. In the top of the eighth, Boston got its first two hitters on base with an error and single. Two outs later, Youkilis drew a walk off battle-tested reliever Bradford to load the bases. Maddon countered with a daring move. He called on virtually untested lefty rookie Price to face Game 5 nemesis Drew, a left-handed, .280 hitter. Price got ahead in the count 1-2, then fired a 94-mph fastball that had Drew swinging at air, and every Rays fan in attendance—or following on TV and radio—exhaled collectively.

Jason Bay, a player Friedman had hoped to acquire from Pittsburgh at the July trade deadline before Boston intervened—walked to start off the top of the ninth with Price still on the mound. But David, in a display of his greatness to come, got Mark Kotsay and Jason Varitek looking at strike three.

The Rays were now one out away as Lowrie stepped to the plate to pitch-hit for Alex Cora. Lowrie's two-base hit had resuscitated the Red Sox two games earlier, but he swung at the second pitch, bouncing the ball to Aki, who raced over and stepped on second base for the force—leaping in the air jubilantly in one of the franchise's indelible images. Rays players and coaches in the dugout sprinted onto the field to hug and high-five their teammates in an exuberant and emotional scene, before cavorting in the compulsory champagne bath awaiting in the clubhouse.

The Rays had done the seemingly impossible. They'd reached the World Series. Magrane and I made our way to the makeshift stage outdoors on the plaza, surrounded by ecstatic fans, already thinking about the next milestone in this unprecedented and improbable ride—a date with the Philadelphia Phillies in the World Series.

The national media had descended upon Tropicana Field during the ALCS in impressive numbers. For the Series, set to begin on October 22, 2008, the media turnout was insane—including a massive contingent of Japanese press staying in town to cover their new favorite son, Aki.

The Phillies had disposed of the Los Angeles Dodgers in five games, so they came to town a bit more rested than the Rays. But many columnists and baseball writers on hand for the opener felt the upstarts from Tampa Bay had the edge in the series, due to the offense that had come alive in the playoffs—spurred by Upton's record-tying seven homers in the post-season and Longoria's six—and the intimidating din of the Trop, where the Rays would have four chances at victory, if needed.

They had earned that right with the American League's All-Star Game victory in July, when the AL squad eeked out a 4-3 victory in 15 innings in Yankee Stadium. The Rays' players on the team more than carried their weight, with Longoria doubling in one of the runs, Navarro adding a single and a walk and Scott Kazmir earning the win with a shutout inning in the 15th. Maybe it was a good sign that Philadelphia closer Brad Lidge got the loss. By rules, the winning league secured home-field advantage in the World Series for its eventual pennant-winner—in this case, Tampa Bay.

Once again, Joe Magrane and I were set to host the pregame and postgame shows just outside the stadium. But thanks to the Rays and the radio crew, Andy Freed and Dave Wills, we got to call a few innings of the Series on radio during the home games—something that we very much appreciated.

Unfortunately, Game 1 became something of a mirror opposite of the All-Star Game, with Kazmir taking the loss in a 2-0 outcome and Lidge saving the game for Cole Hamels. Chase Utley's two-run homer in the first was all the scoring the game offered, quite an anti-climax following the week-long buildup and heightened expectations at home.

But Game 2 was a completely different story. The Rays regained their composure, scoring twice in the first, once in the second and once in the third for a 4-0 lead. The Phillies got on the board in the eighth with an Eric Bruntlett homer off Price, and then threatened in the ninth when Carlos Ruiz led off with a double and Jayson Werth reached on a Longoria error, bringing home an unearned run. Price then shut the door by striking out Utley and coaxing lefty slugger Ryan Howard to ground out—sending Tampa Bay to Philadelphia tied 1-apiece.

That's when the feel-good story took a turn that—even as I reflect upon it today—remains a prime example of how bad weather and badly behaved fans can ruin a promising World Series, regardless of which team winds up on top.

The shift of the Series to Philly will forever be remembered as the week when the bottom fell out on the Rays—amid torrential and bitterly cold rainstorms of almost biblical proportions. This phase of the Fall Classic was also accompanied by the less than hospitable treatment of Rays wives and family members in the stands by a faction of Phillies fans.

The Phillies have long been a top-tier, first-class organization and the majority of their fans—like those from any area—are simply passionate about their team. Though this is a city where fans once made news for booing and flinging snowballs at Santa at an Eagles game, Philadelphia has a long and storied history as a solid sports town. However, the assault unleashed on the Rays families in the stands during the '08 World Series blemished the reputation of a great fan base.

As Carla recalls, "We went up early to visit some of the sights, like the Liberty Bell and Independence Hall and enjoy all the iconic American sights Philadelphia offers. But that good feeling didn't last long. Upon our arrival at Citizens Bank Park that night, the situation quickly deteriorated."

Many of the Rays' wives and family members wore Tampa Bay logos on their hats, shirts and jackets. They soon learned that displaying their allegiance to the visiting team only made them targets.

"Shortstop Jason Bartlett's wife, Kelly, was wearing a papoose carrier strapped to her body with their baby son resting inside while she was settling into her seat in the family section seat," Carla continues. Suddenly she had several Phillies fans in her face. Rocco Baldelli's father, Dan, stepped in and was escorted out after trying to protect her by getting in between Kelly and a male Phillies fan harassing her.

"Trevor Miller's wife, Pari, was wearing a cap with a 'TB' logo when a guy walked up to her and poked his finger hard in the front of her hat, forcing her head back, and yelling, 'What the 'blank' is that?' None of us felt safe wearing our own logos through the rest of the Series."

Traveling secretary Jeff Ziegler, a former St. Petersburg police officer, made sure MLB security was present to offer protection and escort family members exiting the park after the game. Still, as Carla recollects, "when the family bus left for the team hotel, loud popping noises erupted—it turns out that someone had set off firecrackers underneath the bus. Then, as we pulled out of the lot, the streets were lined block after block with people making obscene gestures at us." It was a sad display and unbecoming for such a great American city.

Joe, Todd and I caught our own grief outside the stadium during the pre and post game shows. There was no security guarding our set, and fans crowded around, yelling and being generally obnoxious and disruptive. We removed the "flags" from our

Fox Sports Florida microphones and carried on. There we were, bundled up in our mufflers and top coats, powering through it, ignoring the loudmouths and rain in the background.

One moment of comic relief in the middle of all this came when Keith Olbermann, the former ESPN commentator-turned-political talk show host on MSNBC, walked by. Magrane recognized him and called him over to be an impromptu guest on the show. But our employer, Fox, was no fan of Olbermann and later demanded to know who was responsible for his unscripted appearance. We flatly put the blame on Olbermann, saying something to the effect of "He just walked on - we didn't even want him. He just forced his way on." And, of course, we all stood by our story.

That little faux pas was nothing compared to the meteorological ordeal we faced, from the moment we arrived at Citizen's Bank Park. A cold, nasty rain began in the afternoon and never let up, causing MLB and Fox Sports executives to consider postponing the contest as late as 9 p.m. Finally, the rain abated enough for the game to start 90 minutes late, at 10:06 p.m., the latest start in Series history.

After the contest finally got underway—following a National Anthem performed by a Pennsylvania 18-year-old beginning to make waves, Taylor Swift—the Phillies jumped to a 2-1 lead in the second against Garza. In the sixth, they made it 4-1 when Howard and Utley hit back-to-back homers. This didn't look promising. Just when you began wondering if the Rays were going to show up at all, a Crawford single and Navarro double in the seventh sparked a two-run rally, pulling their team to within one, 4-3. Suddenly, it was a game again.

Then, in the top of the eighth, Upton walked, stole second and third, and tied the game 4-4 on a throwing error by the catcher, Carlos Ruiz. The Rays were back in business, and you could see the excitement ripple through their dugout. But trouble began anew when Bruntlett led off for the Phillies in the bottom of the eighth, getting hit by a J.P. Howell pitch, and moved to second on a Grant Balfour wild pitch.

Maddon ordered the next two batters to be intentionally walked, pulling the infield in to play for the force out at the plate. In one of Joe's trademark inventive moves, he even moved Zobrist in from right as a fifth infielder. But Ruiz squibbed a roller down the third base line. Longoria charged and dived at the ball, but had to rush his under-handed throw and the ball sailed off the mark. Bruntlett was safe and a perfectly awful night was over with a 5-4 loss—at 1:47 a.m.

Game 4 began on Sunday with the temperature reading 54°F, but feeling 10 degrees colder. From the start, you could see how much the tiring, frustrating loss had taken out of the Rays, now down in the Series 2-1. The Phillies scored in the first and built a 5-1 lead in the fourth against a battered Sonnanstine—and Phillies pitcher Joe Blanton even got in the act with a homer. Blasts from more expected sources, Werth and Howard, made it a runaway, 10-2. Just like that, the Rays and their miracle season were on the ropes, one step from elimination. The team had come back from the brink numerous times during the season, but given the hostile elements and crowd, this was the toughest spot yet.

The weather was miserable and getting worse when Game 5 began Monday night. You wouldn't want to walk your dog in this weather if you could avoid it. It began with a gusting drizzle, with the thermometer already down to 47 degrees and falling—more what you'd expect for an NFL *Monday Night Football* game on a sloppy gridiron than a critical game of the World Series. The conditions immediately gave Kazmir problems, as he loaded the bases with two walks and a hit batsman in the first, then yielded a two-run single to Shane Victorino before getting out of the jam.

Being down 2-0 out of the box was definitely not what the Rays needed under such difficult circumstances. But Kaz settled down and, in the top of fourth, Peña doubled off Hamels, and Longoria singled him home to narrow the deficit. The nasty weather began to get even worse, with rain blowing sideways from the harsh wind, but play continued through five innings.

In the top of the sixth, battling the deteriorating conditions and odds, the Rays did something remarkable. With two outs, Upton legged out an infield single in the hole at short and proceeded to steal second base. Down in the count 1-2, Peña then lined an opposite field single to left and B.J.—doing his best not to slip and go sliding on his face—sprinted home on an infield that now resembled a chocolate soufflé, tying the game 2-2 in a stunningly clutch comeback. After Longoria flew out to center to end the inning, the umpire crew led by Tim Tschida huddled and, with pools of water beginning to cover the infield, announced that the game was being suspended.

Major League Baseball commissioner Bud Selig convened a hastily arranged press conference on the lower level of the stadium to handle a barrage of questions from the media about the unusual decision to suspend play. While regular-season games are official after five innings, or even four-and-a-half with the home team leading, post-season games come under the purview of the Commissioner. Selig didn't intend to let the Series end in a game curtailed by rain, and announced that play would resume the next day in the bottom of the sixth.

This caused a major logistical headache for the Rays and all of us associated with the team. We'd checked out of the Westin Hotel in Philly earlier in the day, planning to fly home after the game. But the hotel wasn't able to make room for us to check back in that night. Jeff Ziegler scrambled into action, calling 20 hotels in the region. Many reservationists actually thought he was joking with them—asking to book 80 rooms on a moment's notice.

Finally, he got lucky. The one place that could accommodate our large contingent that night was in Wilmington, Delaware, 25 miles to the southeast. The one bright spot in this mess was that our destination was the luxurious Hotel du Pont. So, we set off in our own version of Crossing the Delaware, savoring the moral victory of tying the game late. It was 2 a.m. when everybody arrived at the hotel. We piled inside, thoroughly exhausted, but thrilled that the Rays had somehow survived to play another day.

When we awoke Tuesday morning, however, the cold rain continued to drench the Philadelphia area, washing out any chance of playing a baseball game. There wasn't much else to do but stay inside, eat in the hotel restaurant, watch TV, visit in the lobby with other members of the organization, and wait for Wednesday night, when the game was now scheduled to resume. Some players ventured outside—Balfour reported back that he'd found a great burger joint, and Garza even went to the stadium to work out. But mostly, we laid low and waited, hoping that the Series would return to the friendly confines of the Trop for Game 6.

The long delay had the effect of rejuvenating the Rays' spirits, but it didn't take long for the Phillies to dampen them in a World Series contest now extending into its third day of play—after a 46-hour delay. Balfour took the mound to pitch the bottom of the sixth, and yielded a leadoff double to pinch-hitter Geoff Jenkins. He moved to third on a sacrifice bunt and scored on Werth's bloop hit when Aki—sprinting into shallow center with his back to the ball—barely missed making an over-the-shoulder catch and Philadelphia was back on top, 3-2.

But one of the few great Series moments for Tampa Bay followed in the top of the seventh. Rocco Baldelli—fighting through the effects of the rare condition that abruptly pulled the rug out from an exceptional baseball future—stepped to the plate with one out and drilled Ryan Madson's first offering into the left-center seats to tie the game 3-3. It was an electrifying moment, and gave the Rays new life.

Then came the play that saved the Phillies from a return to St. Petersburg—and secured the championship. It happened just after Jason Bartlett singled, and moved to second on a sacrifice bunt by Howell. The next batter, Aki, ripped a hard grounder heading up the middle for what looked like an RBI single and a 4-3 Tampa Bay lead.

But second baseman Utley raced to his right, made a backhanded stop and pivoted as if to make the throw to first. Instinctively, though, he knew he would never have thrown out the swift Iwamura, so he double-clutched in mid-air and one-hopped a throw to the plate. Bartlett was tagged out easily and a golden opportunity had been snatched away.

The acrobatic, heads-up play prevented the Rays from taking a 4-3 lead and vital momentum. In the bottom of the inning, Philadelphia bounced back when Pat Burrell led off with a double. He was lifted for pinch-runner Bruntlett, who scored the decisive run on a one-out single by Pedro Feliz. The Rays mounted a rally in the top of the ninth, when Navarro singled with one out and pinch-runner Fernando Perez stole second. But following Zobrist's fly out to right, Lidge struck out Hinske, ending Tampa Bay's dream season.

When it was all over, you couldn't help but wonder how different things might have been if there had just been normal autumn weather in Philadelphia. The Rays were an athletic bunch—Aki, B.J., Crawford, Bartlett, Zobrist and others. And the terrible conditions effectively neutralized their speed. Seeing the team come up short was incredibly disappointing. But what an amazing story it had been. In fact, I still regard the 2008 season as a great story even without the World Series championship. Had the Rays won, their accomplishment would have ranked as one of the greatest stories in baseball history—going from 96 losses the year before to a world title.

It wasn't to be, but I consider myself blessed to have been a passenger on such an unforgettable ride.

## CHAPTER FIFTEEN

# "If You Think It Makes You Look Hot, Wear It"

When I look back at the run the Rays staged between 2008 and 2013, what they accomplished was nothing short of unbelievable. It's hard to quantify the degree of difficulty involved for a small-market major league baseball team to reach four postseasons, along with a World Series, within six years—all while playing in the beastly American League East, and juxtaposed with a decade-long legacy of losing.

My view is if the people connected with this organization were to stay in the game for another 30 years—from the manager to the players to the front office to the folks at the turnstiles—they would never again experience an extended run like this one. I've seen lots of baseball in my career, and, without a doubt, the achievement was absolutely astounding.

I don't intend to delve into every factor that helped shape the stretch after 2008, or examine all the frustrating moments—and there were plenty in the following year—that foiled the potential of an even greater streak. But as an old play-by-play man, it seems only fitting to provide you with a look at some of the highs, lows and in-betweens that put the Rays in a position to win as a franchise—and put me in a position to chronicle the successes and failures, the exultation and anguish, and the human interest stories that make baseball a mirror of everyday life.

## 2009

There was no reason to think the Rays could not contend again when the '09 season rolled around, even though the roster was missing an array of faces that had become so familiar during the inspired World Series run.

Gone were Eric Hinske, Cliff Floyd, Rocco Baldelli and Trever Miller, all of whom had moved on as free agents. It was sad to see Rocco go, but he was no longer in the Rays' plans and the native New Englander signed with the team he'd grown up rooting for, the Red Sox. He'd have a shot at contributing to Boston's lineup in a part-time role—strange as it would be to see him in the uniform of Tampa Bay's bitter 2008 rival.

Edwin Jackson was dealt to the Tigers for promising young outfielder and Tampa native Matt Joyce. But perhaps the biggest change heading into the season was the addition of designated hitter Pat Burrell, the former Philadelphia long-ball threat, whose double in Game Five of the Series had helped beat the Rays and give the Phillies the championship.

Burrell, who signed a two-year deal worth $16-million, was among the best proven home-run hitters on the 2009 free-agent market. The 32-year-old right-handed hitter was brought in to become Tampa Bay's fulltime DH—and make up for some of the power lost with the departures of Hinske and Floyd. That seemed like a reasonable expectation, considering Burrell had banged 29 or more homers in the four previous seasons, including 33 the year before. Unfortunately, Pat provided an unforeseen power outage—but more on that in a moment.

Change wasn't limited to the playing field. My longtime broadcast partner, Joe Magrane, had moved on as well. After 11 seasons, Joe wanted a new opportunity. He'd served admirably as the baseball analyst for NBC's 2008 Summer Olympics coverage during the previous August, and now he'd been hired to do color commentary for the new MLB Network. It would feel strange not to be sharing the booth with Joe anymore, after having been through so much with him during the course of the franchise's history. But I was well-acquainted with the incoming talent—my old pal and occasional partner with ESPN, Kevin Kennedy, who had signed on for 100 games as the primary analyst. Former big-league southpaw and Rays pitching assistant Brian Anderson was hired to handle 50 games—after doing a terrific job subbing when Magrane was in Beijing for the Olympics. Todd Kalas, our in-game reporter extraordinaire, was even down to work as an analyst for some games as well.

Kevin had been working with Fox Sports in Los Angeles, co-hosting a national weekly baseball show with Jeanne Zelasko. And as fate would have it, he was on the verge of accepting a color job covering the Washington Nationals. But Kevin liked the idea of teaming up again—and also being able to stay within the Fox Sports family. SportsChannel Florida had by now morphed into Fox Sports Florida, and the network signed an eight-year exclusive contract in 2009 to broadcast 75 Rays games, with another 75 on its sister network, Sun Sports.

The timing hadn't been right for Kevin to go for the job in 1998, and I can't imagine working those first 11 years with anyone but Magrane. But now everything lined up perfectly—he'd even be able to continue to serve as co-host of his Sirius/XM Radio baseball talk show. Kevin recalls it like this: "I told my agent at the time, 'If I could work with Dewayne again and be at a Fox affiliate, that would be outstanding.' Then, after I accepted the job, Dewayne sent me an email that read, 'Well, it's about time.' "

I felt great about the new broadcast team. But as it soon became evident, 2009 would be a far different year from the watershed '08 season. It reminded me of a young ballplayer who has a great rookie year, but feels pressure to equal the performance in the second year—and winds up falling short of the mark. Granted, the Rays still finished with their second-best record in club history, 84-78. But the season was a disappointment in light of heightened expectations. Along the way, a series of bad breaks offset some outstanding performances and undermined the team's hopes of a return to the post-season.

Perhaps it was a sign of rough sailing ahead when the season opener at Fenway Park had to be postponed because of stormy weather. It was the first time the Rays had an Opening Day game washed out—and felt a bit like déjà vu coming only five months after the World Series weather fiasco in Philadelphia.

One of the first problems the Rays encountered in 2009 had another Philly connection. Burrell never fully adjusted to the DH role, which requires an entirely different mindset and preparation routine, and he simply didn't know American League pitchers nearly as well as National League hurlers. That's not uncommon for a veteran hitter changing leagues late in his career. The more he pushed himself to find his groove, the more he seemed to struggle. There was no getting around the formidable hole he created in the meat of the lineup. Burrell wound up batting .221 with just 14 homers in 412 at bats, far from the pop the Rays needed and expected to get—especially for the price they paid.

Burrell was far from the only unforeseen factor in things not working out. Another unanticipated problem occurred in late May in a game against the Florida Marlins. Second baseman Aki Iwamura, who had demonstrated his immense worth on offense and defense in 2008, was injured trying to turn a doubleplay when Chris Coghlan plowed into his leg. Aki suffered a torn ligament in his left knee and was lost for most of the season, and—in truth—would sadly never be a factor with the Rays or any team again.

And then came the devastating blow that occurred in a Labor Day game at Yankee Stadium. Carlos Peña was on a league-leading home run pace with 39 shots—within easy reach of surpassing his team record 46 from 2007. But he was struck in the hand by a fastball from New York's fire-balling ace, CC Sabathia, and suffered two fractured fingers. You could almost feel Carlos' intense pain as he writhed in agony at the plate, lost for the season with 25 games to play. The fact that he finished in a tie for the American League home run lead at 39 with the Yankees' Mark Teixeira shows you the type of blistering tear he was on.

The Rays were in no position to win the AL East at that point, trailing New York by 16.5 games, but they still had a shot at the Wild Card spot. Losing Carlos, their prime power source, was a terrible setback. They fell that day 4-1—their fifth straight defeat in what became an 11-game losing streak, leaving them just one game above .500 and out of the running. Any realistic hopes the Rays entertained for the Wild Card faded in that stretch, undone partially by the lack of a reliable closer. With Percival lost to injury, the committee approach in 2009 blew an unsightly 22 saves.

Lost in the shuffle of the downslide were some exemplary efforts—such as Ben Zobrist's sensational, career-best season with 27 home runs, 91 RBI, 91 runs scored, a .297 batting average and a team-leading OPS (on base plus slugging percentage) of .948; Longoria's superb sophomore season with 33 homers, 113 RBI, a .281 batting average and a Gold Glove; and Crawford's wall-climbing catch in the All-Star Game en route to yet another fine year at .305 with 185 hits and 60 stolen bases, including a modern day record-tying six steals in one game.

And, yes, there were also a few efforts that would have been nice to forget, like Chicago White Sox lefty ace Mark Buehrle's perfect game against the Rays on July 23, 2009—preserved on the final at bat, when centerfielder DeWayne Wise made a leaping catch at the wall to rob Gabe Kapler of a home run and keep Buehrle perfect.

In 2008, it was precisely the kind of ball that would have gone out of the park for the Rays. But there was no such magic left in '09—a season that also saw the Rays trade struggling starter Scott Kazmir to the Angels in late August, holding an 8-7 record with a 5.92 ERA at the time. As difficult as the year proved, one aspect of it never wavered—the unflinching optimism of Joe Maddon, named 2008 AL Manager of the Year for his phenomenal work in leading his team to the Series. Joe kept the troubles in 2009 from completely weighing down his players, and the fact that they finished at a respectable six games over .500—for a second straight winning season—was testament to his touch with the young team.

The year before, he had introduced the first themed road trip, and those colorful and humorous team charter flights became a full-blown tradition in 2009—reflecting the manager's unorthodox, hip and fun-loving style, and his desire to keep the atmosphere on the team loose, regardless of external pressures. Players, coaches, staff and, of course, Maddon donned elaborate outfits that adhered to whatever theme had been selected for a given road swing. The one that got the most attention in 2009 was the "Ring of Fire" road trip to Toronto and Detroit, dedicated to Johnny Cash. Joe, ever the showman, even dyed his hair black for the excursion.

He was quoted in the local papers, explaining the move this way: "I felt we were just way too uptight around here. I had to loosen things up a bit. ... We got to the World Series last year by being free-spirited about the whole thing, openly risk-taking, and not worrying, all that kind of stuff. The black hair is symbolic of all those things." Maddon simply refused to dwell on negatives, and kept the clubhouse mood on an even keel in spite of the challenges. For the record, the Rays avoided falling "down, down, down in a burning ring of fire" on the Toronto-Detroit trip, coming away with four wins in the seven games.

If there was one constant in the seasons to come, that was it—not just Joe's innovation as a baseball strategist but the creative way he set the tone with his players. He expected everyone to be accountable—to themselves, and to the team—but was never one for enumerating and enforcing rules. Joe wanted his guys to show up on time and be ready to play, leaving them plenty of latitude to govern themselves in between. This was the manager who one day summed up the dress code for his players in a single phrase: "If you think it makes you look hot, wear it." He had no use for making the players don a jacket and tie on flights—unless that happened to overlap with theme-trip attire.

Joe once remarked to me that there is enough stress in baseball without adding more with silly, unnecessary rules. He said it made no sense to require major league players to wear suits on chartered flights. "Nobody sees them," he said. "I'd much rather have discipline on the field."

## 2010

There were other lively theme trips this season, but the biggest excursion was the one back to the playoffs. The costumed travel continued to be a trademark part of the ride—such as the "BRaysers" jaunt, when the team wore specially created preppie blue plaid sports coats (that combined the words blazers and Rays), and a "Loudmouth Pants Rowland" road swing. The latter was named for 1917 White Sox manager Clarence Henry "Pants' Rowland, whose team was no-hit twice in the season but still reached the World Series. Like Roland's team, the Rays suffered the indignity of being no-hit twice—a perfect game tossed on Mother's Day in Oakland by Dallas Braden, followed by former teammate-turned-Diamondback Edwin Jackson, who won a 1-0 decision in spite of throwing 149 pitches and walking eight batters. Adding to the oddity was that we called the action that night from an unusual perch in the centerfield stands. We didn't have a great view of Edwin's many pitches, but, under the circumstances, it was just as well.

Rather than worry about it, Maddon embraced the double whammy and staged a "Loudmouth Pants" road trip, with everyone donning the craziest-looking slacks they could get their hands on. The Rays ultimately weren't able to match Rowland's feat of reaching the World Series, but 2010 was a distinct improvement over the year before.

For one thing, the Rays got to savor a no-hitter for a change, on July 26, 2010 at Tropicana Field, when Matt Garza faced the minimum number of batters, allowing only a second-inning walk, and shut down the Detroit Tigers—with the help of a grand-slam by Rays' newcomer Matt Joyce against his former team. Garza's first no-hitter in team history emerged as one of the highlights in a season marked by the usual wave of comings-and-goings, as Friedman continually re-shaped the roster within the constraints of his limited payroll.

He cut his losses early on with Burrell, who got off to another slow start and was designated for assignment by mid-May. Adding insult to injury, Burrell then signed with the San Francisco Giants, and hit .266 with 18 homers in just 289 at bats in 2010, helping the Giants win the pennant and the World Series. Go figure.

Some new faces didn't pan out particularly well, as veteran Hank Blalock was signed to replace Burrell, but was cut by late June. Catcher Kelly Shoppach, who'd hit 21 homers with a .261 batting average for Cleveland in 2008 and was regarded as a solid defender, was brought in to add depth behind the plate. But he wound up on the disabled list with a knee injury early on, and finished with a .196 batting average.

On the flip side, Friedman acquired closer Rafael Soriano from the Braves and signed him to a one-year, $7-million deal—and Soriano proved worth every penny. He won the closing job in camp and went on to record a league-high 45 saves, along with a 1.73 ERA.

Left-handed-hitting catcher John Jaso emerged as a reliable bat in the lineup, hitting .263, and his discerning eye and good base-running instincts even prompted Maddon to make the unusual move of elevating Jaso to lead-off man for 45 games. Joyce showed power potential as a part-timer against right-handed pitchers. Sean Rodriguez, acquired from the Angels in the Kazmir deal, began what would be an extended run as a role player and sometimes-starter for Maddon with his hustle, hard-nosed play and defensive versatility.

And, Baldelli—after his one-year stint in Boston—returned to the Rays' fold as a special assistant helping with Tampa Bay minor leaguers, expressing hope he could successfully manage his condition and eventually return to the field. That desire became a reality when he signed a minor league deal with the Rays in mid-July, and began working his way back into game shape.

This was also the season that Carlos Peña, in a spite of one hot streak that included a club-record home run in six straight games, began struggling mightily on offense. Carlos was always prone to a high strikeout tally, and that was no different with 158 whiffs—topped only by B.J. Upton's 164. This time, however, Carlos' batting average fell below the Mendoza Line at .196, even as he hit a team-high 28 home runs and continued to provide airtight defense at first.

Speaking of B.J., the club's No. 1 pick from 2004 continued to have a rocky relationship with many Rays fans, who felt he didn't always display the requisite hustle. That issue was thrust into the spotlight in 2008 when Maddon actually benched B.J. in August for not running hard enough to first on a ground out. Lack of effort was a cardinal sin in Joe's book. And in late June of 2010, Upton—whose long, loping strides in center sometimes appeared as less than all-out effort—casually chased down a line shot by Arizona's Rusty Ryal in the left-center gap at the Trop. The hit wound up as a triple and, in between innings, the lackluster display became the cause of a heated scene in the Rays' dugout.

I was told Evan Longoria simply made a passing remark to Upton, saying, "That was no triple." And, in a show of immaturity that was not altogether unfamiliar, B.J. took major umbrage, triggering an all-out yelling match in which teammates had to pull Upton away.

The moment was significant because the Rays had a dearth of experienced leadership, unlike the abundance that helped propel them in 2008. Cliff Floyd, in particular, had been a positive resource for B.J.—whose locker was located only several feet away—during that World Series season. But Cliff was long gone, as were veterans like Hinske and Percival. Peña was struggling too much to assume the role effectively. And Evan, while not a demonstrative guy by any means, made an attempt in his own way to step up as a leader in that dust-up.

You don't want players yelling at each other in the dugout, but the incident didn't have the negative effect on team equilibrium it could have. Upton apologized, was benched for a day (though Joe, perhaps to help B.J. save face, said the decision to sit him was unrelated to the incident) and the Rays came out of the blow-up just fine. Maddon praised his players for self-policing the situation—and closed the door on the matter.

With that, the team rolled on, winning 20 of its next 28 to keep the pressure on the first-place Yankees. The pitching staff carried more than its share of the load. Price blossomed in his third season en route to a 19-6 record with a 2.72 ERA to lead a staff in which three pitchers surpassed 200 innings (including Garza's fine season at 15-10 with a 3.91 ERA and his no-no, and Shields' off-kilter showing at 13-15 with a 5.18 ERA).

On September 1, Baldelli completed an inspiring return to the majors, when the Rays promoted him from Durham to serve as a DH, pinch-hitter and backup outfielder. How much Rocco could contribute was a matter of conjecture, but it was great to see him back in a Tampa Bay uniform as the team continued its pursuit of the division title.

On September 8, the Rays fell to 2.5-games behind New York after a 11-5 thumping in Boston. I remember that day because we were ready to fly to Toronto for a three-game series—and I suffered a pinched nerve in my neck between doing the game at Fenway and the flight to Canada. I don't know when or how it happened, but it was so painful and made me so uncomfortable that I had to broadcast those three games in the Rogers Centre virtually lying down.

The persistent pain—extending all the way down my right arm—drove me to see a chiropractor and then a Rays' doctor, to endure a series of cortisone injections and even submit to an MRI. Despite all that, the pain didn't let up until I'd undergone rehabilitation therapy throughout the final month of the season.

Meanwhile, the Rays battled their way to the AL East lead with two weeks left, but—with just three games remaining—slipped to second and into the Wild Card spot behind New York with a 7-0 loss at Kansas City. Two tense games were left with the Royals, and they won them both, while the Yankees lost their last two—propelling the Rays, not so long ago baseball's laughing stock, to their second division title in three seasons.

That set up an ALDS collision with the Wild Card Texas Rangers, a team Tampa Bay had beaten in four of six contests in 2010. But at the trade deadline in July, the Rangers had acquired left-handed pitching sensation Cliff Lee, the 2008 Cy Young Award winner with Cleveland, and Lee suddenly loomed large in the best-of-five showdown.

He outdueled Price in a 5-1 series-opening victory at the Trop, though you could say the Rays lost their best chance after loading the bases with one out off Lee in the first—then went quietly with strikeouts by Peña and Baldelli. In Game 2, the Rangers roughed up Shields early and cruised to a 6-0 win, suddenly pushing the Rays to the brink of elimination after a pair of home games.

But Maddon—in his familiar style—stayed calm and confident, and that rubbed off on his players as they faced long odds in the loud, oppressively hot environs of Rangers Ballpark. They rebounded with wins of 6-3 in Game 3 and 5-2 in Game 4, forcing a pivotal fifth game back in Tropicana Field for the right to advance to the ALCS. The Trop was re-ignited with new hope as Price squared off against Lee once again. But with the score tied 1-1 in the third, Nelson Cruz stole third and scored when Shoppach's throw to Longoria sailed into left field, and Lee clamped down once again for decisive 5-1 win.

It was a disheartening conclusion to an excellent season, knowing the Rays could just as easily have advanced to the ALCS against the Yankees. But there was one consolation. Maddon and his team had firmly established themselves as a consistent force to be reckoned with in the heavyweight AL East. After such a legacy of losing, this was an accomplishment of major proportions.

I should add a footnote to the series. I wound up on the "DL"—watching the whole thing from home on television. Due to my pinched nerve, my bosses at Fox Sports/Sun Sports let me take off the postseason. Although, as you recall, I wouldn't actually have broadcast any of the games once the networks took over in the playoffs. It was a good thing I had the added rest, because my neck didn't really get better until Christmas. Being home had its benefits, too. Steph and Dan—who'd welcomed baby Zach into the world in 2007—had their third beautiful child, a daughter named Elizabeth (nicknamed Evie)—soon after the ALDS ended.

I had plenty of time to get acquainted with my adorable granddaughter, and to play with my two active grandsons. With Carla in my life, and everyone in the family thriving, there was so much to be thankful for. I still thought about Dee all the time, but knew she would have been glad to see us happy and moving on so well.

## 2011

I had a new fulltime partner in the booth for the new season, analyst Brian Anderson, whose youthful, hair-on-fire style (despite shaving his head) added a lively dimension to his strong insights from the perspective of a former big-league pitcher. B.A. and I clicked well, with a style that often had me playing the role of straight man to his off-the-wall humor, an easy rapport infused with serious analysis of the action and ample interludes of kidding around. Brian remembers the first game we ever did together in Oakland when he was filling in for six games during the '08 campaign. He graciously credits me for calming his nerves, though I thought he did a fine job without any help from me.

"I was really nervous—I'd done some three-man booth work with the Indians, with Matt Underwood and Rick Manning," B.A. recalls. "I was kind of the third wheel. That's why I was so eager to do those games with Dewayne. I figured, 'Six games—what's the big deal?' But all of a sudden, I show up in the booth and it's a completely different animal. When you're the color guy, and there's no third-wheel for you to lean on, the pressure is really on you. And I remember Dewayne just encouraging me, saying, 'Just do your thing. Don't worry about it and let's just have some fun.'

"Maybe he sensed that I was nervous. But he was very reassuring and didn't overload me with information. The idea was that he'd lead the way and I'd follow along. Still, for me, that first game was the worst—an absolute grind to get through it. I went back to the hotel, thinking about what Dewayne had said to me about having fun. All I had to do was prepare well and follow his lead. The next day, I went in with a completely different attitude and that's where it really clicked. That's when I started to think,

'Wow, this is really enjoyable.' And what made it even better was the chemistry we developed and later built on."

By 2011, B.A. and I were completely in synch, mixing our observations and explanations with a healthy dose of levity. The only thing out of whack once the games began to count was the team itself. My pinched nerve was fully healed by now, but the season began as a real pain in the neck for the Rays after a winter of renewed excitement.

The club had to say farewell to one of its best players ever, Carl Crawford, who cashed in on his free-agent status with a seven-year, $142-million contract with the arch-rival Red Sox. In doing so, he passed on a $108-million, six-year deal with the Angels—a team I believed would have been a far better fit for C.C., with its spacious left field, than the intense and somewhat claustrophobic atmosphere in Fenway. But he opted for the biggest bucks, and—before the season was done—learned the hard way that money doesn't always buy happiness.

In addition to Crawford's expected departure, the Rays chose to part with Peña rather than extend an offer to their slumping first baseman, even with his laudable glove and power. And from a personal perspective, we were sorry to see Dan leave the Rays. He signed a one-year contract with the Red Sox, the team of his childhood as a native Rhode Islander and gave Crawford some company from Tampa Bay.

Friedman needed to address the roster holes left by the departures of Crawford and Peña and responded by making quite a January splash—signing a pair of veteran free agent offensive stars, outfielder Johnny Damon, former Red Sox and Yankees star in pursuit of his 3,000th hit among many other milestones, and feared hitter Manny Ramirez, with 555 career homers and plenty of baggage to go with them. Damon proved to be a marvelous addition to the roster, both with his bat, clubhouse energy and leadership. Manny—not so much. Ramirez, always as much of a renegade as one of the game's great hitters, had been suspended for 50 games in 2009 for violating baseball's drug policy by taking

HCG, a women's fertility drug intended to enhance testosterone production.

The Rays, in need of more offensive punch, decided Manny was worth the risk. But to say things did not go well would be a colossal understatement. The team lost its first six games and then—out of the blue—Ramirez, in the midst of a hapless 1-for-17 start, abruptly announced his retirement from baseball. Suffice it to say that was a very bad first week. News quickly surfaced that Manny was facing a 100-game suspension for another drug violation, and chose to call it a career after 19 seasons rather than attempt a comeback.

The silver lining in the wake of the Ramirez mess was that the Rays turned to two new players for help. First baseman and home-grown product Casey Kotchman, who had signed as a free agent after seven big-league seasons, was promoted from Triple-A Durham. And outfielder Sam Fuld, acquired from the Cubs in a multi-player trade in the off-season for Garza, became a regular outfield presence with Damon moving to DH.

Kotchman immediately established himself as a defensive wiz at first of Peña's elite caliber, and also became a standout offensive performer, batting .306 and making up for a lack of power by leading the team in hits with 155. And Fuld, playing both left and right, took full advantage of his opportunity—soon dubbed "Super Sam" for his series of diving and leaping catches and a spectacular start with the Rays otherwise known as "The Legend of Sam Fuld."

The turnaround began in the seventh game—the first without Ramirez—when Dan Johnson pulled, for lack of a better term, a Dan Johnson. On a cold Friday night in Chicago, he blasted a three-run homer in the ninth inning to cap a five-run rally that beat the White Sox, 9-7, for Tampa Bay's first win of the season. That Sunday afternoon, Fuld made one of the best catches many of us had ever seen—sprinting full-out into the rightfield corner, diving parallel to the ground and sprawling onto the warning track to rob Juan Pierre of what might well have been an inside-the-park grand slam, or without question a bases-clearing triple.

Fuld bloodied his arms and legs on the rough surface, and, though the Rays lost, his inspired play added more fuel to the Rays' fire amid the early turmoil.

Three weeks later, they had evened their record at 11-11. And by early May, they'd climbed—at least temporarily—into first place. It was quite a turnaround after stumbling so badly out of the gate, and Fuld's unexpected contribution in that first month helped pave the way.

Returning to home territory in Boston the day after his ESPN Web Gem catch in Chicago, he purposely passed up a chance to hit for the cycle in his final at bat. Playing in front of family and friends, Fuld—acquired primarily as a defensive specialist—started the game in storybook fashion with a homerun, double and triple. Then, in the ninth, he drilled a liner to left for an easy two-bagger in his team's eventual 16-5 rout of the Red Sox. Giddy teammates yelled from the dugout for Fuld to stop at first for a single, but he insisted on advancing to second base and forgoing the rare career feat. Yet that only added to his growing "legend." By April 18, Fuld had become a feel-good national story, leading the AL in batting at .396—earning the nickname "Super Sam" and becoming an Internet sensation. Even after he tailed off offensively by summer, his diving catches remained a mainstay of the evolving season.

While Longoria battled injuries and an uncharacteristically sub-par offensive season, Damon stepped up as a clutch, tenacious hitter at .261 in 150 games, and Joyce enjoyed an All-Star season, hitting .277 with 19 homers. The pitching staff gelled with Shields often brilliant in amassing a 16-12 record—including a career-best 225 strikeouts, a club-record 11 complete games and a 2.82 ERA. Jeremy Hellickson followed his brief introduction in 2010 with a 13-10, 2.95 ERA showing that earned him AL Rookie of the Year. And Kyle Farnsworth, signed in the offseason to bolster the bullpen, developed into a reliable closer with 25 saves to go with a 5-1 mark and 2.18 ERA.

But I have to hand Maddon plenty of credit for steadying the ship, considering the season might easily have gone down the tubes early on. When the Rays lost their first six games, he buoyed spirits by toasting the team on the plane to Chicago by proclaiming, "Here's to the best 0-6 team in baseball." And naturally, Joe continued to orchestrate one team-building theme trip after the next—a 1950s-style hat day when the Rays took the train from New York to Boston, in a nod to the old method of baseball travel; a "grunge" outfit theme on a flight to the grunge music capital of Seattle; a Beach Boys flight on an ensuing charter to Anaheim; and a Pajama Party look on the overnight flight from LA to Baltimore. It was classic Joe, along with his penchant for blasting his favorite rock, Motown and country albums from his manager's office before games—and sipping wine from his well-stocked collection following victories.

After losing the first two games in September, the Rays were staring at the seemingly impossible—trying to make the playoffs despite being nine games behind Boston in the Wild Card Race. No team had ever reached the post-season trailing by that great a margin in September. But the Red Sox were in the midst of a major meltdown, and Tampa Bay was more than glad to contribute to their misery, gaining crucial ground by taking six of seven games against Boston that month. With three games to play, the Rays pulled into a Wild Card tie with the Sox—by beating the first-place Yankees in the second game of a four-game, season-ending series at the Trop.

In Game 161, often forgotten in the pages of Rays' history, the Yankees moved ahead 3-2 with a run in the top of the sixth and had the bases loaded—when catcher Russell Martin hit a grounder to third. Longoria scooped it up, stepped on the bag for the force and fired the ball to second baseman Zobrist for the second out, and Zo then fired to Rodriguez to complete a dramatic triple play, keeping Tampa Bay close.

In the bottom of the seventh, the Yankees brought in a reliever familiar to the Rays—Rafael Soriano—to protect the 3-2 lead. But after walks to Upton and Longo, Joyce crushed a 1-0 pitch deep into the right field stands for a three-run homer that gave the Rays a must-win 5-3 decision—setting the stage for history in Game 162.

You know the rest of that story.

After the home run heroics by Dan Johnson and Evan Longoria, coupled with Boston's demise in Baltimore, the Rays were back in the postseason for the third time in four years. They jetted to Texas on an emotional high, while Maddon and pitching coach Jim Hickey laid the groundwork for an unconventional move.

They elected to start rookie lefthander Matt Moore, who had only been promoted from Triple-A Durham a month earlier, but looked sharp against the Yankees in his one career start. That lone start represented the fewest by a Game 1 pitcher in MLB postseason history, but Matt performed brilliantly: seven innings of two-hit ball against notoriously hard-hitting Texas. A homer by Damon and two by Shoppach did the rest in a 9-0 upset demolition of the Rangers and ace C.J. Wilson.

But any thoughts of the Rays emerging as a team of destiny, a la 2008, soon began to fade. Texas overcame a three-run deficit to win Game 2, 8-6. They came back from a 1-0 margin in Game Three, aided by a two-run, sixth-inning shot by Mike Napoli off of Price, for a 4-3 victory at the Trop. And Adrian Beltré's pair of homers off Hellickson, in the second and fourth, proved too much for the Rays to overcome in a 4-3 setback and another heartbreaking, postseason loss to the Rangers.

It was painful to see the season come up short once more against Texas, no matter how potent the Rangers' bats were, or how big the team's payroll was. The mere fact that Maddon and his group of gritty players made it this far—especially considering the hole in which they started, and the gap they overcame at the end—still ranked as a towering baseball achievement by any measure, packed with some of the most exciting baseball moments you'll ever see.

## 2012

By comparison, this season was quite the letdown. The fact that the Rays finished 90-72 just illustrates how far they had come—winning 90 games and yet paling in comparison with three of the previous four seasons. Maddon was the hands-down choice for his second AL Manager of the Year award and was rewarded with a three-year, $6-million contract extension running through the 2015 season. And things actually got off to a fine start. Carlos Peña, re-signed after a season with the Cubs, celebrated his return in the season opener against the Yankees with three hits and five RBI, including a first-inning grand slam in a 7-6 victory.

The Rays won the second game 8-6, with Peña adding an RBI single, and completed a promising sweep of the Yankees with a 3-0 win—featuring a homer and double by their old first base fixture, back with an apparent new lease on life. But as with so many facets of 2012, high hopes gave way to a less enticing reality. Peña would hit .197 with a team-high 182 strikeouts and only 19 homers.

Another source of early optimism was Luke Scott, the former power-hitting outfielder for Baltimore. Following season-ending surgery with the Orioles in 2011, Scott signed on with the Rays for $5-million to become the team's designated hitter—spelling the end of Damon's short run with the Rays. But Scott was hampered by injury and, other than a strong month of July, never got on track, hitting .229 with 14 homers. Longoria suffered a fluke injury in late April, partially tearing his hamstring sliding into second, and would miss 85 games. If there was any question about what Longo meant to the Rays, they floundered at 41-44 in his absence, compared to 49-28 when he was in the lineup.

Infielder Jeff Keppinger wasn't much of a talker, but spoke loudly with his bat, leading the team with a .325 average. One weird moment involving Keppinger, however, somehow typified the herky-jerky season—he suffered a broken big toe after being struck by a foul ball in the dugout, and was forced to the DL. This became a campaign in which Friedman added a cavalcade of players in hopes of finding a spark—Ryan Roberts, Brandon Allen, Brooks Conrad, Ben Francisco, Drew Sutton, and even taking a flier on former Yankees great, Hideki Matsui. With dozens of Japanese writers following his every move, Matsui managed only 14 hits with two homers and a .147 batting average in 95 at bats—though I absolutely don't fault Friedman for rolling the dice on him.

The Rays tried any and everything in 2012—and ultimately tried our patience. The one saving grace was the performance of the pitching staff. David Price became the club's first 20-game winner at 20-5, and its first Cy Young Award recipient. Shields received precious little run support but still compiled a 15-10 record and 3.52 ERA, with Moore, Hellickson and Alex Cobb all reaching double digits in wins.

Yet one of the biggest stories was found in the bullpen. Fernando Rodney, a castoff from the Angels, grabbed hold of the closer role early and never let go—entertaining fans with his archery pantomime act, which consisted of launching an imaginary arrow sky-high after every game he saved. That added up to 48 invisible arrows, but more noteworthy was his devastating fastball and change-up combination that landed Rodney in baseball's record books. He finished with an ERA of 0.60, breaking Dennis Eckersley's 0.61 mark as the lowest by a reliever in the history of the game. I wasn't a huge fan of his Robin Hood shtick—I lean a bit more to the low-key Midwestern style. But I certainly appreciated his rare achievement and the entertainment value he provided for fans in a frustrating season.

Game 162 was quite a different story from the one that unfolded in 2011. B.J. Upton closed the controversial book on his Rays tenure, before jumping into free agency—receiving a surprisingly warm ovation from his often-critical fans. Longoria picked up where he left off—hitting not two but three home runs this time in a 4-1 win over Baltimore. His effort was like an exclamation point punctuating Longo's value to the team—and underscoring just how much his absence had hurt in a season that never quite got on track.

## 2013

The big story of the offseason was Tampa Bay's trade with Kansas City, sending Shields and reliever Wade Davis to the Royals, in exchange for top rookie outfield prospect Wil Myers and pitcher Jake Odorizzi. Following his mid-June call-up from Durham, the mop-topped Myers justified Friedman's faith in him—hitting .293, while playing rightfield and winning the AL Rookie of the Year Award.

By now, the Rays had given up thinking one-time prospect Reid Brignac would emerge as their starting shortstop. He was dealt to Colorado, and Friedman signed a one-year deal with Yunel Escobar, who had worn out his welcome in Atlanta and Toronto. But in 2013, Escobar emerged as an excellent, everyday starter at short, with decent offensive production. He made his share of dazzling plays, highlighted by an acrobatic, behind-the-back glove flip to Zobrist, turning a sure Dustin Pedroia single into a doubleplay against Boston.

His occasional hot-dogging at short—with the little jump-shot move after making a putout—was tolerable, but, in retrospect, a sign of trouble on the horizon. One of the best developments was the addition of first baseman James Loney, a superb defender and a truly professional hitter, as evidenced by his .299 batting average with 33 doubles and 13 homers.

Healthy again, Longoria played in 160 games and, despite a batting average that dipped to .269, powered the offense with 32 homers. Super-utility man Zobrist settled in primarily at second base and was a vital part of the excellent infield, while also remaining a steady producer on offense, with a .275 batting average and team-high 72 walks.

Centerfielder Desmond Jennings had his share of thrilling offensive and defensive moments, but still fell short of expectations with a .252 batting average and just 20 stolen bases in 28 attempts. It became increasingly clear that D.J. was less effective as a leadoff man than lower in the lineup, where he seemed to feel less pressure. It also became evident that Luke Scott, who had re-signed with the team with a cut in pay, was not the answer.

Luke continued to battle injuries and finished with a disappointing .242 batting average in 253 at bats and just nine homers.

Once again, the Rays pitching kept it competitive. Price began the season on the disabled list with a strained left triceps, but returned to pitch well at 10-8 and with a 3.33 ERA. Matt Moore, overcoming some command issues, rolled to a 17-4, 3.29 showing, while Cobb was his best yet at 11-3 with a 2.76 ERA, and rookie Chris Archer made a fine showing with a 9-7 record and 3.22 ERA.

But what distinguished this Rays team more than any individual performance was the Herculean team effort when it counted most. Down to two games left in the season, they lost 7-2 in Toronto, and dropped into a tie with Texas for the newly created second Wild Card berth. On the final day of regular-season play, they rebounded with a 7-6 win over the host Blue Jays, while the Rangers beat the visiting Angels 6-2—forcing a one-game playoff and a Game 163 in Texas.

You couldn't have scripted this any better. It wasn't the playoffs, but the atmosphere was as tense as any division series showdown. For the third time in four years, it was Tampa Bay vs. Texas in a matter of postseason survival. The Rays arrived from Toronto Sunday night after their victory. And on Monday evening, they pinned their hopes on the left arm of—who else?—David Price, whose big-game legacy was on the verge of being defined by Texas. This time, however, David was magnificent. He fired a complete-game, seven-hitter in a deceptively tight 5-2 win, lifting his team into the Wild Card Round against the Cleveland Indians at Progressive Field.

For the third time in three days—in three different host cities—the Rays were in a must-win situation. Designated hitter Delmon Young, reunited with his original team in the offseason, took the edge off by hammering a third-inning solo homer to left field for a 1-0 Tampa Bay lead. Cobb did the rest, holding the Indians scoreless through 6.1-innings, with relievers Joel Peralta, Jake McGee and Rodney preserving what ended as a 4-0 win and a trip to the ALDS against Boston.

The Rays headed to Fenway with a blast of momentum, while the AL East champs had lost the final two games of the regular season. In the early going of Game 1, it looked very much as if Tampa Bay might stay on a roll—following solo homers by Rodriguez in the second and Zobrist in the fourth for an encouraging 2-0 lead.

But in the bottom of the fourth, everything changed, courtesy of a bizarre play in the Rays' outfield. After a lead-off Pedroia single, Myers had an Ortiz fly ball in his scopes—but simply stopped running, mistakenly thinking Jennings was coming over from center to make the play. What should have been an easy out became a ground-rule double. After a pop out, former Rays' regular Jonny Gomes, now a regular Tampa Bay nemesis, bashed a two-run double and Boston never looked back in a 12-2 win. Myers' rookie gaffe underscored how costly it can be when you give a team four outs, instead of three, in the postseason. With their confidence renewed, the Red Sox rolled with relative ease to the ALDS title in four games.

Like any playoff elimination, losing to Boston stung—especially after mounting such a valiant charge to reach the playoffs.

## 2014

Naturally, hopes ran high that the Rays would continue the trend in '14—and various national preseason prognostications even predicted a World Series appearance. But right out of the box, they lost two key members of their starting rotation to injury—Moore was lost for the season with a torn a ligament in his pitching elbow, and Cobb went on the DL for six weeks with a strained oblique.

After a 10-10 start, the season quickly spun out of control. The situation was made worse when the trumpeted return of Grant Balfour, now in the closer's role, immediately went south. On top of that, on June 4 came the very sad news that Don Zimmer, the beloved Rays Senior Advisor since 2005, and the acclaimed baseball man with 66 years in the game, had passed away at age 83. The news hit all of us in the organization very hard. The team soon added "Zim" patches to the jerseys as a tribute to his memory, and his moving memorial service fittingly took place on the infield of the Trop before a game, with family, friends and fans paying their respects. I was so honored to serve as the master of ceremonies, a reminder of our days together in Chicago.

But the swoon was on full force with no relief in sight. By June 9, the Rays had lost 13 of 14 games and owned the worst record in the majors at 24-41—conjuring memories of the bad old Devil Rays days at 17 games under .500.

The previous season, Maddon had made a habit of bringing a procession of pregame visitors to the clubhouse to lighten the mood—penguins, a magician, a merengue band, salsa dancers and even a 20-foot-long python. In 2014, one special guest of Joe's garnered national attention—a local Seminole Tribe medicine man had offered his services to reverse the team's fortunes, and was invited from time-to-time to say mystical blessings throughout the Trop.

More recently, it's come out in the press that not all the players were keen on Joe's eccentricities when it came to loosening up the clubhouse, and some longed for a more traditional baseball environment. In my view, these gimmicks were his way of filling a void on the team of vocal veteran leadership—in an ongoing attempt to diffuse the pressures of a long season and the inevitable bumps along the way.

The Rays desperately needed a spark, and the energetic, all-out play of rookie rightfielder Kevin Kiermaier helped light a fire under the team. Kevin had taken over after Myers—who'd gotten off to a poor start at the plate with an undisciplined approach to pitches—collided with Jennings in right-center and was lost for three months. McGee emerged as a reliable closer with Brad Boxberger supplanting Joel Peralta as set-up man—forming the "Jake & the Box" shutdown combo. And little by little, the Rays began to turn things around—even after Friedman made the tough decision to trade soon-to-be free agent David Price to Detroit for young lefty Drew Smyly. Despite being written off, the team came back against the odds and, on August 15, evened its record at 61-61.

It was tempting to think Maddon and company were about to pull off another miracle. You could envision a way for it to happen. But it wasn't to be. The Rays lost their next game and never reached .500 again, finishing out the year a frustrating 77-85. As I look back on the season, I just don't think the offense was good enough to have supported a full comeback—not when you score an AL-low 612 runs.

Basically, the Rays struggled to be adequate. They were subpar in all of their numbers—and not the team defensively that they had grown accustomed to being. There was a tremendous dropoff with the infield, particularly shortstop from 2013 to 2014 in the play of Yunel Escobar. Catcher was another obvious trouble spot, with new acquisition Ryan Hannigan battling injuries and hitting only .218 and Jose Molina hitting .178. Basically, if you look at the season statistics across the board, it's why the team that many observers picked in spring training to reach the World Series turned out to be less than mediocre.

In the customary post-season press conference, Friedman and Maddon expressed the view that the team only needed a few tweaks to return to contention. When reporters asked Joe about his upcoming contract negotiations with the team, the man who embodied the Rays' way reaffirmed his desire to stay with the club for the long-term, remarking, "Hopefully, it's going to last many more years."

I suspect you know what happened next. But at the time, nobody saw it coming.

# EPILOGUE

Seismic news shook the foundation of the Rays in October 2014. First, it was announced that Andrew was becoming President of Baseball Operations of the Dodgers—and two weeks later came the aftershock: Joe was exercising a barely known out-clause in his contract to pursue other managing opportunities.

I was as surprised as anybody. As usual, I'd attended the final session with the media at the end of season, when the two men responsible for the team's direction had looked back on the angst of the past campaign, and ahead to the possibilities of the next one.

Judging from how Andrew and Joe spoke in late September about the tweaks needed to return the Rays to the postseason in 2015, nobody in the room had any reason to suspect they wouldn't be back to try to get the job done. They had been linked inextricably for nine seasons. And they shared a vision built on metrics and matchups, helping to engineer a new reality for the Rays—one they seemed eager to improve on.

But change is as much a part of baseball as it is in everyday life. And business is a big part of both. If a person gets a chance to make considerably more money for what they do best, and take care of their family at an entirely different level, it's easy for me to understand the allure. I have no qualms about anybody going for a better deal, if it's within reach. Take care of yourself and your family. Contribute to causes you believe in. And don't look back.

Andrew was presented with an overwhelming opportunity on October 14, when the Dodgers hired him for a reported $35-million over five years. The job gave him control over baseball's largest personnel payroll, compared to one of the game's more modest roster budgets in Tampa Bay. Even then, I'm sure it was a difficult decision for him, given his loyalty to owner Stu

Sternberg. But what trumps financial security for his children and his children's children?

Good for Andrew for making the move.

Of course, in so doing, he triggered the now-famous opt-out clause in Joe's contract, a two-week window to leave the team that could be activated by certain events—including the departure of Friedman from the organization.

In spite of the tension and ill feelings surrounding Joe's sudden departure—following differences that arose in negotiations with the Rays over a new contract—I have no issue with his decision to exercise his escape clause to explore other managing opportunities that might be available.

Obviously, he found a big one with the Chicago Cubs, signing a deal for $5-million in each of the next five years. It's unfortunate his transformative tenure with the franchise ended on a less-than-harmonious note. From my perspective, I understand Joe's desire to survey the baseball landscape, and—at 60 years of age—seek the best possible situation for himself and for his family.

Before coming to Tampa Bay, he had put in his time out of the limelight, spending more than 30 years in the background with the Angels—as a minor league manager, as a bullpen coach, as the guy who ran spring training, and as a bench coach to manager Mike Scioscia. The Red Sox said "no" to him as their new manager in 2004, the Rays said "yes" in 2005—and the rest is history.

I genuinely enjoyed Joe in his years with Tampa Bay. And he can be the King of Chicago if he finds a way to overcome history, and help the Cubs win their first World Series in more than 100 years. I wish him well and I'll be watching—and I feel the same about Andrew in his quest to return the Dodgers to the top of baseball.

Naturally, though, I'm most interested in what transpires with the ball club I've covered these last 18 years—and the new regime led by Andrew's successor and longtime colleague, Matt Silverman, and rookie manager Kevin Cash.

When Joe and Andrew left, a lot of fans wondered if the sky was falling. But here's the thing: Matt has been around since Stu took control of the franchise in 2005—a full season before Maddon was hired. As team president, he always had an especially keen interest on the baseball side. He demonstrated right away that he didn't need time to master any learning curve. Judging by how he dove right in and made an array of significant moves, building a new framework for the team within its fiscal realities, I'd say he's done an admirable job of hitting the ground running.

And his hire of newcomer Cash, hailed in all corners of baseball as a sharp baseball mind, with great communication skills and a bright future, bodes well for the franchise. What a great human-interest story Kevin is: a local kid who grew up playing baseball in Tampa on a team that made it all the way to the Little League World Series, a Gaither High School graduate, a Florida State University product, a catcher—albeit briefly—on the roster of the 2005 Devil Rays, and a young man getting his first chance to manage at any level.

Some people have wondered how serving as a bullpen coach for Cleveland manager Terry Francona could qualify him to lead a major league team. Yet if you think about it, a bullpen coach who really takes the job seriously is perfectly suited to make the jump.

With the Indians, Kevin did a lot more than just answer the bullpen phone and tell a reliever to start warming up. As a former catcher, he continually helped players with his insights and input—often, according to Francona, when he didn't even realize how helpful he was being.

With the Rays, he has the built-in benefit of having an excellent pitching coach in Jim Hickey, who rides herd on the starters, and bullpen coach in Stan Borowski. Handling a pitching staff is not an easy job—a challenge I regard as one of the toughest facing a manager on a game-by-game basis. This is especially true of the bullpen. Think of how many games are won and lost by a team's relief corps. It's true now more than ever. Based on everything we know about Kevin Cash, he has a chance to be an outstanding manager—especially judging by the way his team surpassed expectations with a strong start to the 2015 season. Kevin has also shown himself to be a very capable and willing manager in baseball's new age of information and analytics, while also attempting to balance a traditional approach to the game.

I enjoyed hearing how Kevin, as a Little Leaguer, would constantly come home from games and pepper his father—a former minor league player—with questions about baseball strategy and why various decisions were made in different situations. Clearly, the game engaged his curious mind at a young age—just one of the ways baseball offers so many great lessons for youngsters.

That made me think of my two grandsons, 10-year-old Gabe, and 7-year-old Zach—and the important lessons baseball teaches kids, as it once taught me. As often as my schedule allows, I watch them play Little League games. Gabe primarily plays shortstop or pitches, and spends a lot of time—as all his fellow position players do—waiting for his chance to make a play. The nature of the game is that it is filled with down-time. And it doesn't give a player a chance—every minute or every second—to make a contribution. But, as in life, you have to be prepared for the moment your chance will come, and be ready to try and do your best when that happens. That's something Gabe and Zach are learning.

The difference between success and failure often occurs in that period—the down-time—when you're waiting and preparing yourself. In baseball, as an infielder or outfielder, there's so much opportunity to lose your concentration and waver during those long stretches, when—more than anything—you need to be vigilant.

The more you remain focused and prepared, the greater chance you'll have to succeed when your chance comes—in baseball, or any endeavor you undertake. You don't know when that ball is going to be bouncing to you at short. Most of the time it won't be, but you'd better be ready. That's one of the things I love about the game. It teaches you discipline, and perseverance, being poised for that next opportunity—whenever it may come your way. If you can experience baseball as a kid, it's a wonderful educational tool to prepare for the road ahead.

My own love for the game as a child was rooted in being a participant but also a listener, captivated by the voices crackling over the airwaves on my transistor radio and eager to scour all the stats I could in *The Sporting News* (no different, when I think about it, from the way Gabe and Zach absorb all the baseball updates they can from MLB's Quick Pitch and myriad baseball broadcasts on TV).

What a journey it has been since my childhood love affair with the game. Along the way, I've been fortunate to have watched many a player position himself for success by mustering an extra level of commitment and hard work—guys like Nolan Ryan, Don Mattingly, Jamie Moyer and Evan Longoria. I felt privileged and inspired to have covered Andre Dawson, as he virtually willed himself to overcome the pain of his bad knees to re-emerge as a star with the Cubs, and to learn the story of Carlos Peña's parents, leaving behind home in the Dominican Republic to live in an unheated attic in Boston, all to give their kids a better chance of success—and an opportunity their son Carlos refused to let slip away, working tirelessly to earn his shot in the big leagues.

Baseball has even put me in the path of a sitting and future U.S. president. In late September 1988, President Reagan made a surprise visit to Wrigley Field, donning a Cubs warmup jacket and throwing out the first pitch as the crowd—and Harry—went crazy with excitement. The Secret Service had its dogs check out the broadcast level to sniff out any threatening items. For some reason, the hounds focused on my briefcase, which contained my usual stash of a chocolate chip cookie or two. I have to admit, it was truly a thrill to see the President up close and feel the air of electricity in the building.

Three years later, I was in the press box at Arlington Stadium before a Yankees-Rangers game, doing my usual pregame preparation when the Managing General Partner of the home team popped his head into my booth—George W. Bush. This was before he was even the Governor of Texas, let alone the President of the United States. But I get a kick thinking back to how just the two of us talked for a while about baseball and ways the future Commander-in-Chief wanted to build his team. He was very cordial and asked me if I thought the Yankees would be willing to trade centerfielder Roberto Kelly for rightfielder Ruben Sierra. I told him I thought it wasn't likely—the Yanks valued Kelly too much. So, in a sense, I guess you could say I've served as a presidential advisor along the way.

Of course, I've also been fortunate to have shared the booth and crossed paths with the highly talented and colorful group of broadcasters you've read about in this book. I learned from many of them in my formative years behind the mic and I remain grateful for my association with so many fine folks over the past five decades.

I wouldn't be where I am today without one of them, Gene Elston, whose kindness and patience with an eager—and somewhat forward—young kid opened the door to a career and life in major league baseball. As I write this, I'm happy to say that Gene celebrated his 93rd birthday in March 2015—nine years after being awarded the Ford C. Frick Award from the National Baseball Hall of Fame, giving him a permanent home in Cooperstown for his work behind the mic. I'll always remember what Jack Buck told me one day as we were working behind the scenes to support Gene's election to the Hall of Fame: "Nobody ever paced a baseball broadcast better than he did."

Gene joined another broadcasting giant in the Hall with whom I was privileged to work—the incomparable showman of the airwaves, Harry Caray. Gene also took his place alongside the late, great Bob Prince, whose decision to leave the Astros opened the door for me to the majors, and who was so gracious to me in my tryout for the job as his replacement.

You might be wondering about what became of Milo Hamilton, who found himself as the odd man out at WGN, as a would-be successor to iconic Jack Brickhouse—after Harry came on board and took over the show.

Milo, who turned 87 in 2014, did just fine for himself. After working with Gene in 1985 and 1986, he took over as the lead play-by-play man in 1987 and stayed on the job until 2012—the longest run of an impressive career that landed him in the Hall of Fame in 1992. And there's even a street in downtown Houston named in his honor—Milo Hamilton Way. Holy Toledo!

I count myself lucky to have had my own longstanding relationship with a major league baseball team, the Tampa Bay Rays, as a member of the Fox Sports Florida and Sun Sports team. Whether broadcasting their games in the lean years of 1998-2007 or the exhilarating ride from 2008 to the present, I couldn't have asked for a better job—or a better corner of the world to live with my family.

I get to earn a living calling the games of a first-class organization, then drive home to the beautiful Sand Key beachfront overlooking the Gulf of Mexico. In the study of my condo, you'll find a wide assortment of photos, books and icons of my years in baseball, including a small section of actual Wrigley Field seats.

They are a wonderful reminder of my years at WGN, broadcasting Cubs games, where the frequent losing inspired me to coin a sign-off phrase I've used through the years after a defeat: "We hope you've enjoyed the broadcast, if not the outcome." A section on one wall includes photos of those two special 3,000th-hit moments I was able to describe on the air: Wade Boggs homering to reach the landmark plateau for the Devil Rays in 1999, and Derek Jeter reaching the milestone with a blast for the Yankees in 2011. Wade playfully made sure to sign the picture by thanking me for calling "the first" of those two extraordinary moments.

I treasure a picture hanging on the wall of a Stan Musial statue that never was made, a reminder of my childhood years learning from the rich tradition of the St. Louis Cardinals—and signed by both Stan the Man and the artist, Amadee Wohlschlaeger. One of my favorite pieces is a distinctive LeRoy Niemann seriograph of Nolan Ryan, recalling one of my unforgettable highlights in Houston when Gene and I called Ryan's record-breaking fifth no-hitter. I proudly display a photo of my son-in-law, Dan Wheeler, sporting the Rays' blue uniform from his days with the franchise, and both a photo and autograph of Babe Ruth accompanied by words to live by: "Don't let the fear of striking out get in the way." And it means a great deal to have Don Zimmer's autograph on a team baseball from the 1989 Chicago Cubs and their NL East division-winning club.

But of all the mementos, the ones that bring me the best feelings and most comfort are the assorted photos picturing members of my wonderful and growing family, each of whom is a blessing beyond words—Steph and Dan and their three kids, Gabe, Zach and Evie; Alexa, who is engaged to a terrific guy named Mike Gherardini (and who, on March 25, 2016, will walk down the aisle in the bridal gown her mother wore when we were married—on the same day and month as our wedding); an array of nephews and nieces; dear friends who have felt like family; and two loving women, Dee and Carla. Some guys are lucky enough to be graced by one amazing woman. To have shared a life with two such women is something for which I'm forever thankful.

I look forward every day to the next step in the adventure that Carla and I enjoy—her work at Quantum Leap Farm north of Tampa, which uses equine therapy to help wounded veterans, first responders and people of any walk suffering from trauma or illness; our frequent travel from city to city; and our deep involvement and constant fun with our extended families.

And I still look back on the rich life Dee and I had together, as well as her lasting impact on anyone fortunate enough to have known her. She certainly lives on in Steph and Alexa. There are so many examples, but I always have to smile at one story in particular, involving Steph and Dan early in their marriage.

Dan was pitching for Triple-A Richmond, and one night had a really bad outing as a starter, getting knocked around and yanked in the second or third inning. After the game, he and Steph were driving back to their apartment. Dan was pretty upset and not saying anything—and Steph, who hates silence, the way her mother always did, turned to him and said, "Well, are you hurt—or do you just suck? Because if you're hurt, that's one thing. But if you just had a bad night, then don't give me the silent treatment. You just go get it done the next time." That was her mother talking—the strong, straightforward way Dee always took on life.

I've taken on life equipped with a faith that has always guided and sustained me. And the road that guided me to Dee—leading us through many years of a wonderful marriage with two great daughters—was paved by our faith and spiritual beliefs.

In the same way, that road led me through grief and loss after Dee's passing to a new life with Carla. Maybe it's not surprising our special song is the Rascal Flatts hit entitled *Bless the Broken Road*—which beautifully notes how the heartaches, losses and detours along the way can be part of God's greater design to take you straight to where you need to be. Looking back to 1977, if Dee and I hadn't missed out on our first choice of a house in Houston by a mere 10 minutes, we would have moved in and never met the Berry family—never had so many of connections that changed the course of our lives.

And almost nine years ago, as Carla and I sat on the balcony until the wee hours of the morning, who knew that we would transcend our pain to experience this wonderfully fulfilling relationship between two people? We never expected this to happen—but here we are, happy and grateful.

As the title of this book suggests, the people you have read about in these chapters have prepared themselves for success by virtue of hard work. But they have also achieved success because of faith and grace. It occurs to me that we are enamored by and enchanted by the intellect. It is a major force in achieving our material success. However, by definition, the intellectual exercise—driven by reason, rationality and the scientific method—is finite and limited by human experience. That is where faith and the allowance of grace appears as a driving force.

The road I am traveling continues for me now in so many satisfying ways. I still get excited about heading to the ballpark—ready to describe the next story in the ongoing narrative of a Rays' baseball season. I'm sure there are some young boys and girls out there watching, caught up in the magic of baseball the way I was as a child—part of the game's endless appeal from one generation to the next.

When I thought about why I wanted to write a book in the first place, the reason had to do with kids more than anything else. I wanted something to show my grandchildren and let them know a little more about their grandfather. And after I'm gone, I want them to be able to show this book to their kids and say, "Here's what your knucklehead of a great-grandfather did." And maybe they'll see something in their own lives—a way of working hard to achieve whatever goals they choose to set—a way that will put them, when their turn comes, in a position to win.

# Photo Album

**LEFT:** This is the wedding picture of my paternal grandparents—Perry Francis Staats and Alma May Shell in 1909. They were married in Hahn, Missouri. My grandfather's wisdom, guidance and strong work ethic had a major influence on me.

**RIGHT:** There is no way to adequately express how much I owe to my parents—Perry Henry Staats and Beulah Marie. Here they are in a classic 1950s-era photo shortly after I came along.

**RIGHT**: The highlight of my athletic career—a no-hitter at age 12. My proud grandfather carried a copy of this clipping in his shirt pocket. Note the incorrect spelling of both my first and last name in the newspaper caption—keeping me humble.

**BELOW**: My first TV station job was at KPLR in St. Louis. We could easily have been the inspiration for *Anchorman*'s Ron Burgundy or *WKRP in Cincinnati*. Left to right in this 1976 shot is sports reporter Al "The Mad Hungarian" Hrabosky, me, news anchors Bill Thomas and Nancy Scanlan and art critic Gentry Trotter. In the background is the massive satellite dish that gave our nightly newscast an edge.

NO-HIT PITCHER Dwayne Stadts, 12, of the U11 team who hurled one of two no-hit games this season in the East Alton Little Leagues. Although Stadts struck out 18, his mates lost the contest in nine innings, 2-1 to the Wilhite team.—Journal Photo.

**LEFT:** The Astros' broadcast team: Gene Elston and engineer Bob Green (back row); me and former pitcher Larry Dierker (front). Bringing Larry aboard as the analyst really completed the crew. He and I quickly developed a comfortable on-air chemistry.

**LEFT:** Steph got to model Astros ball caps for a cap-night promotion. The team photographer, Harold Israel, thought it would be a great idea to pose Steph amid all these hats for various promotional material.

**BELOW:** Interviewing Pirates great Willie Stargell before a Houston-Pittsburgh game.

New broadcast team for Astros — Dewayne Staats (l), Gene Elston

**ABOVE**: Soon after I joined the Astros, Gene Elston and I were featured in a 1977 article in the *Corpus Christi Caller-Times*.

**BELOW**: "The Summer We Fooled 'Em"—during the 1981 baseball strike, Gene and I, along with our engineer Bob Green, went to a studio to re-create great games in baseball history to fill air time.

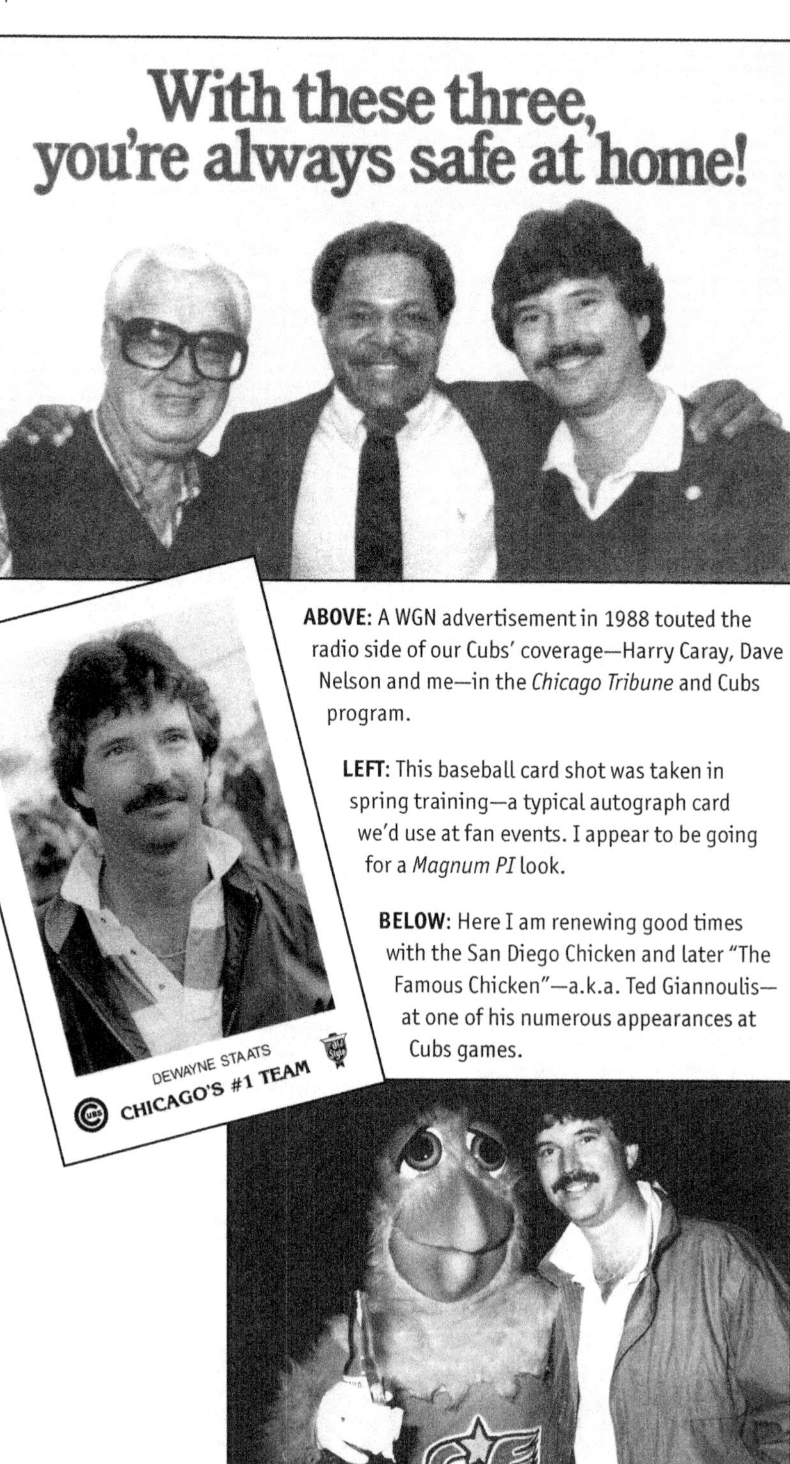


**ABOVE:** A WGN advertisement in 1988 touted the radio side of our Cubs' coverage—Harry Caray, Dave Nelson and me—in the *Chicago Tribune* and Cubs program.

**LEFT:** This baseball card shot was taken in spring training—a typical autograph card we'd use at fan events. I appear to be going for a *Magnum PI* look.

**BELOW:** Here I am renewing good times with the San Diego Chicken and later "The Famous Chicken"—a.k.a. Ted Giannoulis—at one of his numerous appearances at Cubs games.

**ABOVE:** Moderating a session with Harry at one of many Cubs Conventions we attended to mingle with die-hard fans.

**BELOW:** Our broadcast team donned tuxedos for the first night name in Wrigley Field history in 1988. Steve Stone and I had several special visitors to the booth, including Bill Murray (standing) and Bob Collins (front row), a popular morning drive guy on WGN radio.

**ABOVE:** Harry Caray, Steve Stone and I hammed it up for this WGN ad promoting our telecasts.

**RIGHT:** During an August 8, 2014 Rays-Cubs game at Wrigley, I did a guest spot (on my birthday) singing *Take Me Out to the Ballgame*, exhorting fans to sing loud enough so that Harry could hear them up above.

**ABOVE**: Hanging with good pal Ned Colletti of the Cubs' front office, along with sensational Cubs broadcasters Vince Lloyd and Lou Boudreau.

**BELOW:** That's me with Cubs radio partner Dave Nelson, a man for whom I have such immense respect—as a broadcaster and human being (he currently sits on the board of an organization that provides housing for orphan children affected by AIDS in South Africa).

**ABOVE:** Hall of Fame Detroit Tigers baseball broadcaster Ernie Harwell joined Tony Kubek and me in the MSG Booth at Yankee Stadium as part of his farewell tour, even calling an inning with us—what a thrill.

**BELOW:** A family portrait during the Yankee years: Alexa (6) and Steph (12), with Dee and me, on a summer vacation—during a weeklong break in the season—in St. Thomas.

**TOP**: Taking a quick break in the booth with Tony and a West Coast stage manager during a Yankees game.

**MIDDLE**: Enjoying a moment with former Mets and Yankees executive Arthur Richman, brother of UPI sports columnist Milt Richman, and a great baseball personality—along with Yankees first base coach Lee Mazzilli.

**RIGHT**: At the mic with ESPN.

SPORTS *of the week*

# Staats on the 2d Half

With the Rangers and the Knicks sharing the city's sports spotlight well into June, the Yankees performed in relative obscurity during the first half of the season. Now, the focus of fans is on baseball as the second half of the season unfolds under threat of a players' strike.

This afternoon at 4:30, Dewayne Staats will be at the MSG microphone in Seattle to cover a Yankees-Mariners game. This is Staats' fifth season in the MSG booth, and the lack of attention during the first half of the season didn't bother him.

BOB RAISSMAN

"You have to remember I got a real taste of that when I was in Houston [where he was voice of the Astros for eight seasons]." Says Staats: "You got into September and everyone was talking football. My approach is the same whether the Yankees are the focus of attention or taking a seat behind the Knicks and Rangers."

Staats believes the Yankees benefited by being out of the limelight. "Concentration is a big part of this game. The more attention you have focused on you, the more demands on your time to talk to the media," Staats offers.

Staats believes that Yankee fans will see a similar style of play as the season presses on.

"I don't think [Yankee manager] Buck [Showalter] has any secret plan or strategy," he continues. "He has managed from the first week of the season with an eye toward September; he has managed with the whole season in mind. The club is constructed for the long haul.

"The Yankees have interchangeable parts," Staats continues. "Buck has been able to rest guys for a couple of days and switch other guys into the lineup. The Yankees are very maneuverable, very flexible."

The Bombers played well during the first half despite what Staats characterizes as an inconsistent pitching staff. "But you must remember that pitching across the board in baseball wasn't that good," Staats notes. "The Yankee pitching staff wasn't as good as it could've been, but when you compare it to the rest of the league — the world grades on a curve — they were pretty good."

No matter how well the Yankees play, their efforts could be wasted if there is a strike.

Staats expects a job action, but not until late in the season. "I tend to think they might get the second half in. I think the players want to collect as many paychecks as possible, then put the postseason in jeopardy," he says. Would this preclude the Yanks from making a trade, which could put them over the top? "I think there's some validity to that theory, but it wouldn't surprise me if the Yankees make a trade even though they may be staring a strike in the face," says Staats. "From the Yankees' perspective, the idea was to get in first place as fast as they could and stay there, because you don't know when the season will be cut off by a strike." ■

ED MUDRAWSKI

NEW YORK VUE · DAILY NEWS **59**

Bob Raissman, a media critic of the *New York Daily News*, always liked the work Tony and I did in the MSG booth—and I got a big kick out of the caricature, too.

**LEFT**: I love this shot of Dee, taken during a trip to Vegas. She and I made time to see the Hoover Dam on the Colorado River.

**RIGHT**: While still working for WGN, I received my distinguished alumnus award plaque from Southern Illinois University Edwardsville in 1987—then dashed off to the ballpark to a Cubs-Cardinals game in St. Louis.

**LEFT**: My daughter Alexa and Shannon Magrane, daughter of my Tampa Bay partner Joe Magrane (and a 2012 *American Idol* star), were on hand for a bobblehead night featuring their dads in 2006. Joe and I threw out the first pitches simultaneously that game (Shannon caught Joe's pitch and Alexa caught mine).

**LEFT & MIDDLE:** I enjoyed 11 fun and memorable seasons in the booth with freewheeling partner Joe Magrane, whom I had covered when he pitched for the Cardinals. We knew we'd arrived when we got our own bobblehead night.

**BOTTOM:** Making the rounds at a charity smoker event in the Trop's cigar bar with original Tampa Bay Devil Rays owner Vince Naimoli and Eric Newman of the J.C. Newman Cigar family.

**ABOVE**: Todd Kalas and I have worked together since the start of the Devil Rays-then-Rays franchise—he's a truly gifted broadcaster and has been a great friend through the years.

**RIGHT**: Wade Boggs provided one of the unforgettable moments in franchise history by blasting a home run for his 3,000th career hit—the first player ever to achieve the feat.

**LEFT**: A friend sent me this cartoon incorporating a signature sign-off line I've used since my days covering the Cubs: "We sincerely hope you enjoyed the telecast... if not the outcome."

**ABOVE:** With my partner, former big-league pitcher Brian Anderson, at a 2015 game in Seattle. We've worked together regularly since 2010, and it's been a blast.

**BELOW:** On a West Coast swing in 2011, our stage manager placed a curtain between us during a late-night telecast in Oakland—as a spoof following an erroneous media report that there was tension over a disagreement we had on a call. We finally had to stop when B.A.'s mother called and said, "What's going on?" We didn't want to distress her, so we tore down the curtain and had a brotherly embrace of reconciliation.

**ABOVE:** The beach-front wedding party reception when Carla and I were married (left to right: Brandon Berry, Dan Wheeler, Mark Berry, Gil Engler, Carla's nephew Davis Gaudette, Carla, her niece and flower girl Sarah Tarrance, Gayla Berry Gaudette, Deanna Najvar, Stephanie and Alexa.

**RIGHT:** My son-in-law, Dan Wheeler, and his son Gabe at Doubleday Field in Cooperstown, N.Y., when Dan represented the Rays in the Hall of Fame Classic game and Gabe (10) served as batboy.

**BELOW:** Dan and Steph's other two children, Evie (4) and Zach (7), paid a visit to the booth at Tropicana Field—and tried out the headsets.

**TOP:** With Carla on the balcony at our Sand Key, Florida home overlooking the Gulf of Mexico.

**MIDDLE:** My wonderful grandkids—Gabe, Evie and Zach

**LEFT:** One happy guy

Here we are with our horse, Doc, at Quantum Leap Farm, an non-profit equine therapy and retreat center outside of Tampa. Carla and Doc work at this amazing facility, serving injured and sick children and adults, including many military vets and first responders suffering from PTSD. This shot was taken by Quantum Leap staff photographer Mark Lalli, a retired service member and Wounded Warrior. For more information about QLF, visit quantumleapfarm.org.

HOUSTON SPORTS ASSOCIATION, INC.
P. O. BOX 288
HOUSTON, TEXAS 77001
PHONE RI 8-4500

14 SEPTEMBER 1966

Dewayne Staats
816 Ewing
East Alton, Illinois 62024

Dear Dewayne:

It is rather hard to put down in detail how to become an announcer. I would suggest you get as much education as possible and while doing that try to get work on some commercial radio station to get experience.

I do not know how Aspromonte got the nickname 'Slats'. Frankly, I have never heard him called that.

Here is the opening day lineup for Houston in their first game in the National League: Aspromonte 3B, Spangler CF, Mejias RF, Larker 1B, Pendleton LF, Smith C, Amalfitano 2B, Buddin SS, Shantz P.

Enclosed you will find some of the other items you requested.

Best wishes,

Gene Elston

encls.

One of the letters that helped encourage me to pursue my career in broadcasting. I wrote to Gene Elston, the voice of the Houston Colt.45s and later the Astros, frequently as a youngster, starting in 1964, when I was 12. And he showed his kind, generous spirit in writing back. I'll always be grateful to Gene for his guidance and inspiration. Eleven years after writing to him and receiving this response in '66, I was working in the booth alongside him in the career of my dreams.

# ACKNOWLEDGEMENTS

I gratefully acknowledge the Creator for a life filled with family and friends referenced in this book and the many more who have impacted my life. Thanks to my paternal grandfather, who helped me see beyond the immediate, and to both sets of grandparents who never gave me reason to question their unconditional love. To my father, who by example, taught me the value of honesty, a full day's work for a full day's pay, and the responsibility of caring and providing for your family. To my mother, who helped me realize it can be done and worked to make sure her son got off to a great start and gave me two wonderful sisters.

To Dee for her love and unconditional support and her willingness to buy into my childhood dream. For the immeasurable gift of two daughters and all the time invested, often singlehandedly, nurturing and riding herd on both of them. She taught us all how to live and laugh and how to face earthly mortality with faith and dignity. I will always believe she fought so hard and lived for us until we told her it was all right to take the next step.

To Carla, who rescued me and is living proof that love and lightning can strike twice. She renews me daily and completes our family, providing love, caring and insight to the girls and grandchildren... who delight in "Lala's" presence.

I offer my gratitude and full endorsement to award-winning author and journalist Dave Scheiber. His professional talents are eclipsed only by his stature as a man, husband and father. His guiding hand and hard work in this project were invaluable.

I salute Gene Elston, who provided me with childhood memories of baseball on the radio that have endured a lifetime. His mentoring has made possible a life beyond my dreams. reaching both the professional and personal realms.

Guidance during my time at East Alton-Wood River High School was provided by speech teacher Tom Fearno and English Department Chairman Richard Claridge. Both pointed me in the direction of Southern Illinois University Edwardsville. SIUE and student radio station WSIE FM provided me with an opportunity to learn and show what I could do.

Dick King of the Oklahoma City 89ers was willing to offer a young man an opportunity. Ted Koplar of KPLR TV in St. Louis was willing to take a chance on a 22-year-old announcer with no television experience.

Tal Smith, Art Elliott and Dean Borba of the Houston Astros were bold enough to make me the youngest major league baseball broadcaster at the time, even though I had no big-league experience.

The Chicago Cubs and WGN, MSG and the New York Yankees, and ESPN elevated my game and exposure. For that I am in the debt of Dan Fabian, Wayne Vriesman, Dallas Green, Chuck Swirsky, Bob Gutkowski, Chet Simmons and George Steinbrenner.

My time in Tampa Bay has been a long-term blessing. The initial ownership group under Vince Naimoli, in conjunction with broadcast executive Dean Jordan, brought me into the fold and for that I an extremely grateful.

My time and career has been enhanced during the Tampa Bay Rays era under the direction of principal owner Stu Sternberg. Stu's keen interest in our broadcasts in concert with Sun Sports/ Fox Sports Florida's commitment and executive guidance has lifted our product to a level on par or surpassing any other major league production.

The men and women who work behind the scenes on our broadcast crew are the best and I am consistently proud of them and their excellent work. They make coming to work a joy. I am equally indebted to the many partners I have been blessed to have worked with through the years and hope our story gives them their due.

My present partners, Brian Anderson and Todd Kalas, and I have been together long enough to develop family-like bonds. I am grateful for their company on a nightly basis. I also delight in the work and company of Rich Hollenberg, Emily Austen, Doug Waechter and Orestes Destrade, who we often see on our pre- and post-game coverage.

I gratefully acknowledge a nearly 50-year friendship with Roger Lewis, who was so helpful in getting this project off the ground.

I humbly offer my gratitude and respect for John Simmons, who is truly an American success story matched only by his philanthropic heart. You may recall my earlier mention of the Laclede steel mill, where my father worked when I was a little boy and my maternal grandfather, Carl Berrong, also worked. Well, it turns out John's father worked there, too. And when the mill hit hard times and went bankrupt in 2001, John provided the finances to resurrect it as thriving Alton Steel, a lifeline to the city of Alton and surrounding communities. John's belief in and support of our story made this project possible. On behalf of our family I thank you.

And, finally, to the viewers and fans who throughout the years have been so kind and engaged, I thank you for loving our game and our broadcasts. My guiding light during every broadcast has been the awareness that you are allowing us into your space every time you tune us in and my goal is to make it worth the investment. Thank you from the bottom of my heart.

***—Dewayne Staats***

First and foremost, my thanks to Dewayne Staats for the opportunity to help bring his life story to the written page. Dewayne is first-class as both a broadcaster and person – and it was an absolute pleasure collaborating with him to make this book a reality. I also extend my gratitude to Dewayne's many former and present colleagues who graciously contributed their time for interviews, as well as members of Dewayne's wonderful family: his wife Carla and daughters Stephanie and Alexa.

I'd be remiss in not thanking my late father, Walt Scheiber, who instilled my passion for sports in general and baseball in particular. My dad, who grew up loving the New York Giants in the 1930s the way Dewayne rooted for the Houston Colt .45s in the 1960s, isn't here to read *Position to Win*. But I feel certain he would have enjoyed learning about Dewayne's remarkable journey in baseball and approach to life's many challenges. Speaking of parents, I owe a big debt of thanks to my mom, Barbara Scheiber, a professional writer and editor by trade who still has her fastball and played a key role in the editing of the manuscript from start to finish. My kudos to photographer Mike Sexton for his terrific front and back photos, and graphic artist Susan Spangler for her bang-up book design.

Of course, I give an enthusiastic shout out to my wife Janie and our ever-expanding family for their constant support and enthusiasm as I worked away at all hours, holed up in my little home office. Finally, a tip of the hat to AstrosDaily.com, which provided helpful background on the Astros' seasons of 1977-84, and the folks at baseballreference.com – a site that has everything you could possibly want to know about any game, any inning or any player, and then some, and helped enormously in my research.

*—Dave Scheiber*

# ABOUT THE AUTHORS

Dewayne Staats marks his 40th season broadcasting major league baseball and 18th with the Rays. A fixture on the Emmy Award-winning Fox Sports/Sun Sports telecast, Dewayne is closing in on his 6,000th career broadcast as one of the game's most respected play-by-play announcers. He has worked alongside Hall of Fame announcers Gene Elston on radio and TV with the Houston Astros (1977-84), Harry Caray for WGN radio and TV calling games of the Chicago Cubs (1985-1989), and Tony Kubek for the MSG Network covering the New York Yankees (1990-94). He also spent three years doing play-by-play for ESPN in a variety of sports.

Dewayne began his career as a sports reporter for WSIE Radio as a student at Southern Illinois University at Edwardsville, where he graduated in 1975, earned Distinguished Alumnus of the Year honors in 1987 and was inducted into its Alumni Hall of Fame in 2010.

He was named a finalist for the Ford C. Frick Award, presented annually by the National Baseball Hall of Fame, in 2012 and 2013. The National Sportscasters and Sportswriters Association honored him in 2013 as Florida Sportscaster of the Year. Dewayne actively supports Quantum Leap Farm in Odessa, Fla., where his wife, Carla, works as a counselor. He has two daughters, Stephanie Wheeler and Alexandra Staats, and three grandchildren: Gabriel (10), Zachary (7) and Evie (4).

Dave Scheiber, a national award-winning journalist and coauthor of the critically acclaimed *Covert* and *Surviving the Shadows*, is a past first-place winner in one of the industry's most prestigious writing contests—the National Headliner Awards. He was also a member of a *St. Petersburg Times* investigative team nominated for the Pulitzer Prize, for a series that won the National Education Writers

Association first prize; and a first-place winner for investigative reporting and feature writing in the Associated Press Sports Editors competition.

His work has appeared in a wide variety of publications—from cover stories in *Sports Illustrated* to the *Washington Post* to Fox Sports, where he wrote about the Tampa Bay Rays, Buccaneers and Lightning. Scheiber most recently worked as a writer in marketing for All Children's Hospital Johns Hopkins Medicine, specializing in telling human stories and earning a Mark of Excellence Award from the Florida Hospital Association. He resides in St. Petersburg, Florida, where he and his wife, Janie—parents of six children—perform with the Ocean Road Band, a popular classic rock band in the Tampa Bay area.

CPSIA information can be obtained
at www.ICGtesting.com
Printed in the USA
LVOW04s0320091115
461664LV00025B/571/P

9 780692 487969